Socialism in Russia 3010602

C000193293

Also by John Gooding

RULERS AND SUBJECTS: Government and People in Russia, 1801–1991

Socialism in Russia

Lenin and his Legacy, 1890–1991

John Gooding

palgrave

First published 2002 by
PALGRAVE
Houndmills, Basingstoke, Hampshire RG21 6XS and
175 Fifth Avenue, New York, N. Y. 10010
Companies and representatives throughout the world

PALGRAVE is the new global academic imprint of
St. Martin's Press LLC Scholarly and Reference Division and
Palgrave Publishers Ltd (formerly Macmillan Press Ltd).

ISBN 0–333–96426–8 hardback
ISBN 0–333–97235–X paperback

This book is printed on paper suitable for recycling and made from fully managed and sustained forest sources.

A catalogue record for this book is available from the British Library.

Library of Congress Cataloging-in-Publication Data
Gooding, John, 1940–
    Socialism in Russia : Lenin and his legacy, 1890–1991 /
John Gooding
        p. cm.
    Includes bibliographical references and index.
    ISBN 0–333–96426–8 — ISBN 0–333–97235–X (pbk.)
        1. Socialism—Russia—History. 2. Socialism—Soviet Union–
–History. 3. Russia—Politics and government—1894–1917.
4. Soviet Union—Politics and government. I. Title.

HX313 .G66 2001
335.43—dc21
                                                        2001052347

10 9 8 7 6 5 4 3 2 1
11 10 09 08 07 06 05 04 03 02

Printed and bound in Great Britain by
Antony Rowe Ltd, Chippenham, Wiltshire

Contents

Preface

This book will try to answer three basic questions about the socialist experiment in twentieth-century Russia. Why did socialist ideas in their Marxist form come to be implemented in Russia, a country that seemed entirely unsuited to them? Why did the experiment lead to such suffering and upheaval and fall so far short of achieving its original goals? And why did the attempt to rescue the experiment from an apparent cul-de-sac bring about its rapid and ignominious collapse?

At the book's heart lies the paradox that the attempt to build a socialist society was first made in a country that anyone acquainted with Marxism would have expected to come more or less last in the queue. For socially and economically, as well as politically and culturally, conditions in early twentieth-century Russia were far removed from those which Marx had seen as a necessary preparation for socialism. This was a backward society which had yet to pass through the bourgeois stage; backward, pre-bourgeois societies do not, or so it seemed, achieve socialism. Yet if Russia provided poor soil for achieving socialism, it provided very good soil on which to attempt it. Russians in fact had every reason for wanting socialism, even if they had little apparent chance of getting it. The country might not have mustered the necessary preconditions, yet no society in Europe *needed* socialism more, none fell so far short of equality and freedom, and nowhere else were socialists so singlemindedly dedicated to their ideal. Russia might lack a stable bourgeois-capitalist regime; what it had instead was an incompetent semi-feudal autocracy which looked as if it could be toppled like a house of cards. And if committed socialists were few there, the masses of the people could be seen as having been prepared for socialism by the communal principles of village life, as being in essence and by instinct socialist already, even if the word 'socialism' was unknown to them.

Such ideas were not good Marxism (though Marx himself in later life developed a certain sympathy for them). However, they formed the unacknowledged substratum of Bolshevik thinking and, in particular, of Lenin's thinking. Russia might not have what was necessary for fully realized socialism, but its very peculiarities would enable a socialist-oriented government, could such be established there, to clear the ground and put the missing preconditions in place. The country would thus get to socialism by a distinctive path of its own. The journey begun in October 1917 continued, in the event, for seventy-four years. There would be great achievements during this three-quarter century; there would also be enormous suffering and sacrifice – but what lay at the journey's end would not be socialism.

The central figure in this account of the failed socialist experiment in Russia is Lenin. He was an active participant for only the first third of the century under review, but his influence would be pervasive throughout it. There are, to be exact, three Lenins in the book. There is the living Lenin, who created Bolshevism, led the Bolsheviks to victory in 1917, and directed the Soviet state during its most formative period: powerful, charismatic, driven, a man struggling to reconcile the contradictions implicit in the attempt to achieve socialism in these unfavourable conditions. There is the posthumous Lenin as Stalin fashioned him, dead but eternally alive, an inescapable, godlike presence, the embodiment of party omniscience and might, and the ultimate authority in the Soviet universe. And then there is Lenin as a subterranean school of thought, and in time the perestroika reformers, perceived him: a Marxist idealist, an anti-Stalin and fundamentally a democrat. Both posthumous figures were carved out of the original; both had some claim to represent him; neither fully captured him. Lenin number three would make a major contribution to bringing the experiment begun by Lenin number one to its sorry ending. Yet many of the questions raised, and so crudely and contradictorily answered, by the living Lenin have not ceased to be relevant to the country in which he asked them. Whether from the Mausoleum or from a modest grave, Lenin will continue to cast his shadow over Russia and the Russians.

* * * *

What follows has taken some three years to write, but the issues it discusses have been turning over in my mind for thirty years or more. My thinking about socialism in Russia owes an incalculable amount to a wide circle of my teachers, friends and pupils. I will single out only a few. Zhenya Lampert, who first got me interested in socialism in Russia. Mark Sandle, who read sections of the manuscript and made valuable comments and corrections (but is not of course to blame for the blemishes which remain). Mary Buckley, whose spirited interest in all things Soviet has been a constant stimulation. Elspeth Reid, an unfailing friend on the Russian front. To all I am immensely grateful. My greatest debt, however, is to my wife, Katharine, who does not talk history with me but has done so much to make the life in which I can write it.

JOHN GOODING

Introduction

1

The history of socialism in Russia is very largely the history of the attempts by a minority, first as revolutionaries and then as rulers, to fit the masses of the people to its shifting ideas of what was necessary for socialism. Amidst the swirl and clash of these ideas, certain fixed points of course stood out. A socialist society would be one that replaced exploitation and inequality by social justice. It would be a society in which everything necessary for the general wellbeing would be owned in common. It would be a community rather than a cluster of competing individuals, and its members would live and work together in harmony. It would bring about conditions that enabled each person to realize his or her potential to the full. And it would be a society that succeeded in reconciling freedom and equality, one in which people could pursue their individual ends without jeopardizing the wellbeing of others.

That the Russian masses were ready for socialism and basically suited to it was something most nineteenth-century Russian socialists believed fervently. And this was not simply wishful thinking on their part: the traditions of village life in Russia were very different from those in the west, and they did seem to point in the direction of socialism. Russian peasants suffered from a harsh climate, infertile soils, rapacious landlords and a state which until 1861 had imposed serfdom upon millions of them. Even after they were freed from serfdom, the peasants remained a profoundly deprived class and one that was segregated in effect from the rest of society. These conditions had over the centuries created among them a way of life that was cooperative rather than competitive, collectivist rather than individualistic, a way of life whose underlying belief was that each person was necessarily dependent upon his fellows and bound to them by reciprocal obligations. If peasants were not to perish in the harsh world of tsarist Russia, it was vital that they all pull together. The basic rules of the Russian village were mutual support, mutual responsibility, and fair shares for everybody. Each should have enough to get by – but nobody should have too much. Each should act socially responsibly and nobody should imperil the general welfare, and stern action would be taken against anyone who did flout the unwritten code. The Russian village was as a result a community based upon more or less universally accepted principles of equality and social solidarity, the like of which could not be found anywhere in the west.

Although subject of course to state and landowner, the village was in everyday matters a largely self-governing community. The *mir*, as the community was known, made its decisions at a village assembly which every adult could attend and at which all heads of household had a vote, while day-to-day business was conducted on the community's behalf by an elected headman. Collective decision-making and mutual responsibility were so ingrained in the peasants that even when they left the village to work elsewhere they carried its principles with them. In the new surroundings they would form an *artel* or communal association, elect a headman, make all significant decisions collectively under his guidance, and live together, sharing work, wages and hardships.

The most important of the *mir*'s functions was to divide up arable land among households, and it did this in accordance with either their work capacity or the number of mouths they had to feed. What households received, however, was not a single chunk of land but a large number of narrow and widely scattered strips – in this way good, bad and indifferent land was shared out equitably. And the principle of equity was maintained in most areas by a periodic redistribution of strips in accordance with the changing needs of households. These egalitarian practices did not in themselves, it must be said, create a socialist community. Where the agricultural system of the village fell short, as Karl Marx and other commentators on the Russian village pointed out, was that each household cultivated its own strips independently and kept the produce for itself.[1] Under a properly socialist system, the land would have been farmed collectively, as a single unit, and the produce would have been pooled for common use. Yet if the agriculture of the village was not fully socialist, it did have a clear tendency towards socialism. What was crucial in this respect was the absence of private property, that is, of any hereditary and absolute right to the land, the periodic redistribution of strips, and the unquestioned acceptance that this basic productive resource should be shared out in accordance with need. The Russian peasant might not act in all respects like a socialist and would almost certainly know nothing about socialism; but it was tempting to think that communal tenure and the lack of private property had taken him, without him realizing it, at least half way to socialism.

The embryonically socialist community of the Russian village existed, however, within a wider society that was anything but socialist. The *mir* did its best to protect the peasant against the injustices and inequalities of tsarist Russia, yet had itself been shaped by that which it was reacting against and unavoidably replicated some of its features. In this hostile environment, the whole emphasis had to be on sheltering the peasant and enabling him to survive, not on encouraging his self-development. These circumstances inevitably turned the peasant into a team player rather than someone who thought of himself as an individual with a career to make and rivals to beat; and the team for which he played – peasant Russia – was one that consistently found itself with its back to the wall. The village's egalitarianism tended as a result to be repressive, concerned with behavioural conformity, and inclined to pull people down rather than to push them up. The weak and the needy were helped, but the talented, the ambitious, the eccentric and anyone who simply wanted to 'do his own thing' were held firmly in check. When in the years before the First World War the government tried to persuade peasants to break away from communal agriculture and better themselves by setting up on their own, very few took the opportunity and those who did were treated as pariahs. Economists and government advisers had come to view communal agriculture as hopelessly unproductive, as dooming the countryside to poverty and endemic disorder, but the peasants themselves continued to see the community as their one and only shield against adversity. Solidarity and conformity were essential; defying the community went against a deeply ingrained instinct. The equality of the Russian village was an equality of grinding poverty, which the peasant resigned himself to as an unavoidable evil. What he could not accept was differentiation within the community; and he did at least have the satisfaction, as things stood, of knowing that, however badly he might live, his lot was little if at all worse than his neighbours'.

The security and solidarity created by the *mir* came, therefore, at the price of stifling initiative, of killing individuality, of depriving the peasant of any sense of himself as someone with certain basic rights which did not come from the community and might at times need to be asserted against it. Life within the community was collectivist in that it more or less excluded the pursuit of socially significant individual desires – except with regard to the land. It was a life with very little privacy; the Russian language did not, as it happened, even have a word for privacy. It was a life without the wide area of personal freedom which people in the west had come to take for granted. Very few of the decisions concerning himself lay in the peasant's own hands. Russian peasants yearned for freedom (*volya*), and their folklore was rich in tales of rebel leaders who had risen up to free them and slain numerous landowners but ultimately gone down to defeat and death. Yet freedom meant something quite different to the peasant from what it meant to the citizen of a constitutional state. Being free did not imply living under an accountable, representative government and having personal and property rights that were guaranteed by law. 'Freedom' for the Russian peasant conjured up something else – seizing the lord's land and possessions, casting off forever taxation, conscription and all other burdens imposed by officialdom, and being answerable to no one outside his own community except a distant, benevolent, patriarchal tsar who was no longer surrounded by courtiers and bureaucrats.

Because of this anarchist streak in him, the Russian peasant had had to be held in a firm grip. The main purpose of the government's domestic policy was to corral and contain him. Yet he was also corralled by the very institution that was 'his': the *mir* too reflected the patriarchal and collectivist assumptions which were the cement of the social order. The village's business was admittedly conducted on an open and apparently democratic basis. One western observer was indeed so impressed by these peasant assemblies that here, he concluded, was 'representative constitutional government of the extreme democratic type'.[2] Yet one at least of the necessary ingredients of democracy was notably absent. Russian peasants had no belief in the value of diversity of opinion, and consequently no belief that minorities needed to be protected and given their say. Once a majority opinion had crystallized, those who had wanted something else were expected to swing behind it. A decision that might have been fiercely contested was thus converted into something unanimous, a narrow-majority will into the will of the whole community. The decision arrived at was, therefore, not only binding upon all; it was adopted by each as the expression of his will, as his decision. There was no room for factions, for majority and minority, for continuing opposition by the defeated in the hope of overturning the verdict. Anyone who persisted in a minority viewpoint would be seen as anti-social, an enemy of the community, and ostracized, punished or driven out. There were thus elements in peasant culture that would one day play into the hands of those whose version of democracy emphasized unity and conformity to the extent that it extinguished minority viewpoints altogether and demonized anyone who dared raise his voice against the general line.

The hostility to deviant thought and behaviour within the village was understandable enough. In the insecure world of the Russian peasantry, disputes and feuding were a luxury that simply could not be afforded. Safety for all lay in each being prepared to submit to what the community as a whole saw as necessary. The 'general will' may often have reflected the majority of individual wills; it may sometimes, on the other hand, have been no more than the will of a dominant group or even of an autocratic headman. But a general will, however arrived at, there had to be. Belief in the need for unity followed inevitably from the fact that peasant Russia had always lived on or close to the brink of disaster. In the teeth of adversity and yet also because of this very adversity, Russian peasants had come up with a way of life that was remarkable for its cooperation, its solidarity, its egalitarianism. The soil in which these apparently socialist characteristics developed had been nourished by fear, hunger, a searing sense of injustice. What remained to be seen was whether the peasant community would continue to grow towards socialism, whether indeed its proto-socialism would survive at all, should different and more favourable circumstances come along.

2

That Russia has a special mission for socialism, that its people are innately socialist, was and still is widely believed, and the belief can be traced back as far as the 1840s. It was not of course peasants who were buoyed up by this sense of special destiny. They might dream of a life transformed; but it was their champions among the educated who saw the village community with its equitable division of land and its subordination of personal desires to a general will as the breeding ground of socialism.

During the nineteenth century a numerous educated class developed, drawn in large part from the nobility, but also (and increasingly as the century went on) from the offspring of priests, merchants, petty officials and minor army officers. From the 1860s, the word 'intelligentsia' became applied to the radical part of this class. The member of the Russian intelligentsia – the *intelligent* – tended to be fervent and extremist. He, and sometimes she, aimed to overthrow not only the tsarist state but the whole existing economic, social and cultural order. Beyond that revolutionary overthrow lay equality and freedom – in a word, socialism. And the *intelligent* usually understood freedom in a way not dissimilar from the peasant: to be free was to be subject to a minimum of authority and external constraint and, above all, to be free from obedience to a state. There were some radicals, however, who swung in the opposite direction: this anarchic outlook was in their eyes either dangerous, because it opened the way to chaos, or simply unrealistic, because it disregarded the central direction and the repression of opponents which would be a necessary prelude to socialism. They too believed in life without the state as an ultimate goal, but nevertheless insisted on a massive use of state power as an indispensable means to that end. This contradictory attitude, this mixture of being both repelled by the state and attracted by its effectiveness, was to be an especial characteristic of Marxists.

From the 1880s, Russian revolutionaries turned in increasing numbers to Karl Marx, whose writings, based apparently on the solid foundation of science, made socialism's success seem inevitable. Russians who accepted Marxism and its determinism nevertheless had to live with some uncomfortable implications for their own country. Economic development alone, Marx seemed to say, could create the conditions necessary for socialism. The socialist revolution would be generated not by backwardness and traditional exploitation, however extreme, but by the new forms of exploitation and the new social forces created by modern industry. It was hard not to infer from this that Russia's chances of reaching socialism in the near future were nil. The biblical consolation of the last coming first could not possibly apply in this case. The last and most needy would come last. The history of socialist thinking in Russia would from then on be largely the history of the attempts made by Russians to find an escape from the proposition apparently laid down by socialism's greatest figure: that for a country such as Russia the way to socialism lay through a great deal more pain and suffering, that things could not become better before they had become very much worse.

Those who came to be known as Mensheviks were least successful at avoiding Marxism's bleak implications. Socialist revolution, they admitted, could only be a remote prospect in Russia. The working class was so far small and lacking in socialist consciousness, while the peasants were not a genuine revolutionary force at all. Once the 1905 upheaval had failed to develop into a bourgeois revolution proper, the Mensheviks became more moderate still. Since the country was not yet ready even to clear this preliminary hurdle, the socialist revolution began to look to them very distant indeed. There would first have to be a great deal of economic, social and cultural development, during the course of which the darker aspects of the tsarist inheritance would be gradually eliminated. Meanwhile, all the Mensheviks could do was offer peaceful opposition and work with the more radical liberals. Some of them even gave up the belief in revolution altogether.

Ideas of a peaceful path to a socialism that did not differ drastically from existing society – a socialism that kept private property, classes and the state – were meanwhile catching on in the west. Such ideas, first preached by Eduard Bernstein, seemed to reflect the reality there. Capitalism was stabilizing itself; the gulf between the classes was narrowing; democratic institutions gave the previously disfranchised an effective means of bringing pressure on governments. In relatively cohesive societies in which rich, middling and poor were bonded by feelings of common citizenship, the idea of a peaceful path to socialism made sense. But Russia was not a cohesive society, and the gulf between the classes, already enormous, was growing wider. Reconciliation between the classes and the creation of a state that served the whole community were, in the Russian context, little more than a fantasy. Many Mensheviks, recognizing as much, held on to the idea of an eventual socialist revolution. Yet however revolutionary their doctrine, their reading of Marx forced them to curb their revolutionary instincts. This was not a time for heroics. And when tsarism collapsed in 1917, they would feel obliged to prop up the bourgeois government which succeeded it. They could as a result offer the masses no short-term alleviation whatever of their miseries. For the Mensheviks, revolutionary commitment in fact came a poor second to Marxism. It was left to the Bolsheviks to try to span the chasm which separated this backward and suffering society from Marxist socialism by means of a determined, organized, revolutionary assault.

3

What above all distinguished the Bolsheviks from the Mensheviks was their conviction that backwardness did not condemn Russia to a lengthy and painful period of waiting during which the conditions necessary for socialism would have to be allowed to ripen. Lenin was not in the least daunted by backwardness. A party of dedicated professional revolutionaries, tightly controlled and drilled in Marxism, could, he had decided, very largely make up for the mature revolutionary class which Russia so far lacked. Moreover, it was quite wrong to regard the masses of the people as hopelessly ill-prepared for socialism and unsuitable for revolutionary activity. The peasants in his view constituted a semi- or at least a potential proletariat, while the non-Russians, too, were natural material for the revolutionary cause. These two elements, which together made up the great bulk of the population, might not yet have achieved socialist consciousness, might not even have heard the word 'socialism'. But they were potentially socialist; and it only needed Bolshevik power and Bolshevik policies to turn latent socialism into active support for a socialist programme.

That said, Lenin took care to remain within the framework of Marxist orthodoxy. The next item on the agenda in backward Russia had of course to be the bourgeois, not the socialist, revolution. The bourgeois would, however, neither make nor benefit from 'their' revolution – they feared the masses, Lenin insisted, far more than they disliked the tsar. The revolution would in fact be made by and for the workers, though with the party playing a guiding or vanguard role in it. Lenin and the Bolsheviks thus came up with a bourgeois revolution that, far from being distanced from the socialist revolution, came uncannily close to it in time and in nature. And as things turned out, a mere eight months would elapse between the downfall of tsarism and the Bolshevik seizure of power in October 1917 on socialism's behalf.

The Bolsheviks thus rejected the pattern that Marx seemed to have envisaged for the west – of the bourgeois revolution giving rise to an initially stable bourgeois-dominated regime, under which the economic and other conditions necessary for socialism would be put in place. During 1917 and after it, the Bolsheviks acted on the assumption that in Russia things would have to be done the other way around. The socialist revolution, that is, the seizure of power by socialists, would have to come before the socio-economic and cultural transformation which, according to theory, should have preceded it. In Russia the socialist regime would itself create the conditions necessary for socialism rather than be created by them. Between the revolution and the achievement of socialism, there would, therefore, have to be a transition period of unpredictable length, during which the regime's first task would be to bring the country to the point of readiness for socialism which 'should' have been achieved under a bourgeois government.

The Bolsheviks' seizure of power in October 1917 as a result by no means fitted Marx's idea of a socialist revolution. That should have been a revolution of the masses in a society where capitalism had developed to the full and burned itself out. This was a seizure of power in a country in the early stages of capitalist development by a determined conspiratorial group with the support of a small working class but in the face of the indifference, and before long the active hostility, of the peasant masses. The prematurity of the Bolsheviks' action can be put down in part to impatience – their hunger for power had been sharpened by the incompetence and the unpopularity of the Provisional Government. But the Bolsheviks were more than power-hungry opportunists. Capitalism was in its death throes, Lenin had persuaded himself. And in war conditions so much economic power had been concentrated in the state that the infrastructure needed for the transition to socialism already in large part existed. Worldwide revolution was therefore imminent, but beginning it would be easiest where the capitalist system was at its most vulnerable – in Russia. The Bolsheviks were thus being offered an epochal opportunity, which it would be folly not to take advantage of. Socialism in the radical form they conceived it could not of course be achieved within the foreseeable future by the freely made decisions of the majority. (Lenin's contempt for socialists who let themselves be hobbled by democratic niceties was nothing less than scorching.) But it could be achieved if the enlightened few took decisive action *now*. The way forward in fact was to seize power and use it to reshape both material existence and popular consciousness, to impose, that is, the conditions under which the masses of the people would come sooner or later to a willing acceptance of socialism. Using state power to the utmost, the Bolsheviks would crush all resistance, expropriate the exploiters, create a political system based on the soviets, bring about a massive expansion of the economy, and by means of intensive socialist schooling reorientate the whole mental life of the nation. This was a staggeringly ambitious programme, but the Bolsheviks took power with immense confidence in their ability to carry it through.

Their confidence rested in part on the belief that they would not have to use naked force for very long. The new regime would be given a vast material and moral boost by the victory of socialism in the west. And it would soon elicit a surge of support from the grass roots of Russian society itself. Both of these optimistic assumptions proved to be mistaken, however. There was no socialist revolution in the west. Furthermore, the basis of solid minority support with which the Bolsheviks had begun soon crumbled away, and before long they had virtually the entire population against them. It was a situation that would have been unimaginable to Marx and which the Bolsheviks themselves could hardly have imagined prior to October: a government of Marxists, a government committed to socialism, being kept in power by force alone in the face of near-universal hostility. Yet force proved effective. And naturally enough the Bolsheviks used it not only for self-defence but for the cause that would soon, they were convinced, make force unnecessary – for socialism. If the masses would not willingly lay socialism's foundations, then they would have to do the work under duress.

The most striking case of socialist-oriented coercion came in agriculture. Socialists agreed, as we have seen, that there could be no socialism without communal cultivation of the soil – yet the peasants remained stubbornly wedded to individual farming. During the early Soviet period the Bolsheviks coerced and browbeat the peasants in various ways, but held back from trying to change the whole basis of agriculture. This was not a matter of principle; the task simply seemed beyond them. With NEP, from 1921, Lenin turned to a different approach and set the party on a course of positive conciliation of the peasantry. In 1929, however, Stalin began a programme of forced collectivization, which he pushed through with all the might of the party apparatus, the Red Army and the secret police. His reasoning was clear. Socialism required collectivized agriculture. Peasant shortsightedness was obstructing that and through it the whole socialist enterprise. Therefore the peasants would have to be coerced. It was a particularly brutal example of what had become the underlying Bolshevik thesis – that an ignorant people had to be made to accept changes to which they would never give their voluntary consent. These changes would transform life; before long, the peasants would sing the praises of those who had coerced them and see them as their benefactors.

Bolshevik strategy for the new society was guided of course by Marx, who had thought in terms of two post-revolutionary phases: a 'first' or 'lower' phase would lead on to 'the higher phase of communist society'.[3] Bolsheviks adopted Marx's distinction, but called the phases 'socialism' and 'communism'. In Soviet usage, therefore, 'socialism' indicated a transitional stage still marked by some features of the old society, as opposed to the fully realized new society or 'communism'. Not only did the Bolsheviks relabel the phases; they made far more of them than Marx had. Marx after all had believed that the socialist revolution would not occur until the conditions necessary for socialism already existed. On that reckoning, the transition from capitalism to the new society should have been fairly short. Force would have to be used in the early stages, but he seems to have assumed that any coercive measures applied would have the support of the overwhelming majority. The 'dictatorship of the proletariat', a phrase that would come to describe the iron rule of the Bolshevik elite, would therefore simply have been the dictatorship of the masses over the minority of former exploiters.

For the Bolsheviks, however, the transition was a vastly more important and more problematical matter. Having taken power so prematurely, they were obliged to insert into the scheme something Marx had in all probability not envisaged – a transition to the transition. They gave no particular name to this preliminary phase, perhaps because naming it would have been an admission that they were improvising. And they blurred the question of what exactly constituted socialism by describing Soviet society almost from the outset as a 'socialist society'. What Lenin for one meant by this was that it was a society aspiring towards socialism and preparing the ground for it. He certainly did not think of Soviet society as already having entered the socialist phase, as already living under socialism. That would not be achieved until the masses understood and willed it; it could only be the result of their own voluntary and informed commitment.

The distinction between 'socialist society' and 'society living under socialism' was, however, a fine one, and it proved very difficult to maintain. Having set democracy aside, the party had no way of justifying itself except by emphasizing its achievements as a creator of socialism. It had every incentive as a result to interpret 'socialist society' as a society that was not only en route to socialism but had already made giant strides towards it; and in the mid-1930s Stalin wiped the distinction out altogether when he declared that socialism had, basically, now been achieved in the Soviet Union. What in fact had been achieved was complete control by the state of the economy and all aspects of social life, and the elimination of any remaining elements of popular self-management and self-motivation. The pre-transition phase was thus, formally speaking, put behind; the country was now ready, or so it seemed, to begin the transition to communism. That, however, was very clearly far off, and no leader, apart from the imprudent Khrushchev, would make it sound at all close to realization. Communism as the party, keeping on the whole faithfully to Marx, interpreted it would of course be extremely difficult to achieve since it implied not only fundamental social change but a moral revolution as well. The party anyway had very little reason to hurry: the attainment of communism would after all bring its rule to an end, while failure to keep to any over-ambitious timetable for communism would embarrass and even discredit it. The optimal target-date for communism was some imprecise midway point between the utterly remote and the fairly near future; and there the communist goal remained, an increasingly implausible spectre on an ever-receding horizon, until the whole Soviet enterprise was finally abandoned.

4

At this point something more needs to be said about the relationship between socialism and communism. For Marx, these had been the successive and closely linked phases of a single 'formation'. The difference between them was of degree rather than kind; the second would simply be a more highly developed, a perfected, version of the first. That was how Lenin understood the relationship, and that was how it continued to be presented in Marxist-Leninist ideology: communism would grow naturally and more or less imperceptibly out of socialism, without any break or disruption. During the pre-transition, however, Soviet society had acquired a character very different from its intended communist culmination. The dictatorship of the proletariat had become in effect the dictatorship of the party over the rest of society. All rival organizations and voices had been silenced; even within the party itself democracy was extinguished and the rank-and-file were required to give unquestioning obedience to the leadership. That was understandable enough in conditions of civil war. Yet once the war had been won, controls had been further tightened rather than eased. With the formal achievement of socialism in the mid-1930s, one might have expected that the state would at last begin to 'wither away'. Quite the contrary: Stalin found pretexts to make it more pervasive and more powerful still. Life without a state and without 'bossing' thus remained as remote from the Soviet citizen as the rainbow; and even the ordinary freedoms of life in a bourgeois society were denied to him.

Equality suffered similarly. Naturally enough it was declared an aim – with the rider that full equality could not be achieved until communism. Inequality of material conditions nevertheless persisted; and under Stalin, who attacked the equalizing tendency as unMarxist, the inequality became much more pronounced. Moreover, during the 1930s a new, highly privileged ruling class emerged, which was rewarded for its services to the Leader much as the old ruling class had been rewarded by the tsar (though unlike the old ruling class it was also subject to the ravages of the purges). The equality the mass of Soviet citizens enjoyed was thus an equality of material deprivation rather than of abundance, an equality of helplessness before the powerful, an equality of exclusion from the elite and the decision-making process.

The socialism which had been created on Soviet soil did not therefore point towards a communist fulfilment, and if anything pointed *away* from it. This was a socialism which reflected more of the Russian past than it anticipated of the communist future. It had little or nothing in common with the equality and freedom of communism and could hardly prepare the way for them. Socialism and communism, intended to be consecutive phases, the twin parts of a seamless single formation, had been turned in effect into polar opposites. And if the two were linked, it was not by their common qualities but rather by their differences – the idyll of an equally shared abundance and a life without external constraints acted in a sense as a psychological compensation for the privations and the repression of everyday existence. Before the revolution, many ordinary Russians had been consoled in their wretchedness by the dream of an entirely different order of things; after it, the hardships of life were made more bearable by an assiduously promoted vision of a new world that lay on the horizon – and would always remain beyond reach.

Yet the original Bolsheviks had not been hypocrites and Machiavels – Lenin most certainly had not been. They were, with exceptions, dedicated Marxist socialists who had devoted their lives to realizing Marx's vision. However, they had been driven by the logic of their situation as Russians, or so it seemed to them, into making their revolution prematurely, and they accepted as an unavoidable evil the difficult and unpredictable road to socialism that lay ahead of them. They had armed themselves with beliefs appropriate to their task – the vanguard party, the dictatorship of the proletariat, the absolute, scientific correctness of the truths they stood for. There would be no room in the Bolshevik state for diversity of opinion or for creative opposition, even if it came from a socialist standpoint. Having taken power by force, the Bolsheviks would rule by force. Faced with an ignorant and hostile population, they would impose all the changes necessary for socialism. The bottom line, of course, was that they would relinquish power once the masses proved ready for it. In the meanwhile, socialism was being grafted onto the tsarist heritage, and socialist enlightenment was mingling with the darkness it was intended to disperse.

The Bolsheviks, needless to say, rejected that heritage. They were democrats (after their own fashion), they were rationalists and enlighteners, they were internationalists; and they saw their task as nothing less than the creation of a worldwide socialist community in whose Russian part almost nothing that had been thought of as characteristically Russian would remain. But faced with the unexpected hostility of a population whose potential for socialism they had grossly overrated, they were forced to act like traditional Russian rulers, crushing any flicker of resistance to their dictates. They could not even begin to accomplish their task, in fact, unless they, a tiny minority, imposed themselves and trampled, or seemed to trample, upon the very principles that guided them. They were as a result caught within the paradox that the ends they willed could not be achieved except by means that directly flouted those ends. Their dictatorship could indeed be justified on Marxist grounds, but the sustained dictatorship of a handful over the vast majority was incompatible with any notion of socialism, Marxist or otherwise. Hoist on the petard of their own overweening ambition, how could the Bolsheviks extricate themselves? The way they found out of their difficulty – and the only realistic alternative to surrender – was to acculturate. By the early 1930s, they had come up with a model of socialism that was more or less perfectly adapted to the environment. The autocratic state had now taken on a distinctly patriarchal form; Stalin was a father to his people, and one who interceded more vigorously against their enemies than any tsar ever had. Traditional collectivism had been strongly reinforced, and the dominance of group interests over individual ones was more explicitly justified than ever before. Anyone who threatened group solidarity by striking out on a line of thought or action of his own was now in danger of being denounced – and punished severely – as an enemy. Christianity had more or less gone, but a surrogate faith had replaced it; life in the atheist Soviet state had taken on a quasi-religious character, with ornate rituals, solemn liturgical incantations, feast days, promises of a secular heaven and hell, and a morality almost Manichean in its black-and-whiteness. Bolshevik internationalism had, moreover, gone the way of Bolshevik democratism and rationalism. The task of creating socialism in a hostile capitalist environment, of defending the fortress of socialist virtue against external enemies (and internal traitors), of setting an example which the so-called advanced countries would one day follow – all of this flattered the patriotism which the Bolsheviks' original internationalism had so badly wounded and stirred anti-westernism and even a certain national messianism.

Yet in time Stalin's heavily russified socialism would fall victim to its own success as a modernizing agent. It would become decreasingly effective as a system for stimulating economic growth; it would also, for a significant section of the population, become culturally outdated. Modifications were made under Khrushchev and Brezhnev, but they failed to change the basic structures and values of Stalinist socialism. By the 1980s it had developed into a crushing economic liability. It had become an anachronism in a society that had left its peasant origins behind, was now preponderantly urban and well-educated, and had a sizeable sector that approximated to a middle class. Moreover, its claims to be a genuine socialism had been quietly disputed for some time by a considerable body of intellectuals, who believed that the country had abandoned the true socialist path at the end of the 1920s. It was against this background that Mikhail Gorbachev and a motley coalition of reformers began their attempt to create a new socialism with its roots in Bolshevism's pre-Stalinist traditions, a socialism that was culturally de-russified, economically productive and democratic. They would 'go back to Lenin'; and the great perestroika reform began as a revival, after years of neglect, of the Leninist heritage.

5

Going back to Lenin – what a strange idea! Had Lenin in the meanwhile disappeared from sight? Not at all. The Soviet citizen had lived under his more or less permanent gaze, and no significant transaction, public or private, had taken place without him. This Lenin, the Lenin of official propaganda, the Lenin on plinths, had been awesome in his power and his intellect. His clenched fist and jutting chin had warned that the party – *his* party – would not tolerate the slightest flicker of opposition. However, there was also another Lenin, very different from this all-conquering and omniscient icon: an unofficial, even underground, Lenin not known at all to the general public, yet familiar and important to intellectuals who questioned the regime's socialist pretensions. It was this Lenin that the reformers would go back to.

This was not the Lenin whose furious impatience had driven the Bolsheviks to seize power in October 1917, nor the ruthless strategist who had enabled them to survive the battles of 1918–20. The Lenin who mattered to the regime's critics had been seen most clearly during the months before his death when, brooding on his life's work, acutely aware of the new society's failings, he had written the pieces that would become known as his 'political testament'.[4] It was not, however, only the dying Lenin that the critics went back to. They focused on a side of his political personality that had tended to look beyond *realpolitik*, beyond the acts of repression and compromise made necessary by the country's unreadiness for socialism and its hostility to Bolshevik rule. This Lenin had been troubled by the discrepancy between socialist ideals and Soviet reality. He had never let go of his conviction that socialism could not be created by decree, that it could only be brought about by the willing and informed efforts of a people that desired it. With NEP, his idea of cultural revolution and his new approach to the nationalities he had grappled with the basic problem of the revolution – the need to end the alienation between party and masses and to create between them a genuine accord based on a common commitment to socialism. By wiping that problem from the political agenda, subsequent regimes had put socialism proper beyond reach. And there lay the fateful appeal of Lenin to upholders of what this book will call the Alternative Tradition. For their Lenin, a Lenin freed, as they supposed, from regime-serving distortions, a Lenin who had fought with considerable success to resolve the contradictions of the revolution – this Lenin could still inspire a reorientation that would save the socialist experiment in Russia. And thus the ground was prepared for the denouement of the tragedy.

6

The collapse of the Soviet state of course provided historians with a marvellous vantage point from which to view the whole experiment. And the finale naturally encouraged those who saw the experiment as having been fundamentally flawed and doomed from the outset. If things had gone that badly wrong, they were surely bound to have gone wrong; the tragic course and the denouement were due not to accident but to intrinsic design faults – to some 'original sin'. Among the works that adopted such an approach, two were of especial importance: Martin Malia's *The Soviet Tragedy* and Andrzej Walicki's *Marxism and the Leap to the Kingdom of Freedom*.[5] Each was written with the certainty and the judgementalism which came naturally to western commentators in the wake of the Soviet collapse; and each was in its way a masterpiece. Walicki's stood out as a work of magisterial scholarship, while Malia's was a literary tour de force which will live on as a monument to an era and a cast of mind long after its usefulness as a reading of the Soviet experiment has evaporated. Both were exercises in intellectual history, and both were inspired by the same underlying thesis: that the Soviet tragedy had to be understood as the product not so much of Russia's backwardness or of its peculiar political culture as of the destructive effects of Marxist ideology. The aims of Marx's socialism, the authors argued, were not only unrealizable but self-contradictory, since the pursuit of freedom and equality as Marx envisaged them required suppression of the market, of private property, and of civil society itself. The Bolsheviks were, as a result, the prisoners of an illusion whose inevitable outcome was unremitting coercion, suffering for the vast majority and the ultimate collapse of the whole experiment. The failure of socialism in Russia, as Malia put it, 'stems not from its having been tried out first in the wrong place, Russia, but from the socialist idea per se'.[6]

This, then, was an interpretation that pinpointed coercion as the mainspring of the Soviet endeavour. Coercion, both authors insisted, flowed logically from the 'ideocratic' essence of the system – from the regime's commitment, that is, to the secular theology of Marxism. The Marxist-Leninist enterprise was 'inherently impossible'; attempts to realize it had therefore to rest upon 'the massive application of force'; such an application could only produce 'a preposterous surreality'. The Soviet experiment, Malia declared, turned totalitarian 'not *despite* its being socialist but *because* it was socialist'.[7] The system could not in consequence tolerate any reforms that might jeopardize the party dictatorship. As for the belief that Marxism-Leninism might be reconciled with democracy, that was a flight of fancy with no foothold in reality.

All of this did not rule out the possibility that party members might be led astray by a false understanding of the system and might at times even struggle against the 'logic' of the system. Lenin and Gorbachev could both, in their different ways, be taken as exemplifying such struggle. These rebellions, however, either were no more than superficially radical and in essence still conformed to the system (Malia's and Walicki's interpretations of Lenin's), or else they broke the bounds of the system altogether (Walicki's interpretation of Gorbachev, whom he saw as leading 'a true "moral revolution" ... not only an antitotalitarian but also an anticommunist revolution'[8]). What neither historian would allow was the existence of a serious and sustained reformist tendency. This created an especial problem in the case of Lenin, given the powerful fascination his 'last struggle' and 'testament' have exercised for posterity. If the leader's final thoughts were not only unradical but confused and even 'pitiful', as Malia argued, then the 'fetishization' of his ending was not easy to explain, could only indeed be written off as 'bizarre'.[9]

There had of course, the authors allowed, been reformist attempts, periodic bouts of 'soft communism'. Malia for one went so far as to take from Moshe Lewin, the outstanding historian of Soviet reformism, the idea of Soviet history as a series of alternating episodes, a 'two-act play'.[10] In Malia's hands, however, the 'two-act' approach yielded an interpretation wholly different in spirit from Lewin's. The bouts of 'soft communism' (NEP, Khrushchev, perestroika) appeared as short-lived reactions against the more brutal exigencies of the system on the part of people who continued to accept its essence, whereas for Lewin the reforming aspiration was not simply a within-system response to the fundamental Soviet prototype but had reflected an alternative vision of a libertarian, pluralistic, market-based socialism with roots not only in the writings of Marx, Engels and Lenin but also in the early practices of the Soviet regime itself.

What, then, was missing from these monumental obituaries of the Soviet experience was the Alternative Tradition, those generations of reform communists who saw Stalinism as a perversion of socialism and honoured, and no doubt idealized, Lenin for his attempt to forestall it. The reform communists were, admittedly, few in number and mistaken in their assumptions, yet without them and their illusions we cannot explain where the perestroika movement came from and why, before crashing to defeat, it scored such stunning successes. For the Soviet system was brought down by more than those who rejected or cynically exploited it, and by more than the ongoing process of its own decomposition. The collapse was precipitated by the triumph of a reformist coalition inspired and validated by Lenin's last-gasp rethinking, which would challenge and rapidly dispossess the party dictatorship in the name of a socialism that was held to be truly socialist precisely *because* it was democratic. The October revolution would be brought to fulfilment by democracy, plan and market would be reconciled, Soviet socialism would be saved by the realization of its democratic potential – these were the myths of perestroika. The reformers got it wrong and by attempting to achieve real socialism simply destroyed the travesty, but without them the course of history would have been other than what it was.

1

Before Lenin

1

Socialism in Russia began with Alexander Herzen, who escaped from Russia in 1847 to seek revolution in the west but in exile discovered the socialist potential of the country he had left behind. Herzen had all the makings, it might have seemed, of a liberal. Nearly all his friends were from the liberal cultural elite. He himself had strongly libertarian convictions. It was to be free and to fight for freedom for others that he had left Russia and would suffer the miseries of permanent exile. For all that, Alexander Herzen emerged not as a liberal but as a socialist who fiercely assailed liberalism and the bourgeois civilization it upheld. And yet his socialist beliefs were significantly different from those of his great contemporary, Karl Marx. They were to be the source of the distinctively Russian socialism which became known as 'populism'.

It was Herzen who worked out populism's basic ideas. He rejected the path of capitalist, industrial development being followed in the west and argued that Russia's very backwardness would enable it to take a quicker and less painful route to socialism. He poured scorn on the idea of a bourgeois-dominated liberal state as a necessary preliminary to socialism – such a state could only perpetuate the existing evils of society and postpone a socialist solution to them. These passionate repudiations led on, however, to a passionate positive assertion. Russia, Herzen insisted, could create a socialist society in its own way out of its own resources. It would do this thanks to the village community, which had instilled a socialist outlook into the peasants and safeguarded them from influences that would have made socialism far more difficult to achieve.

These were to be the guiding ideas of most Russian revolutionaries until the 1880s. Elements in them would remain an inspiration for many revolutionaries until the October Revolution. All would be rejected by Russian Marxists as romantic, unscientific nonsense. They would nevertheless exercise a powerful, if subliminal, influence on those among the Russian Marxists who eventually took power in Russia and set the country on course towards socialism.

Herzen's originality lay in his rejection of the assumption, made by almost all previous Russian radicals, that if Russia was to achieve a better life, it had to follow in the footsteps of the west. Those deviations from the western pattern which others bemoaned as backwardness, as something shameful, he by contrast held up as an asset. Russia did indeed have no large manufacturing towns – but who would want to live in smoke-ridden, inhuman London, the city of his exile? Was London with all its miseries really an acceptable model for the future of mankind? Russia was equally fortunate to have been spared the bourgeoisie, that rapacious and philistine class which in 1848 had ridden to power over the bodies of the socialists. Herzen savaged the bourgeois with a mixture of aristocratic contempt and radical venom, and he exulted in their absence from Russia. 'We are not bourgeois,' he insisted, ' we are peasants. We are poor in towns and rich in villages.'[1] As a peasant people untouched by bourgeois civilization, the Russians were lucky enough not to be shackled by the mental fetters which constrained the peoples of the west. They were not held back by any sense of legal propriety – the rule of law meant nothing to them. Nor were they deterred by any property consciousness, since they neither desired property for themselves nor respected property rights in others.

The advantages supposedly conferred by capitalist development and bourgeois domination were , or so Herzen preached, in reality the very opposite – major obstacles to the attainment of socialism. And so with a deft flick he turned the Marxist approach upside down. Socialism would come in Russia as a result not of development but of backwardness, not of economic advance and modernization but of peasant misery and pre-capitalist communalism. The last would come first; Russia would get to socialism by a better path, a path of its own, a path which its alleged disadvantages alone would make possible. The attitude was expressed in a nutshell by Nikolai Chernyshevsky, the other major figure in early Russian socialism, when he remarked that history was rather like a granny – it was 'terribly fond of its grandchildren'.[2]

The belief that Russia might leap ahead of the west, that it was a young and fresh country with a future rather than an exhausted one living off the glories of its past, that the very miseries of its history indicated the likelihood of a brilliant consummation – all this had a galvanizing effect on Russian radicals. Later ones were, admittedly, more respectful towards Marx than Herzen had been. *Capital* was even published to acclaim in Russia in 1872 (having been let through rather surprisingly by the censors, who took the view that it was too dryly scientific and too irrelevant to Russian conditions to cause mischief). What his Russian admirers saw Marx as depicting, however, was a capitalist hell, a contemporary inferno, which Russia could and therefore should make every effort to avoid.

In rejecting capitalism the populists of course rejected the liberal-capitalist state with its beguiling rights and freedoms. They did so categorically. Many went so far as to regard the autocracy as a lesser evil than its liberal alternative. Why so? Because the autocracy by its very conservatism and ineffectiveness acted as a brake on developments that could only make socialism more difficult to achieve. For populists, the liberal state was a fine-looking facade, which masked bourgeois domination and exploitation of the masses. Like Marx, they saw liberalism as a means of legitimizing bourgeois power and perpetuating social inequality; where they differed from him was in denying that the liberal state was a necessary stage on the way to socialism and therefore, for all its evils, an advance over absolutism. The only acceptable progression, for the populists, was from the autocracy straight to socialism, bypassing the liberal stage altogether.

But there were other reasons, too, for the populists' attitude – among them, a sense of guilt. Many came, like Herzen, from the landowning class, from what would become known as the 'conscience-stricken gentry'. The values and tastes that made freedom matter to them they saw as a product of their privileged upbringing and education, which the peasants had paid for with their sweat and blood. To fight for a parliament and civil liberties would be to put their own refined, and perhaps over-refined, needs before those of the masses – it would be simply immoral. Nikolai Mikhailovsky spoke for many when he said: 'We renounce the increase of our rights and our freedoms, since we see these rights as instruments for the exploitation of the people and the multiplication of our sins.'[3] Peasants needed bread and decent living conditions, not paper rights and a parliamentary talking-shop which would merely inflict further hardships upon them and postpone still further the day of their liberation.

Behind the populists' rejection of the liberal, capitalist path lay their desire to link up with the peasant world from which their ancestors had cut them off. Deeply national, if not nationalist, in outlook, they set the western model aside because it seemed an irrelevance or even an obstacle to the task that mattered to them – building an integrated national community. Russia could regenerate itself out of its own resources, out of traditions created by its people over the centuries; it did not need, and might be damaged by, any imposition of ideas and ways of life from the west. Attempts to fit Russia to the western pattern would anyway, populists persuaded themselves, be futile. Herzen's most devastating blow against his Russian liberal friends was to remark that the tsar's persecution of liberalism had been superfluous. In Russia, he insisted, liberalism was an 'exotic flower' which would never take root, 'being quite alien to the national character'.[4]

There was, however, an element of paradox about the populists' contempt for parliaments and civil liberties. Not being able to say, read, write and do what they wanted was of course a cruel deprivation for them. Nowhere else in Europe was the freedom of the individual so flouted; nowhere else, one might have thought, would the educated have clamoured so much for it. And Herzen for one drew a sharp line between the liberal state he detested and freedom of the individual, which for him was a sacred principle underlying all his endeavours. 'The liberty of the individual is the greatest thing of all', he believed, 'and it is on this alone that the will of the people can develop.' It was a recurring lament of his that in Russia the individual had 'always been sacrificed to some social concept, some collective noun, some banner or other'. Moreover, he had bleak forebodings of what might happen to freedom in a post-revolutionary, peasant-dominated Russia. It was only the few, not the masses, who desired freedom. What the masses loved was authority, what they wanted was a government that acted on their behalf. 'To govern themselves doesn't enter their heads.'[5] The commune, he saw clearly enough, had repressed individuality rather than fostered it; what peasants understood by equality was simply 'equality of oppression'. He even had a prophetic nightmare of 'new barbarians' sweeping to power with the support of the masses, wiping out not only the bad but the good, and crushing freedom more effectively than before. Yet if Russia had failed to solve the problem of reconciling the needs of the social whole with those of the individual, so too had the west, which had approached the problem from the other end and in effect sacrificed the community to the appetites of a greedy few. The hope Herzen clung to was that in a post-revolutionary Russia these conflicting needs could somehow be reconciled within a renovated commune.

That, however, was no more than a pious hope, and Herzen could never quell his fears that communal life would destroy freedom rather than enhance it. During the revolutionary upsurge of the 1870s, many populists got around the problem by believing that they had to shed not only their privileges but some of the refined tastes and cultural needs they had developed as a result of privilege. Rapprochement with the peasants was the necessity of the moment; that might lead in time to a shared new outlook in which their individualism and the peasants' communalism would be synthesized. A few went further still, rejected the very idea of individuality, and insisted on the need for intellectual as well as socio-economic levelling – the complete subordination of the individual to the social whole. Herzen might have had some sympathy for the first approach, but he would have had none at all for the second. Freedom was vital to him; he would not have accepted a counterfeit, still less have agreed to its destruction for some supposed greater social good. Yet he had rejected the one sure way of preserving freedom – the institutions of the liberal state – as both immoral and impossible. The future of Russia, for better or worse, lay with the muzhik. And mostly for better. The peasant commune might have serious flaws, as he, Chernyshevsky and others pointed out, yet it lay at the heart of populism's great affirmation – that the Russians were already in essence a socialist people, that out of their own resources they could create a fully socialist society.

It was not Herzen who first 'discovered' the remarkable features of the commune. The discovery had been made by a Prussian conservative, Baron Haxthausen, who caused an enormous stir just before Herzen left Russia by publishing a study which praised the commune as a unique institution whose egalitarian and collectivist features would protect the country from the social upheavals afflicting the west.[6] It was Herzen, however, who first put a radical gloss upon the commune ; far from safeguarding the existing order, he suggested, it was a time-bomb ticking away underneath it and preparing an utterly different future. The commune had saved the Russian people – saved them from the Mongols, the landowners, the bureaucrats and, above all, from the institution of private property. What mattered most about it was the distribution and periodic redistribution of land according to need. Thanks to that, the Russians were 'primarily a socialist people'. Thus the aristocrat looked from his distant exile at the peasant village he would never see again.

Nikolai Chernyshevsky, a humble priest's son who was able to study the commune from close quarters, took a less idealized view of it. Communal tenure was, he admitted, more primitive than the private ownership of land which had replaced it elsewhere in Europe. And he anticipated – and influenced – Marx's later thinking about the commune by insisting that communal tenure of the land was by no means enough for socialism: nothing less than communal *cultivation* of the land would raise productivity to the level necessary for general wellbeing. Chernyshevsky was nevertheless confident that the positive features in the commune would get the better of the negative ones; thanks to them, Russia would take its own, distinctive path to socialism. This was to be the fundamental belief of a generation of Russian revolutionaries, and it would not be seriously questioned until the 1880s.

2

The peasants, then, were socialist by instinct, even if they had never heard the word 'socialism'. They might idealize the tsar, but they hated the landowners; and they felt cheated by the 1861 emancipation, which had left most of them worse off in material terms than before. All that was needed to unleash them as a revolutionary force, or so it seemed, was to turn their latent socialism into a conscious belief. That might well, some populists warned, require a lengthy process of education. There were, however, two strong arguments against delay. One, which gained in urgency as the 1870s went on, was that backwardness was a diminishing asset. The regime was still 'hanging in the air', with little or no support outside the landowning class. But the country was changing fast; capitalism was penetrating in the wake of the railways; before long, the regime might have a solid foundation of bourgeois support. Time was therefore not on the revolutionaries' side. Moreover, ignorant though the peasants might be, they were clearly ripe for revolution. They merely needed to be told the plain truth about how badly they were treated and how much better they would live under socialism. And in this belief thousands of young radicals scattered among the villages of Russia in the mid-1870s with the aim of inciting the peasants to revolution.

The 'movement to the people' failed dismally, however. The peasants turned out to be indifferent if not hostile towards their would-be liberators; there were even cases of them handing young radicals over to the police. The gulf in mentality between the two sides seemed unbridgeable. And the one revolt which did get off the ground merely underlined how great the gulf was, since in this case the peasants had been stirred to action by a fabricated charter in which they had been urged to revolt against the lords by, of all people, the tsar himself!

The failure of the 'movement to the people' forced a fundamental rethink. The belief that the people were ripe for revolution, that with a little prodding they would rise up and free themselves, had been exposed as wishful thinking. The idea of a grass-roots revolution had, temporarily at least, to be ruled out. If there could not be a revolution from below, then there would have to be one from above; if the people could not free themselves, then the enlightened few would have to free them. What this suggested was that the peasant masses could not be made socialist without a preliminary strike – without a revolution carried out for them by the handful who were already socialist.

Even before the fiasco of the 'movement to the people', some radicals had pooh-poohed the idea of a popular revolution in which the educated minority played no more than an auxiliary role. Revolution, Peter Tkachev for one had insisted, could only be made by a dedicated and professional minority; it required not only socialist consciousness but organization, discipline, hierarchy and subordination. More than that: once successful, the conspirators would have to use their power ruthlessly. Seizing power would in fact be relatively easy, provided the revolutionaries acted before the bourgeois had entrenched themselves. The real revolution, however, would consist in the socio-economic, political and cultural transformation which followed the take-over; and that the masses would at first neither welcome nor understand.

Doubts about the people's capacity to make a revolution thus led on to an elitist-authoritarian radicalism, such as practised during the French Revolution by the Jacobins. Tkachev was by no means a pioneer in this respect: the Jacobin case had been argued in Russia half a century earlier by Pavel Pestel. It was no good, Pestel had urged his fellow conspirators, to overthrow the autocracy only to replace it by a liberal political system which featherbedded the landed classes. What was vital was to keep the traditional powers of the Russian state but use them for quite new – and radical – purposes. There could be no social justice in Russia without a lengthy and profound transformation, which could only be pushed through by a dictatorship – by a small group of zealots working in accordance with a carefully detailed blueprint. Such thinking, while undoubtedly influenced by Jacobinism, also owed much to Russia's own political inheritance. Power in Russia would still be absolute and unaccountable if the Jacobins got their way. The difference was that from now on the government's immense power would be used on behalf of the masses.

Tkachev's views were too extreme to win much support in a

movement that still believed in a revolution made not only for but by the people. By now, however, many accepted that only revolutionaries acting decisively at the centre could get the revolutionary process going , and this shift towards Jacobinism was reflected in the creation, in 1879, of a formidable new organization. The People's Will began from the assumption that revolution could be instigated only by dedicated professionals organized in a party that was tightly disciplined and controlled by a small executive committee. Previous populist groups had insisted as a matter of principle that all members should be treated as equal. The People's Will discarded this principle as unworkable. Its leaders were not democratically elected and they acted in secrecy even from their own members. The immediate aim of the organization was to precipitate a coup d'état by assassinating Tsar Alexander II.

Once the coup had succeeded, the People's Will would have moved quickly to obtain a popular mandate, and it would have arranged the election, by universal suffrage, of a constituent assembly. The leaders intended to campaign vigorously in the election, and they counted upon obtaining overwhelming endorsement of their socialist programme. But what if they failed to get it? Tkachev, for one, had cast serious doubt on whether the masses were socialist-minded yet; so too, from a very different standpoint, had a leading anti-Jacobin, Georgy Plekhanov. Should the electors rebuff it, would the People's Will accept their verdict and retire to the sidelines? Or would its leaders then decide to act in the 'best interests' of the masses and to guide them firmly towards the socialism they needed but were not yet mature enough to want? Almost certainly the latter, said Plekhanov. The attempt at revolution would in fact probably miscarry, he guessed. But a successful coup d'état could not be ruled out; and should the conspirators manage to seize power, then their lack of popular support would force them to impose a dictatorship.

The dictatorship of a few on behalf of a socialism which the majority of the population did not yet appreciate was still, as it happened, some decades away (though Plekhanov, to whom this way of achieving socialism was abhorrent, would experience it during the final months of his life). In March 1881 the People's Will carried out the first part of its project when it succeeded in assassinating Alexander II. Its terrorist act led, however, not to revolution but to the triumph of reaction, much as Plekhanov had predicted. The new ruler, Alexander III, tougher and more conservative than his father, clamped down savagely, despatched five leading conspirators to the gallows, and within a short time appeared to have crushed the revolutionary movement completely.

3

The disaster of March 1881 seemed to vindicate those who, like Plekhanov, considered that Russia was not yet ripe for revolution and that premature attempts would be counter-productive. Revolution could be made only by the masses and only when they were ready and willing for it. Until such time, revolutionaries would have to content themselves with preparatory work.

So far most of them had been spurred on by the belief that delay would only increase the difficulty of making a revolution. March 1881, however, simply confirmed Plekhanov's belief that delay was vital, that without it there could be no revolution. In the wake of the disaster he and his group had in fact shaken off their fear of capitalism, their belief in a special, non-capitalist path for Russia, and gone over to Marxism. Russia, Plekhanov argued, had now embarked fully on the path of capitalist development, and that path would in time create the conditions necessary for socialism. True, socialist revolution in Russia was still a distant prospect: what lay immediately ahead was the bourgeois revolution, which would destroy tsarism and greatly speed up capitalist development. But if the Marxist path was slow, it was also sure; and Plekhanov for one took comfort from the image of the Marxist as one who had boarded 'the train of history' and knew that he was travelling as fast as possible in the correct direction.[7]

Plekhanov would go down as the 'father' of Russian Marxism, and for the rest of his life he would stoutly defend Marxist orthodoxy against attempts to dilute or distort it. Yet he had by no means given up the principles that had underpinned his earlier revolutionary activity. As a populist he had stood out against 'voluntarism' – the belief that heroic assertion by individuals could help a society to leap over otherwise necessary stages of development. Marxism simply confirmed and deepened his resistance to the voluntarists. As a populist he had similarly stood out against what would become known as 'substitutionism' – the idea that a person or group could temporarily substitute for and act on behalf of a class or a whole nation. That, too, he continued to oppose as vigorously as before. Socialism was impossible without an advanced working class, a proletariat. 'Such a proletariat', he insisted, '*will not allow* even the sincerest of its well-wishers to seize power.'[8] Socialist revolution, in short, could be made only by the masses, not by a handful of revolutionaries on the masses' behalf.

Despite being a gradualist and an opponent of revolutionary hotheads, Plekhanov by no means took a purely passive attitude towards the unfolding of events. History might be moving towards socialism, but there was everything to be said for giving it a push. The more Marxists could do to advance the cause, the better. In *The Communist Manifesto* Marx and Engels had, after all, emphasized the theoretical and practical contribution which could be made by an advanced group of communists, presumably of intelligentsia background, who 'have over the great mass of the proletariat the advantage of clearly understanding the line of march, the conditions, and the ultimate general results of the proletarian movement'.[9] Marx had, however, said very little more about what this nucleus of advanced workers should do. They would clearly have an educational and inspirational role, and they would coordinate the proletarians' efforts. In 1864 he had been a moving force behind the creation of the First International, with which he hoped to spread class warfare and so speed the coming of socialism.Yet whatever exactly the minority of initiates would do, Marx took it for granted that the breakthrough to socialism could not occur until the proletariat constituted the overwhelming majority of the population. And in the 1890s Engels hammered home the point that socialism would be achieved only when the proletarian masses had become consciously involved in the struggle for it.[10]

In late nineteenth-century Russia, however, 80 per cent or more of the people were peasants. A majority of urban workers was still a distant prospect, and a majority of workers committed to the struggle for socialism a yet more remote prospect. There was even uncertainty about the next item on the agenda, the bourgeois revolution. For the Russian bourgeoisie was not only puny in size: it was timid, deeply divided, and had so far shown very little political muscle. It included skilled professionals who were badly hampered by the lack of civil liberties, yet many of these were state employees and so inhibited from opposition of any kind; and among those who were not, few went beyond modest requests for reform. As for businessmen and entrepreneurs, who might have been expected to spearhead the middle class's advance, they were relatively few and most were either politically apathetic or deeply attached to traditional values and institutions and fiercely hostile to anything that smacked of the west.

This inadequacy of the middle class forced Plekhanov to improvise.

The bourgeois revolution would have to be made not by the bourgeois but by the proletariat. Socialists and liberals would join together in a common struggle against the autocracy, but it was the urban workers who would actually overthrow it. Having handed power to the bourgeois, the workers would then retire to the sidelines – until the socialist revolution itself appeared.

That seemed a neat enough solution to the problem, yet developments during the final years of the century raised a question-mark against this idea of bourgeois revolution made by the proletariat. In its favour was the regime's crash industrialization policy and a consequent massive influx into the towns. By the beginning of the twentieth century, rather more than three million people worked in manufacturing, mining and the railways, and most of them lived in conditions of wretchedness unmatched in western Europe since the early years of the Industrial Revolution. Here, then, at last, was a proletariat, the lack of which had made Marx's socialism-via-capitalism thesis seem irrelevant to earlier Russian revolutionaries. It mattered, too, that this new working class was still closely linked to the peasant masses, and that they – more than 100 million strong – were no longer sunk in the apathy of the 1870s. For most peasants, living standards had steadily worsened since the emancipation; land hunger, if not actual hunger, was by now making peasant Russia desperate. The upshot was that end-of-the-century Russia was very clearly a society in crisis. The impending revolution did not, however, look like being a bourgeois revolution, even in the amended form of it envisaged by Plekhanov. The situation emerging in Russia appeared in fact not to fit conventional Marxist thinking at all. A belated and timid middle class which was unable to carry through its own revolution was looking over its shoulder with increasing apprehension at its supposed working-class allies. The workers, on their side, were by now too numerous, too desperate in their misery, too radical and too imbued with class-hatred to be willing instruments of a revolution that, in the short term at least, would benefit their masters rather than themselves.

Russia thus found itself in a situation that was in some respects premature for the bourgeois revolution and yet in other respects had already passed the point when it seemed feasible or appropriate: the time in fact was from the point of view of Marxist orthodoxy thoroughly out of joint. For even if the bourgeois revolution could be made by others on the bourgeoisie's behalf, it had without any doubt to be made *for* the bourgeois. A bourgeois revolution would give the bourgeois the rights and the political control which the autocracy had so far denied them; and it would grant them these benefits at the expense of the revolution's actual makers, who in conditions of fast developing capitalism would sink into still greater misery.

What this prospect suggested was that the bourgeois revolution had to be fundamentally rethought, if it was not to be discarded altogether. In a country where, for most people, conditions were already terrible and were tending to become worse, the idea of using the masses as a battering ram against tsarism and then heaping further burdens upon them made little sense. Could Russia really not get to socialism without passing through a stage which, conceived in these terms, seemed utterly inappropriate to it?

4

Karl Marx, strangely enough, had late in life come round to the conclusion that quite possibly it could. Until about 1870 he had taken a fairly contemptuous view of Russia, but he had then 'discovered' the country and for the rest of his life he had remained fascinated by it. What attracted him above all in his new field of study was the village community, and he began to play with the idea that, thanks to it, Russia might skip much of the capitalist stage and go direct to socialism. But did not his own *Capital*, a Russian reader enquired, make it clear that 'it is historically necessary for every country in the world to pass through all the stages of capitalist production?' Not so, Marx replied: the inevitability of capitalist development was 'expressly restricted to the countries of western Europe'. The commune might even turn out to be 'the fulcrum for social regeneration in Russia'.[11] True, its potentially socialist features were disintegrating under the impact of capitalism. The commune was in fact 'at its last gasp'. However, one thing – though only one – could still save it as a source of social regeneration. 'To save the Russian commune,' Marx declared, 'there must be a Russian Revolution.'[12]

Not only did Marx long for a Russian revolution. By the end of the 1870s he had convinced himself that one was about to break out – and become a fervent supporter of The People's Will. The revolution he now anticipated would, however, be utterly different from the bourgeois revolution of orthodox Marxism. Far from accelerating bourgeois-capitalist development, the coming upheaval would actually stave off a capitalist regime, and its effect would be to propel Russia in the direction of socialism.

It would of course be a long leap from this impending revolution to a socialist Russia. Yet the revolution in Russia would speed proletarian revolution in the west, which in turn would create more favourable conditions for socialism in Russia. Two other factors would, however, be necessary if the commune was to become the basis of a socialist society. First, the peasants would have to recognize the benefits of collectivized agriculture. Several decades later the peasants would have that imposed upon them; but Marx would hardly have approved the Soviet collectivization, since it flouted his belief that the change needed to be gradual and voluntary.[13] Second, Russian agriculture would require large-scale aid – modern machinery, fertilizers, etc. – so as to 'build into the commune all the positive achievements of the capitalist system'. What was necessary in fact was that the country should 'reap the fruits with which capitalist production has enriched humanity, without passing through the capitalist regime ...'. Such a transplantation of capitalism's achievements would, in Marx's view, be perfectly possible. And were these various conditions for a direct transition to socialism not to be met, then Russia would 'lose the finest chance ever offered by history to a people and undergo all the fateful vicissitudes of the capitalist regime'.[14]

Late in life, then, Marx came up with the idea that Russia might skip the later stages of capitalist development and go straight to socialism, taking advantage of western technology and know-how. This belief that Russia might bypass the bourgeois phase and begin to construct socialism in an essentially peasant society showed insight into what would actually happen. Yet Russian Marxists would never acknowledge any debt to Marx's 'new thinking' concerning Russia, and it would also attract little attention in the west. One reason for this surprising neglect is that Marx did not manage to publish his ideas or even to set them out in any systematic form; another is that in certain obvious respects he was badly mistaken. There was no Russian revolution in the 1880s, no attempt at creating a commune-based socialism. The years following his death in 1883 in fact saw intensive capitalist development and the emergence of an urban working class, which looked like being a far more effective instrument of revolution than the peasantry.

The major reason, however, for the neglect of Marx's insight is that even before the 1881 disaster he and the future Russian Marxists were moving in opposite directions. The possibilities which excited him in distant London no longer excited them. He was embracing the peasantry, the commune and the case for a special path when they were looking elsewhere. Marx was in fact exempting Russia from his universal scheme at a time when the very universalism of his doctrine was what commended it to perplexed Russian radicals. His support for The People's Will and his dismissal of Plekhanov as a tedious pedant must have come as a cruel irony to the 'father' of Russian Marxism. It was hardly surprising that Plekhanov should have kept to Marxist orthodoxy and averted his eyes from an apparent aberration of Marx's that had dealt him a wounding personal blow. In the decades ahead, Russian Marxists would disagree among themselves over many matters; they would, however, hold fast to Marxist orthodoxy, and each would claim to have applied it correctly to the Russian situation. Russia needed first of all to go through the bourgeois revolution, which would have to be made by the workers but could not be made *for* them. Yet this literal application of Marx's teaching to Russia had serious drawbacks. And the man who was to be the chief maker of Marxist revolution in Russia began from the 1890s to work out a strategy that lay between Marx's 'aberration' and Plekhanov's orthodoxy but was closer to the spirit, if not the letter, of the former.

Lenin, born in 1870 as Vladimir Ilich Ulyanov into an educated upper-middle-class family, was the younger brother of a revolutionary martyr. Alexander Ulyanov, who seems to have been a person of outstanding intelligence and integrity, had become a key member of a group of revolutionaries who called themselves 'The Terrorist Fraction of The People's Will'. Their aim was to precipitate revolution by killing the tsar, but their conspiracy was discovered and Alexander, together with four others, was executed in 1887 for his part in it. The future Lenin, if Soviet tradition is to be believed, reacted to his brother's execution by saying 'No, we shall not take that road. This is not the road to follow.'[15] And not long afterwards, according to what became the hallowed Soviet view, the founder-to-be of the Soviet state struck out along the only road that could have led to socialism in Russia: the Marxist one, which diverged sharply from the road to nowhere that had been followed by the populists.

Lenin's commitment to Marxism was, as we shall see, beyond doubt. As a Marxist, he would firmly deny that Russia could bypass the bourgeois revolution. He would dismiss any idea of socialism growing out of the commune, and he would regard the proletariat as the essential instrument of revolution and builder of socialism. Yet like his brother and like Karl Marx, Lenin would have enormous admiration for The People's Will. Like them, he would believe that a small group of dedicated and enlightened individuals could move mountains. Like them, he was convinced that the peasantry could contribute significantly to the revolution and socialism in Russia. But what above all linked him to his brother and the later Marx was his sharp perception of Russia's distinctiveness, of the Russian realities; and the strategy he worked out would be guided by a more or less unerring sense of those realities.

2
The Vision, 1890–1917

1

Lenin has often been seen as a revolutionary first and a Marxist second. In the strictly chronological sense, this is undeniable. Lenin's rebellion came before his Marxism, and was almost certainly begun by his brother's execution. His first guru in the field of revolution was not Marx but the writer his brother had admired most, Nikolai Chernyshevsky, whose belief in a distinctive Russian path to socialism had gone together with fierce hostility towards the liberal-capitalist civilization of the west; and not until the early 1890s did he go over – become converted, one might say – to Marxism.

Though Lenin did not begin his revolutionary career as a Marxist, this does not mean that his Marxism was perfunctory, that it was mere gloss on a pursuit of power by any means. Once converted, Lenin never questioned the basic principles of Marxism as he had originally understood them. Some other Russian Marxists of his generation would abandon Marxism altogether or would go over to a non-revolutionary interpretation of it; Lenin, by contrast, held firm to the fundamentalist vision of a world utterly remade by revolution which had possessed him in his early twenties. Marxism was the rock on which he founded his life – without it there could have been no Leninism.

Marxism, for Lenin, embodied absolute scientific truth. But if he saw it as a science, he also, by implication at least, recognized it as moral truth. As science, it explained the development of human society in a way which made socialism appear the inevitable outcome of the historical process; as morality, it held out a vision in which human beings, freed from oppression and the beliefs that sustained it, were

able at last to realize their humanity to the full. The absolute truth of
Marxism lay at the root of Lenin's notorious intolerance. Marxism was
in his eyes not merely the most preferable variant of socialism; it was
the one and only true socialism, the only one that broke uncompro-
misingly with the rotten bourgeois world and offered mankind
fulfilment and wellbeing. Hence his fierce rejection of other philosophies and value-systems, his contempt for tolerance, for eclecticism,
for any attempt to justify diversity of opinion, for any compromise
with the bourgeois that was not justified by strict tactical necessity.
The world as he saw it was peopled by two kinds of person: the
enemies of socialism and its friends, the latter few in number but
complemented by an immense army of *potential* friends. The enemies
included not only obvious opponents in the form of exploiters and
bourgeois apologists but the still more dangerous category of
socialism's false friends, who claimed to be working for socialism but
in fact deliberately or otherwise betrayed it. As for the masses of potential friends, they had to be worked upon unceasingly until they had
become active participants in the struggle with a conscious and active
commitment to socialism.

Lenin fought in the knowledge that socialism would sooner or later
triumph throughout the world. Knowing that you were on the
winning side was a vital support at times when the struggle might
otherwise have seemed hopeless. Plekhanov's metaphor of the Marxist
as someone who boarded 'the train of history' hinted, however, at the
dangers lurking within Marxist determinism. If the train was bound to
get there, why struggle? Was there any point in struggling until the
'objective conditions' for socialism were in place? Yet in Lenin's case
conversion to Marxism had not abated his revolutionary fervour in the
least. His purpose in life was to overthrow the tsarist regime and create
socialism in Russia at the earliest opportunity ; he did not deviate one
inch from that; Marxism merely made his belief in the justice of his
cause and the inevitability of its triumph all the more copper-
bottomed. 'The idea of historical necessity', he declared in one of his
earliest writings as a Marxist, 'does not in the least undermine the role
of the individual in history: all history is made up of the actions of
individuals ... '.[1] Others might allow the train of history to carry them
along; Lenin issued clarion calls to revolt, and he taught the militants
who gathered around him that the energy of a single individual
could work 'miracles' in the revolutionary cause.[2] Among tsarism's
many opponents, no one could match this would-be miracle-
worker for energy and dedication. 'There is not another man', a rival

revolutionary commented, 'who for twenty-four hours of the day is taken up with the revolution, who has no other thoughts but thoughts of revolution, and who even in his sleep dreams of nothing but revolution.'[3] At the root of this tireless activity lay the conviction that socialism in Russia was not a mere distant dream. If only a small number of revolutionaries would exert themselves sufficiently, then the 'miracle' of a socialist Russia could be achieved quite soon.

2

Yet despite Lenin's rhetoric, the outlook for anyone who wanted to see a Marxist-socialist Russia in the near future was, on the face of it, bleak. Till 1905 the autocracy had not been seriously challenged; and when violence did erupt in that year, it failed to develop into the expected bourgeois revolution. The tsar rode out the storm, and the parliament he conceded turned out to be almost powerless. Russia, it seemed, had not yet got to the starting place for the run-up to socialism. The truths of Marxism might be absolute and irrefutable, but the number of Russians who acknowledged and were prepared to act upon them was tiny. While this remained so, socialism in Russia was surely out of the question. The country would have to be transformed *before* it was ready for socialism, and the transformation was bound to extend over a lengthy period. That at least was the reasoning of those members of the Russian Social Democratic Labour Party (the RSDLP) who had become known as Mensheviks.

Lenin's analysis was, however, fundamentally different. While admitting that socialism in Russia was not imminent, he defiantly rejected any idea that social democrats should wait upon events and in particular any idea that they should leave it to the bourgeois to force the pace. Socialist revolution in Russia was *not* a remote prospect, provided – and the proviso was crucial – that the social democrats organized properly. Organization, however, was their weak point. In this respect the populists of The People's Will had done much better; indeed, their 'magnificent organization' stood out as a model for contemporary social democrats.[4] For The People's Will had created a disciplined and effective party – precisely what the social democrats had not yet done. Such a party, could it be created, would make good what Russia lacked and would propel the country rapidly towards socialism. 'Give us an organization of revolutionaries', Lenin announced in *What Is To Be Done?* (1902), 'and we will overturn Russia!'[5]

But nothing less than the right kind of party would do, and it was this question of the party that caused the fateful split within the RSDLP in 1903 into Bolshevik (Majorityite) and Menshevik (Minorityite) factions. The party, Lenin argued, had to be small, disciplined, conspiratorial and hierarchical: an elite of professional and utterly dedicated Marxist revolutionaries. It would have to be built 'from the top downwards' rather than, as the Mensheviks wanted, 'from the bottom upwards' in the sense that it would expand outwards from a founding core which would continue to keep tight control of all its activities. Once conditions allowed, he agreed with the Mensheviks, the party should be structured on normal democratic lines. But while Russia remained a police state the party could not be both democratic and effective; and the priority, he insisted, was that it should be effective.

Bolshevism was Lenin's response, then, to the tsarist police state; but it was his response, too, to the backwardness of Russian society and the backwardness of the working class in particular. As things stood, the workers were not capable of being an effective revolutionary force. Left to themselves, indeed, the workers were in danger of being led astray by bourgeois propagandists who wanted to prop up the existing society rather than to destroy it. The proletariat's destiny was to act as a vanguard, or advanced detachment, for the exploited population as a whole, but currently it, too, needed a vanguard to guide and lead it. That vanguard could only be the socialist intelligentsia, organized in the party. The workers could neither learn socialism nor organize themselves without help: in both respects they were dependent upon the party, whose task was to teach them, discipline them, and at the right moment lead them into battle.

The Mensheviks, however, rejected this view of a dominant party leading a passive working class as wrongheaded and unMarxist. To them, Lenin was a maverick with a dangerous dictatorial streak; the party they wanted would be larger, looser, more democratic and, they claimed, more genuinely a party of the working class. Rosa Luxemburg, a leading figure in the German social democratic movement, attacked Lenin as a power-hungry would-be enslaver of the working class who had unwittingly absorbed the autocratic tendency, while Leon Trotsky, his future colleague, accused him of being a Jacobin who wanted to put an all-powerful party in the place of the working class. 'Lenin's methods', Trotsky argued, 'lead to this: the party organization at first substitutes itself for the party as a whole; then the Central Committee substitutes itself for the organization; and finally a single "dictator" substitutes himself for the Central Committee ...'[6]

The prophecy proved to be uncannily accurate, and the process of 'substitutionism' would develop much as Trotsky had foreseen it. However, it was not Lenin who was to be the 'dictator' and ultimate usurper. He had envisaged an utterly different course of development; and the first glimmering, at the very end of his life, of the Stalinist denouement plunged him, as we shall see, into a turmoil of rethinking. Admittedly, Lenin did see the party as in some sense substituting for the proletariat. The substitution was, however, intended to be short-lived; and the more successfully the party performed its role, the more quickly by his reckoning it should have made itself unnecessary.

Moreover, Lenin repeatedly attacked the illusion that the party could make the revolution on its own and then impose it. Only the masses could make the revolution; only they could in due course build socialism. To believe that the party should make the revolution on the people's behalf, that a handful of conspiratorial socialists could replace a revolutionary people, was Blanquism (after the French conspirator, Auguste Blanqui), and that he unreservedly rejected. The fight, he urged, 'must be waged not by conspirators, but by a revolutionary party based on the working-class movement'. The essence of the task lay in 'educating, disciplining and organizing the proletariat ...'[7] What was needed in fact was a party that merged 'into a single whole the elemental destructive force of the masses and the conscious destructive force of the organization of revolutionaries'.[8] It was precisely here that the People's Will, which he otherwise admired so much, had fallen down. Its members had been excellent conspirators and their conduct had been heroic: but they had not linked up with the people, and lack of popular support explained why they had failed.

What, then, was necessary was to harness popular passions to a revolutionary blueprint, to unleash the energy of the masses and direct it in the cause of socialism. No party in Europe had yet done this, and the need had driven Lenin to create a highly authoritarian party unlike any other. The party, however, was intended as no more than a facilitator, and its importance should have declined as a proletariat capable of acting on its own emerged. The trajectory of development that Lenin had in mind was thus the very opposite of the one that Trotsky had prophesied. The outcome should not have been that an all-powerful dictator usurped the party but rather that the party, having put the necessary conditions in place, sank back into the masses and became lost from sight among them since they no longer needed control or guidance from above.

3

The urban workers were, or should have been, the heart of the matter, since they, if anyone, were the proletariat. But in early twentieth-century Russia there were little more than three million workers, and most were ignorant and unsophisticated recent immigrants from the countryside. That was why the party had to take them in hand. The workers were nevertheless promising material from the Bolsheviks' point of view. Their very conditions of life made them responsive to revolutionary propaganda; they would be willing and eager pupils. And not only would they readily absorb the socialist message; given party guidance, they would prove a formidable force for revolution. Factory life, Lenin observed, had taught them to act collectively, disciplined them and bred a strong spirit of solidarity among them, and thus it had given them the very qualities that were necessary to make effective revolutionaries. In these respects at least the workers were far superior to intellectuals, who irritated him immensely by their endless bickering, their unwillingness to accept discipline, their preference for airy theorizing as against action.

That said, however, the workers would not make good revolutionaries or good socialists if they were simply the passive instruments of other people's purposes. A bovine proletariat would achieve nothing; and Lenin was astonished and delighted when, come the revolution of 1905, the workers showed far more organizing flair and spontaneous defiance of the authorities than he had expected. Their crowning achievement came with the soviets, or workers' councils, which sprang up throughout urban Russia during the closing months of 1905. Some Bolsheviks reacted against the soviets; Lenin, by contrast, welcomed them, though he stipulated that Bolsheviks who joined them should use them strictly for the party's purposes. And the soviets had more than short-term significance for him; they had given him a first insight into how Russia would be ruled after the revolution.

Yet the soviets had been suppressed and the revolution had petered out. The fundamental reason for the failure was that the working class was still deficient in numbers as well as in quality. Russia did not yet have the proletariat that it needed. And in the aftermath of the failure, the split between Bolsheviks and Mensheviks deepened. Not only did they have different views of the party; they now saw very different paths and timescales by which socialism would be achieved in Russia. For the Mensheviks, the 1905 debacle simply underlined that socialism could not be achieved until the country had gone through all the necessary stages of development. What still lay before it was not only the bourgeois revolution but the whole bourgeois-capitalist phase. After the revolution, social democrats should form an extreme opposition to a government that would almost certainly be dominated by liberals. These would be grim years for the working class and frustrating ones for its leaders; but during them the party would train an elite of skilled and educated workers to be the managers of the future socialist state in Russia.

That, then, was the Menshevik scenario, and Lenin rejected it with anger and contempt. He rejected any suggestion of kow-towing to the bourgeois, who in his eyes were as spineless as they were selfish. He refused to play the liberal-parliamentary game, that hypocritical charade, as he saw it, in which bourgeois interests were advanced under a cover of high-sounding democratic principles. 'Liberal', 'parliamentary' and 'bourgeois' were among the strongest terms of abuse in his vocabulary. But the Menshevik sell-out to the bourgeois was not only unprincipled ; it was also wrong-headed. In their bookish way the Mensheviks were assuming that Russia's path to socialism would in all but detail correspond to the west's. In Russia, however, the bourgeois were incapable of making a revolution and did not even want one, since by now they feared the masses far more than they resented the autocracy. That was why after winning a few concessions they had capitulated in 1905 to the tsar and accepted his continued domination of the political system.

That the workers were incapable of carrying off the impending revolution by themselves was undeniable. They needed a partner. The Mensheviks were utterly wrong, however, in choosing the bourgeoisie for that role. And their stupidity in seeing a revolutionary role for the bourgeois was matched by their obtuseness in failing to see revolutionary potential elsewhere. The workers would indeed make the coming revolution in partnership – but the partner with which they would make it was the peasantry.

4

Lenin's view of the peasant masses as potential allies and potential socialists was crucial. At a stroke it transformed the arithmetic. For the peasants were 80 per cent of the population, and by drawing them to the social democrats' side he therefore made a decisive change, at least on paper, to the balance of forces. Without the peasants, the social democrats could muster no more than a small minority following; but with the peasant millions behind them, they would be the party of the people and the socialist revolution, if not socialism itself, could be put on the fairly immediate agenda.

Lenin's 'recruitment' of the peasants gave a special resonance to the name of Majorityite (or Bolshevik) which he had chosen for his faction. When he coined the name in 1903, he was making a simple debating point: it was his group, or so he claimed, that represented majority opinion within the social democratic movement. But the revolutionary strategy he then developed gave the term another layer of meaning. Not only did the Bolsheviks command majority support within the RSDLP; potentially at least they were the party of the masses of the Russian people. They had, or soon would have, the overwhelming bulk of the people behind them; with that support they could take power and set Russia on the road to socialism. Lenin's 'recruitment' of the peasantry was, as a result, a tactical achievement of the first magnitude – without it the October Revolution could hardly have been attempted and could certainly not have been given any convincing validation.

Faith in the socialist and revolutionary instincts of the peasantry had of course been cruelly dashed in the 1870s and early 1880s. At the beginning of the twentieth century, however, the peasants had broken into an open revolt, which had culminated in a massive onslaught on the landlords in 1905. They might or might not be socialist, but after that it was hard to deny the peasants' capacity as revolutionaries. Something else, too, seemed to favour Lenin's idea of a worker–peasant alliance. The great majority of workers had come recently from the countryside and had kept its mentality – its collectivism, its egalitarianism, its burning hatred of the possessing classes. The workers' peasant heritage was, moreover, being consolidated by a growing influx of peasants into the towns. Four million of them settled in the towns in 1900–14, doubling the urban population. Of St Petersburg's almost two million inhabitants in 1910, only 17 per cent had been born there: almost all were immigrants from the countryside. Nor would the war stop the influx: in 1914–17 the capital's labour-force grew by 60 per cent, most of the newcomers coming from the overpopulated central agricultural regions. The fears, passions and prejudices of these newly urbanized and still deeply peasant workers made them easily receptive to the

Bolsheviks' gospel of class war and their fierce rejection of the whole existing order.

Lenin's idea of workers and peasants acting together to overthrow the tsarist regime thus reflected a reality of Russian life: urban proletarians were very largely peasants beneath the skin. Those who harped on the difference between the two missed how much bonded them – attitudes deriving from a common heritage and common resentments against their 'betters'. The worker–peasant alliance was therefore a natural one, whereas the Mensheviks' idea that the workers should act together for the time being with the privileged – in an alliance that the privileged, moreover, would dominate – went counter to every instinct of the peasant-proletarian.

Yet whatever its advantages, the idea of allying workers and peasants in a common revolutionary endeavour created huge problems for the Russian Marxist, and it would take all of Lenin's ingenuity to keep the idea afloat. For Marxists were notoriously hostile to peasants. They saw them as greedy, reactionary and stupid, and liked to label them as 'petty bourgeois', which suggested all of the selfishness of the bourgeoisie proper without its redeeming education or culture. In Marxist eyes, moreover, the peasantry had no future as a class; and populist views of the commune as an egalitarian and semi-socialist institution which in time would ease the transition to full-blown socialism in Russia were no more than make-believe. The reality was that as capitalism made inroads into the countryside, a minority of peasants would prosper and develop into a bourgeoisie proper, while the majority would become pauperized and would eventually flee the countryside altogether to swell the ranks of the proletariat.

Lenin accepted this basic Marxist analysis of the peasantry and its prospects, and he came out strongly against the populist-type ideas of the Socialist Revolutionaries (the SRs). And yet, unlike the great majority of Russian Marxists, he insisted that the peasants would make a significant contribution to the revolutionary movement and that socialism would be achieved in Russia with the help of, rather than despite, the peasant masses. One sign of his originality in this respect was his use of the word 'proletariat'. For most of his colleagues, proletarians were only to be found in the towns; Lenin, however, from the very start of his career as a Marxist applied the term to the exploited masses *as a whole*. Factory workers were simply the most advanced section of the proletariat; they would lead the way, but social democrats should nevertheless aim to draw 'the whole Russian proletariat into the struggle'.[9] Capitalism, he suggested, had already made such inroads into the countryside that the peasant community had become deeply riven into a bourgeois minority and a mass of pauperized proletarians. What had begun, moreover, as an unsupported impression was soon underpinned by extensive research into economic conditions in the countryside, which he published in 1898 as *The Development of Capitalism in Russia*. Here was apparent proof, massively documented with all the apparatus of scholarship, that capitalism in Russia was very far from being a purely urban phenomenon, that the countryside now contained a sizeable proletariat. By Lenin's calculations, at least half the peasants were proletarian in that they were either landless or had so little land that they had to hire themselves out as labourers. At the other extreme, about one-fifth of the peasant population could, in Lenin's view, be considered bourgeois; and between these two classes came an unstable middling stratum whose members would soon be swept to one or other of the opposing extremes.[10]

With this threefold division Lenin had established the framework for future Bolshevik thinking about the peasantry. There were poor, rich and middling peasants, and the differentiation between them was going on apace. A mass of rural proletarians or semi-proletarians, the potential allies of the proletariat, confronted a minority of rich peasants, with whom they would sooner or later become locked in conflict. Between the two came the middle peasants, who neither hired labour nor hired themselves out: these were the classic petty bourgeois and they were an unpredictable element which might swing either way, depending upon circumstances.

This cut-and-dried view of a peasant community that was rapidly dissolving into mutually hostile groupings was vital to Lenin's strategy for socialist revolution in Russia. And yet, despite his scholarly exertions, it had little in common with reality. Social differentiation was indeed taking place among the peasants, but it had by no means gone as far as Lenin suggested. Perhaps 10 per cent of the peasants could be considered 'poor' or 'rural proletarians', while a tiny number fitted the description of 'rural capitalists'; the great majority, however, were 'middle peasants' who worked on self-sufficient family farms. That the lot of the peasants was grim and getting steadily worse was beyond doubt. Impoverishment was, however, being spread fairly evenly, and so far it had by no means undermined the essential coherence of the peasant community.

That coherence was shown clearly enough in the great rebellion of 1905: it was peasant communities as a whole, directed in most cases by the supposedly moribund communes, that struck at the landlords. Yet despite 1905, Lenin did not in any fundamental way rethink his view of the peasantry; he simply admitted that he had somewhat overestimated how far the capitalist tendency had yet gone, and from then on he emphasized the two consecutive stages, as he saw it, in the peasant movement. First, there would be a *general* peasant rebellion against the landowners. The Bolsheviks should support this and the peasants' basic demand – that all the land should be made over to them and divided up equitably among them. This was a petty bourgeois solution to the agrarian problem, but it could be safely allowed since it would soon be superseded. Rapidly advancing capitalism would speed the process of differentiation among the peasants; and the socialist revolution, when it broke out, would precipitate a class war in the countryside in which the masses of the rural poor would fight for socialism.

How many peasants, and especially how many middle peasants, would take up the socialist cause remained, however, very much an open question, and in his attitude to it Lenin fluctuated between optimism and a cautious realism which underlined the backwardness and petty bourgeois nature of the peasantry as a whole. Yet he had set the argument up in such a way as to yield the answer that he needed. The differentiation of the rural community was going ahead rapidly and antagonism between the two peasant classes, temporarily masked by common hatred for the lords, would be fully exposed once the bourgeois revolution had been carried through. What followed was that the workers could count on considerable, if unquantifiable, support from the peasants for the final showdown of the socialist revolution.

Lenin's attitude towards the peasant question was in fact a blend of sharp-eyed realism and wishful thinking which bent reality to his own needs. That the peasants would be a powerful force for disruption was undoubted. Short-term success, followed by failure, in 1905–6 had only stoked up their anger against the lords and their desire for a final reckoning. Ongoing pauperization and the terrible burdens imposed by the war would only deepen their alienation from the regime. What very much remained to be seen, however, was whether this mighty force for disruption could be converted into a force for socialism. Lenin was assuming that the peasantry was deeply divided. It was not. He was assuming that most peasants were 'poor peasants' who had bitter feelings towards the exploiting minority and were, therefore, proletarians and potential allies of the urban workers. But again he was in error. Most peasants fell into that category whose attitude to socialism would, he admitted, be ambivalent – most were 'middle peasants'. These self-sufficient 'middle peasants' were the backbone of the peasant community and the reason for its continuing coherence. Lenin's blindness towards the middle peasantry had led him into a fateful misreading. Yet without this misreading – without the belief in the peasant masses as potential proletarians – the Bolshevik enterprise would hardly have been undertaken.

5

The peasants were a huge segment of the population to have recruited, but in the years leading up to the First World War Lenin set his sights on yet another major element: the 57 per cent of the empire's inhabitants who, by his own reckoning, were non-Russians.

His thinking about the peasants applied of course to the non-Russians as well. Most of them, after all, were peasants; and in the empire's more advanced parts – Ukraine and the Baltic area, for instance – they too were being driven towards socialism by capitalist development. The minor nationalities nevertheless presented special problems. In varying degrees they had a sense of grievance against their Russian oppressors, and the level of national self-consciousness among them had in recent years risen markedly. Lenin was determined to recruit them for revolution and socialism, but he had become convinced that this could not be achieved unless their national grievances were removed. Forcing the non-Russians into socialism was out of the question; the Bolsheviks had to make them *want* to join the workers and peasants of Russia in the common socialist endeavour. The international society of socialism could only be created by those who genuinely believed in it.

Here again, however, Lenin's desire to cast his net as widely as possible was complicated by his Marxism. Just as Marxism took a dim view of the peasants and their prospects, so it was generally dismissive of nationalism and the nation-state. Marx had famously declared in *The Communist Manifesto* that 'the worker has no country', and he had treated nationalism as a bourgeois phenomenon and the nation-state as something transient. Marxists were internationalists who believed that the large state was best suited to prepare the transition to the stateless internationalism of the worldwide socialist community. As with the peasants, Lenin wholly accepted the broad Marxist analysis: he too was an internationalist who believed that the workers of the world should unite and saw the large state as the best forcing-house for capitalism. As on the peasant issue, however, he came into conflict with doctrinaire colleagues who closed their eyes, as he saw it, to the tactical needs of the moment. The minorities had a strong sense of grievance against the Russians. That grievance was an obstacle to creating a socialist state that embraced all the peoples of the Russian empire, and the Bolsheviks had to do their utmost to remove it.

The crucial issue was the right of national self-determination, which the RSDLP had recognized in a somewhat token fashion in its 1903 programme. By 1912 Lenin had decided that tokenism was not enough. The right to self-determination had to be interpreted as the right to secede from Russia and form an independent state; and when and if the question of secession arose, it had to be decided by 'a universal, direct and equal vote of the population of the given territory ...'[11] In two respects this was a markedly 'liberal' interpretation of self-determination for a Russian Marxist. First, it gave the right to decide the matter exclusively to the people concerned and barred the Russians from having any say in it. Second, it gave no extra weighting to the votes of the proletariat: the matter would be decided on a normal, democratic, one-person-one-vote basis.

That said, Lenin had not retreated one inch from his internationalist and socialist objectives. Allowing freedom of secession was by no means the same as encouraging it; to suggest that it was was as foolish 'as accusing those who advocate freedom of divorce of encouraging the destruction of family ties'. The masses of the minor nationalities understood perfectly well 'the advantages of a big market and a big state'; they would not demand independence unless oppression drove them to it.[12] Lenin's hope in fact was that his nationalities policy would achieve the very opposite of what his impassioned defence of the self-determination principle might have suggested. The right to secede would itself remove the main spur to secession – the minorities' feeling that they were being oppressed. It was vital that they be given a genuinely free choice. It was vital that their separate identity should be respected, that they should be given full cultural and linguistic freedom, that they should not be russified or made to feel like inferiors. Provided these conditions were met, the major psychological barrier to a free union of peoples in a socialist state would be removed. And even if some nations did initially secede, the obvious advantages of joining the Russian-based socialist state and the disadvantages of staying outside it would soon change their minds.

Lenin's optimism on the nationalities question was, in the end, of a piece with his optimism about the peasants. At the heart of this optimism was his belief that the masses of the Russian empire were potential socialists and that, if only the Bolsheviks could create the necessary preliminary conditions, they would willingly, indeed eagerly, take up the challenge of building a socialist society.

6

But first would come the bourgeois revolution. That was basic Marxism. Lenin did not go along with Leon Trotsky, who had given up the idea of two separate revolutions in favour of a single, continuous 'permanent revolution', arguing that once the proletariat had power it would begin the task of building socialism immediately. Yet after the exhilaration of 1905, when the regime had so nearly been toppled by the proletarian onslaught, Lenin twisted and turned uneasily within the orthodox framework. The coming revolution would, he suggested, have a mixture of bourgeois and socialist elements. He agreed with the German socialist Karl Kautsky that 'We are moving towards totally new situations and problems, for which none of the old patterns are suitable.' In September 1905 he even went so far as to declare 'From the democratic revolution we shall at once ... begin to pass to the socialist revolution. We stand for uninterrupted revolution. We shall not stop half-way.'[13] Once the revolution was in retreat he withdrew from this extreme position, and he would not return to it until revolution resumed in 1917. The coming revolution would nevertheless, he insisted, be a bourgeois revolution of the most radical kind. It would be made not only by but for workers and peasants; and its outcome would not be a parliamentary government dominated by the bourgeois but a 'revolutionary-democratic dictatorship of the proletariat and the peasantry'.

The idea of a post-revolutionary dictatorship of the proletariat was another piece of basic Marxism. Lenin attached especial importance to it; it was, he would later claim, 'the very essence of Marx's doctrine'.[14] However, he intended to put the proletarian dictatorship to uses never intended for it by Marx. As Marx envisaged it, the dictatorship would result from the socialist revolution and thus come along once capitalism had run its course. Lenin's dictatorship of workers and peasants, by contrast, would come one stage earlier – not when capitalism was in decay but while it was still rising. It would create the conditions for the socialist revolution rather than be their product. And since it would manage capitalism's efflorescence rather than simply begin with capitalism's fall, Lenin's dictatorship would inevitably last far longer than Marx's and face problems for which orthodox Marxism could give no guidance.

The post-revolutionary regime would, then, be an avowed dictator-ship, but Lenin was anxious that the word should not mislead – this would not be remotely similar to any previous dictatorship. In all the dictatorships of the past, a small minority had exercised power over the masses of the people. This, by contrast, would be a dictatorship *of* the people rather than over the people, a dictatorship exercised by and on behalf of the overwhelming majority, and its coercive power would simply be used against the former exploiters.

Lenin had got a first glimpse of what this post-revolutionary dicta-torship would be like from the soviets in the closing months of 1905. Only a small section of the population had been directly involved, yet for Lenin the soviets nevertheless provided a clear picture of how Russia as a whole would be administered once revolution had triumphed. Wherever they had been set up, the soviets had, he main-tained, drawn the masses into the process of government. The authority they had established was 'an authority open to all ... was accessible to the masses, sprang directly from the masses, and was a direct and immediate instrument of the popular masses, of their will'.[15] Soviet government – government, that is, by the soviets – would be ruthless towards the exploiters and would singlemindedly pursue its socialist objectives. This would, nevertheless, be popular government in both senses of the word. For the first time in history, a government would reflect the wishes of the masses and directly involve them in the tasks of running the country. Parliamentary government, the aim of both liberals and Mensheviks, would be government by and for the bourgeois; soviet government, by contrast, would be government by the people and in accordance with the needs and wishes of the people.

But what would happen in the event of conflict between rank-and-file opinion in the soviets and the revolutionary leadership? Lenin did not say, and he would not engage with this problem until life presented him with it in 1918. Most probably he assumed that the unfolding revolutionary process would avert any such conflict by making the masses consciously Bolshevik-socialist. In any event, there was no suggestion that the post-revolutionary government would be purely Bolshevik – such an idea could not have been aired publicly before October 1917. The Bolsheviks, it was assumed, would share power with other revolutionaries and in particular with the SRs, those 'bourgeois revolutionary democrats' who claimed to represent the peasantry. There were, moreover, clear restraints upon what the coali-tion government would be able to do. Since the country would be at the stage of the bourgeois rather than the socialist revolution, the government would not take over the factories, abolish all private ownership of the means of production, or regulate all economic activity in accordance with a plan. For the foreseeable future, the economy would remain capitalist, even though the capitalists would be strictly supervised. A further restraint was that the new government would be no more than provisional, and one of its first tasks, as Lenin fully accepted, would be to convene a constituent assembly, elected by universal, direct, equal and secret suffrage, which alone would have the right to make fundamental decisions.

Nevertheless, Lenin would be satisfied with nothing less than a dominant voice for the Bolsheviks in the shaping of the new Russia. The provisional government would be put in power, if he had his way, by uprisings which the Bolsheviks would have masterminded, and kept in power by a revolutionary army which was largely Bolshevik-commanded. In such circumstances, the Bolsheviks would hardly take less than the lion's share of government positions. Participation of social democrats in the government would be dependent, Lenin insisted, upon (i) 'the alignment of forces' and (ii) 'control of these delegates by the Party'.[16] If we read 'Bolsheviks' for 'social democrats', this indicates that Bolsheviks would not join the government unless they dominated it and that the leadership would give its delegates very little leeway for making concessions to other parties and interests.

Nor would the constituent assembly be much of a curb upon the Bolsheviks. The idea itself was a hallowed hand-down from the French Revolution – the assembly, elected on a democratic franchise, would reflect the general will of the nation and so have an uncontestable right to make decisions. All revolutionaries accepted the idea, but Lenin from the outset accepted it only with reservations. Fundamental issues such as the land question should, he insisted, be decided *before* the assembly met. Moreover, a democratic franchise was not enough to ensure that the assembly really reflected the will of the people. To satisfy him, the elections would have to take place 'in the right material conditions'; their outcome would have to be an assembly with sufficient power to bring about a new order, not something that resembled the Frankfurt Parliament of 1848 – that 'pitiful assembly of pitiful liberal bourgeois babblers'.[17] More than a decade before a constituent assembly met in Russia, Lenin had thus made it crystal-clear that he would not submit to any liberal assembly basing its claims upon the principles of constitutional democracy. He would make the very minimum of concessions to moderate-revolutionary and liberal opinion. Only Bolshevik policies in their purity could set Russia on the road to socialism; and once implemented, he assumed, these policies would quickly win the support of the overwhelming majority.

Revolution had nevertheless been defeated in 1905–6, and several years of demoralization followed. To make matters worse, the workers of the advanced countries were proving all too quiescent: there was no sign yet of capitalism's crisis, still less of the international socialist revolution. Worker militancy did, however, resume in Russia from 1912; and then from out of the blue came the First World War, which changed everything.

7

In the first place, the war solved a puzzle – that capitalism seemed to have escapd the fate Marx had predicted for it. As the workers of Europe slaughtered one another at their masters' behest, Lenin came to realize that capitalism's final crisis had at last arrived. Capitalism, as it happened, had proved more resourceful than Marx could have predicted: it had found an apparent way out of its contradictions by expanding into the underdeveloped countries and exploiting the cheap labour there. But imperialism had only staved off the crisis; this war was an inevitable outcome of capitalism's contradictions and would bring about its speedy destruction. But not only was capitalism in its death throes; the very concentration of economic power in the state's hands during this, capitalism's final and bloodiest phase, would vastly simplify the transition to socialism. The dog-years, therefore, were over. 'A revolutionary situation', Lenin exulted in June 1915, 'obtains in most of the advanced countries and the Great Powers of Europe.' Europe, he told Swiss workers in January 1917, 'is pregnant with revolution'.[18] The world-wide socialist revolution seemed in fact to be imminent.

The prospect of revolution in the west gave the Bolshevik cause a tremendous fillip. The success of socialism in Russia was unimaginable without its success in the west. Yet Lenin by no means saw the Russian revolution as wholly dependent upon western developments. He had long since believed that Russia might blaze the revolutionary trail. Now he went further; the overthrow of the capitalist world order would begin, he indicated in *Imperialism, the Highest Stage of Capitalism,* not in a developed country but in a country of the periphery, part imperialist but part colony, in which the bourgeoisie was weak and the misery of the workers had not been assuaged by imperialism's profits. Russia was precisely such a country – the weakest link in capitalism's chain. Whether he knew it or not, Lenin's thinking in this respect was remarkably similar to Marx's little-publicized speculations of forty years before.[19] Revolution would begin in Russia; its success would trigger revolution in the west; that in turn would repercuss back upon Russia and make a vital contribution to socialist construction there.

The collapse of the tsarist regime under the strains of war in February 1917 therefore came as no surprise to Lenin. The replacement of the autocracy by a government of liberals disappointed him, yet the conduct of the Mensheviks and SRs of the Petrograd Soviet in supporting this bourgeois government was what he would have expected. Since the outbreak of the war Lenin had cut all his remaining links with the representatives of moderate socialism. By supporting the war efforts these people had merely confirmed that they were the lackeys of the bourgeois and traitors to the international proletarian movement; and in April he would underline his breach with them by suggesting that the Bolsheviks change their name from 'social democrats' to 'the Communist Party'.[20] What happened in Petrograd in February with the connivance of these traitors was exactly the kind of bourgeois revolution that should not have taken place – one that gave power to the bourgeois. Lenin was convinced, however, that the new government would not last. From his Swiss exile he fired off indignant salvoes against it, urging the creation of a government of workers and peasants; and at the beginning of April he returned to Petrograd in order to supervise its overthrow.

Already from exile he had warned his followers that they should not 'force the complex, urgent, rapidly developing practical needs of the revolution into the Procrustean bed of narrowly conceived "theory" instead of regarding theory primarily and predominantly as a *guide to action*'.[21] That said clearly enough that he for one would not let any bookish Marxism get in his way. And when on 4 April he issued a major policy statement – the 'April Theses', as it became known – he sidestepped the hallowed term 'bourgeois revolution'. The country, his statement declared, 'is *passing* from the first stage of the revolution ... to its *second* stage, which must place power in the hands of the proletariat and the poorest sections of the peasants'. [22] But it needed little reading between the lines to realize that the 'first stage', which on Lenin's reckoning was already being left behind, was the bourgeois revolution and that the 'second stage' was the socialist revolution.

Without saying as much, Lenin was finally casting off the restraints implicit in Marx's notion of a separate bourgeois revolution distinct in its timing and in the nature of its tasks from the socialist revolution.

Saying that the socialist revolution was already the order of the day was not the same, of course, as saying that socialism itself lay just around the corner; and from the moment of his return Lenin left no doubt in his followers' minds that they should not expect socialism in the very near future. 'We cannot be for "introducing" socialism – this would be the height of absurdity. We must preach socialism.'[23] Not until people understood, wanted and worked for socialism would it be achieved – achieving it by decree was out of the question. The revolutionary government which Lenin aimed at would nevertheless take extremely radical measures in order to set the transition to socialism in motion. It would abolish the three pillars of the bourgeois state – the police, the bureaucracy, the standing army – and in place of the last it would arm the entire labouring population. While reluctantly keeping on many officials from the former administration, it would bring all officials' wages down to the level of workers' wages. It would confiscate landed estates and nationalize all land. It would amalgamate all banks into a single national bank. And it would assume overall control of the economy, organizing the production and distribution of goods in such a way that they benefited the whole population.[24]

But if any of this was to be realized, the popular support for socialism which Lenin counted upon had somehow to be activated. The masses of the urban and rural poor had to be stirred up, and for that he looked above all to the soviets. The soviets would be 'organs of insurrection, of revolutionary rule'; in addition, they would train the masses 'for participation in all affairs of state'.[25] As living conditions deteriorated and the Provisional Government's popularity slumped, 'All Power to the Soviets!' became the most compelling of the Bolsheviks' slogans. The soviets – 'the real will and mind of the people', Lenin called them – would sweep to power and would create a government quite different from any before: a government of workers' and peasants' representatives, who with the enthusiastic support of the masses would begin to transform Russia in the direction of socialism.

Yet when Lenin had returned to Russia in April, his ambition of overthrowing the Provisional Government in favour of a soviet one and of beginning a direct transition to socialism had seemed outlandish. True, a cheering multitude had met him at the station:

among politicians, however, he stood almost alone. It was not only the Mensheviks who were horrified by the April Theses; so, too, were most Bolsheviks. *Pravda*, the Bolshevik paper, duly printed the Theses, but in an accompanying editorial disowned them for having abandoned the safe ground of the bourgeois revolution; and the Bolsheviks' Petrograd Committee voted them down by 13 votes to 2. The reality was that Lenin stood in isolation on the extreme wing of an extremist party which in February had anyway mustered no more than some 20 000 members. He did not have majority support among his own colleagues, let alone among the urban workers, who favoured the more conciliatory line of the Mensheviks and the SRs, and still less among the masses of the empire's inhabitants as a whole.

Yet Lenin was unwavering in his belief that most people would soon be behind him. The Bolsheviks had been the only consistent and unanimous opponents of the war; as the conflict dragged on, that stand alone would win them more and more supporters. But what would be decisive would be the revelation of how utterly false was the Provisional Government's fundamental premise – that the bourgeois and the toiling masses could live and work together in long-term harmony for one another's benefit. The Mensheviks had preached inter-class collaboration since 1905. They, together with the SRs, had propped up the liberal Provisional Government from the start, and in May the two supposedly revolutionary parties actually entered the government. Nothing, Lenin reckoned, was more likely to drive people to the one party which preached unyielding hostility to the whole existing order and held out a vision of life transformed – of peace, land, bread, and soon of socialism itself – than this coalition government, based on an unprincipled compromise, which ducked or fudged all of the country's crying problems.

By the end of April, Lenin had swung the party behind him. When the First All-Russian Congress of Soviets met in June, the Bolsheviks were still heavily outnumbered with only 105 of its more than 1000 delegates. However, the failure of the Mensheviks and SRs to stop the war, the decline in living standards and the general slide towards chaos led to a massive surge of worker support for the Bolsheviks; so, too, did the repression following a pro-Bolshevik uprising in Petrograd in early July. By the end of July, party membership had risen above 200 000. By early September, the Bolsheviks had majority support in the soviets in both Petrograd and Moscow. The conquest of working-class Russia was almost, it seemed, complete.

The peasants were of course a more difficult constituency for the

Bolsheviks. The peasant soviet movement was separate from the urban one, and when the First All-Russian Congress of Peasants' Deputies met, a mere 14 Bolsheviks were overwhelmed by 537 SRs. Had those proportions been maintained, the Bolsheviks' claim to represent the masses of the Russian empire would have been threadbare. The SRs, however, became hobbled by their membership of the Provisional Government, and their failure to support the peasants' demand for the confiscation of landowners' estates gave the Bolsheviks an opening. By September peasant frustration had passed over into violence. The peasant rebellion, taken together with the emergence of a radical Left SR faction whose position on the land question was close to the Bolsheviks', seemed a clear indication that rural Russia too might support, or at least not oppose, a Bolshevik take-over.

8

With events moving fast in the Bolsheviks' favour, the question of taking power became an urgent one; and on this Lenin found himself at odds with some of his colleagues. Moderates among them held that the Bolsheviks should not assume power unless and until they had nationwide support, as reflected in elections to the forthcoming Second Congress of Soviets (due for late October) or even the much-delayed Constituent Assembly. Moreover, the Bolsheviks should be prepared to share power in government with other socialists who had appreciable electoral support. Lenin, however, strongly rejected both propositions and the 'constitutionalist illusions', as he put it, which underlay them. The Bolsheviks should seize power at the first oppor-tunity rather than wait to be mandated by an elected assembly. They should not share power with people whose views were essentially different – unless those people were prepared to submit to them. And they should use the power they had seized to smash the whole existing state structure and replace it by something entirely different.

This intransigent position of Lenin's reflected arguments he had developed at length in *The State and Revolution,* a major work he had written while lying low in Finland in the late summer. There he had launched a fierce attack on 'opportunists' who were ready to accept the bourgeois framework and deluded themselves that at some future date a socialist one could be peacefully substituted for it. This was an attack upon the Mensheviks and the SRs; but it was also, by implica-tion, an attack upon, or at least a warning to, intellectuals in his own party who showed signs of succumbing to the same illusions. The power that was necessary to create socialism could only, he insisted, be acquired by force. Violent revolution alone could remove the bourgeois state. To think that universal suffrage was 'capable of revealing the will of the majority of working people and of securing its realization' was an absurdity.[26] As Engels had made plain, universal suffrage was nothing more than an instrument of bourgeois rule. The masses could never be freed by the ballot box; only a violent overthrow of the existing system would free them.

Revolution would result in the dictatorship of the proletariat; and Lenin did not hide that, initially, the dictatorship of the proletariat would, in effect, be the dictatorship of 'the vanguard of the proletariat' – in other words, of the Bolshevik Party. That alone was capable, thanks to Marxism, of *leading the whole people* to socialism, of directing and organizing the new system, of being the teacher, the guide, the leader of all the working and exploited people ...'.[27] Having taken power, the Bolsheviks would use it single-mindedly in order to create the infrastructure necessary for socialism. But could they possibly hold on? Could they expand their base of support rapidly enough before their opponents toppled them? Lenin was convinced that they could, and at the end of September he wrote a defiant reply to critics who believed that lasting Bolshevik power was no more than a fantasy. When every labourer, unemployed worker, cook and ruined peasant saw how the proletarian state was helping the poor, then all such, he insisted, would rally to it. And he bolstered his case by citing Engels's belief in what he had called 'latent socialism'. This was a force which would remain hidden and dormant until the revolution; but once people realized that power had passed to the oppressed and was being used on their behalf, latent socialism would be unleashed and become irresistible. A quarter of a million Bolsheviks would run the state; but behind them would stand millions of ordinary people, hitherto excluded from political life, who would become politically conscious and be drawn into everyday administrative tasks, forming in effect a state administration 'of ten if not twenty million people'.[28]

The new regime's success would depend of course in the end upon its success in transforming the material conditions of life, and on this score Lenin had no doubts. Capitalism, he declared in *The State and Revolution*, had been a retarding force on human development. Consequently, 'we are entitled to say with the fullest confidence that the expropriation of the capitalists will inevitably result in an enormous development of the productive forces of human society.'[29] The economic prospects were in fact dizzying: a socialist economy, planned, centrally directed and making full use of the talents of everyone, would prove far more productive than its exhausted capitalist rival and would ensure universal prosperity. The immediate task, of course, was to save the country from economic collapse, and that, Lenin was confident, could be achieved by means of centrally organized distribution of food, clothing and housing. Moreover, the great task which lay beyond that – the creation of a socialist economic system – would be easier than socialism's critics and its more timid supporters supposed. From his study of imperialism Lenin had concluded that the state-monopoly capitalism of the war years had created the very structures that the Bolsheviks needed in order to direct the economy towards socialism. Just as it had produced its own gravediggers in the proletariat, so capitalism had thrown up the institutions – especially the banks – that could be used to supersede it. The economic task was therefore quite different from the political. Whereas the state machine had to be smashed and replaced, the economic apparatus of capitalism had to be preserved and made use of. And to those who doubted whether the Bolsheviks could hold power for long, he insisted on the relative ease with which they and millions of ordinary Russians could take over the economy and direct it in the interests of everyone.[30]

Such was the vision of a Russia transformed which Lenin held out in the weeks before the October Revolution. But if the vision was to be realized, he and his fellow initiates would have to make a supreme act of revolutionary boldness. Socialism, he reiterated ceaselessly, could never be achieved by parliamentary elections or by negotiations with bourgeois or pseudo-socialist parties. The Bolsheviks could count on overwhelming popular support for their programme, but that support could not be activated *until* they had power. Socialist consciousness would be a *result* of socialist practice, of exposure to socialist policies, not socialist policies the result of socialist consciousness. This was the underlying message that Lenin tried to hammer home to his colleagues in the weeks and days before the revolution. Head-counting was, at this juncture, an irrelevance; constitutional niceties were nothing but a snare. The Bolsheviks had to seize power and themselves create the mandate that they needed. The socialist prize was for the taking, but in order to grasp it they would have to show political courage and throw bourgeois scruples to the wind.

Yet Lenin was not deviating from his belief that the Bolsheviks had majority support within their reach. And in order to win over those who had constitutionalist or other doubts, he now crossed the thin line that separated claiming latent from *actual* majority support. That was what made September different from July. Then, he admitted, the Bolsheviks had not possessed majority support. But now, he wrote on 12 September, 'The majority of the people are *on our side'*.[31] From then on he never wavered in this assertion. It was not just the urban workers; most peasants, too, had come over. On 20 September he was more categorical still: a government committed to the Bolshevik programme would 'obtain the support of nine-tenths of the population of Russia, the working class and the overwhelming majority of the peasantry'.[32] Yet he took care not to concede that majority support was a necessary condition for taking power. On the contrary, he made it clear that this was not a matter of principle for him. 'We must not', he told the Central Committee in early September, 'be deceived by election figures; elections prove nothing.' Similarly: 'It would be naive to wait for a "formal majority" for the Bolsheviks. No revolution ever waits for *that.*' [33] And only days before the take-over he admonished the committee that 'The Party could not be guided by the temper of the masses because it was changeable and incalculable; the Party must be guided by an objective analysis and an appraisal of the revolution.'[34]

To put it in plainer language than he chose to use, the Bolsheviks had to take power as soon as they had the chance, whether or not they had majority support. All that mattered was having *enough* support. That they now had.

Two senior Bolsheviks, Kamenev and Zinoviev, however, challenged Lenin's assumption that power was now for the taking. The party, they argued, had neither majority nor sufficient support. The workers were for it, but the peasant masses were against. Any premature action would lead to defeat. Better to wait for the Constituent Assembly elections, due in November, when the party might well win a third of the vote. That would enable it to have the dominant say in a 'governing bloc' with Left SRs and others. Lenin, however, rejected delay. He rejected 'constitutionalism'. He rejected coalitions. The issue came to a head at a Central Committee meeting on 10 October. Lenin urged an immediate uprising. 'We now have the majority behind us. Politically, the situation is fully ripe for taking power.'[35]

By ten votes to two, the committee sided with him. And on 24–25 October, while the Second Congress of Soviets was assembling, the Bolsheviks took power in Petrograd with a minimum of bloodshed.

9

At the congress the Bolsheviks were much the strongest group, yet with some 300 out of the 670 delegates they fell short of an overall majority. Such figures clearly suggested a coalition government with themselves as the dominant element. Lenin, however, would not contemplate any deal with the Mensheviks and the mainstream SRs; and they in turn denounced what had happened as a Bolshevik coup d'état and walked out of the congress. By contrast, Lenin was prepared to have the more radical Left SRs as junior partners in the government for the sake of their likely influence with the peasantry. The Left SRs, however, refused to join the Bolsheviks (though they would change their minds in November), and the upshot was that the remaining delegates endorsed a purely Bolshevik government.

That was not at all what most delegates to the congress had come expecting; out of 366 soviet committees represented at the congress, 255 had sent delegates on the assumption that power would be shared among the various socialist groupings.[36] It was not what some of the most prominent Bolsheviks, including Kamenev and Zinoviev, had expected or wanted. But it was what Lenin wanted, and he got his way. The creation of an all-Bolshevik government indeed brought to a triumphant conclusion the sectarian strategy he had pursued ever since 1903. First, he had set up his own group within the RSDLP; next, he had cut himself off from international social democracy, castigating it for what he alleged was its sell-out to the bourgeois; finally, back in Russia in 1917, he had insisted on a complete break with the existing order and with everyone who advocated even a temporary compromise with it. Only Bolshevik policies pursued by a government with unfettered hands could create the preconditions for socialism. At the Second Congress of Soviets he got exactly what he had wanted.

The October Revolution would be portrayed by many of its opponents as a coup d'état carried out by a clique of unrepresentative adventurers. That was hardly fair to the Bolsheviks: in Petrograd at least they were buoyed up by widespread, if largely passive, support. The 'Majorityites' did not, however, by any stretch of the imagination have the backing of most of the country's inhabitants. They had achieved a dominant position in the urban soviet movement, yet they had little following in the parallel peasant movement, and when a peasant soviet congress met in December their delegates would be heavily outnumbered. The 'Majorityites' represented, in fact, at best a largish minority of the nation – as the elections to the Constituent

Assembly would make crystal clear within a few weeks.

From Lenin's point of view, this minority situation was no cause for concern. Despite his claims to the contrary, he can hardly have expected anything else. What did matter was that the Bolsheviks were now in a position to push through the policies that would shortly bring them overwhelming support. Land for the peasants. Peace for the soldiers. Self-determination for the minorities. Control of their factories for the workers. Bread for everyone. Devastating blows against the exploiters and the state machine which had sustained them. The rapid creation of a state – properly speaking, a 'semi-state' – which would turn people from the passive objects of government into the fully participant and full developed members of a self-governing society. The new government, in fact, would bring about a transfer of power to the dispossessed such as no government had tried or even remotely considered before. It would also save the economy from collapse and lay the foundations for universal prosperity. Against such a perspective, anyone who insisted on head-counting at this particular juncture was guilty, in Lenin's eyes, of inexcusable folly, if not treason to the cause.

The congress which legitimized the Bolshevik take-over was far from a cross-section of the nation, yet the Bolsheviks persuaded themselves that these delegates represented an embryonic general will. They, after all, were very different from the delegates to the moderate-dominated First Congress. 'See how rough and ignorant they look,' was the scathing comment on them of one congress official.[37] The Menshevik Nikolai Sukhanov observed these Second Congress delegates with an equally jaundiced eye. 'Out of the trenches and obscure holes and corners had crept utterly crude and ignorant people whose devotion to the revolution was spite and despair.' Workers and soldiers they might be, yet these men with their 'morose, indifferent faces and grey great-coats' were scarcely any different, he suggested, from the peasant masses.[38]

Meant as a put-down, Sukhanov's comments gave unwitting support to the Bolshevik claim that these delegates spoke for the nation. His point was that such people were not capable of building socialism. What, however, could hardly be denied was that those who jostled in the halls of the Smolny Institute, a former school for aristocratic girls, were the 'dark people', the hitherto downtrodden and excluded, now high on the hope of creating, if not socialism, then at least a life utterly different from any that had been known in Russia before. After the moderates had walked out, the remaining delegates had enthroned the Bolsheviks in power in an atmosphere of ecstatic unity. Could what had happened in the Smolny not be replicated across the length and breadth of Russia? Could the Bolsheviks not shape and speak for a general will of the hitherto excluded mass? And could they not, by doing so, drag the country out of its perennial misery and begin to build a society of freedom and equality which satisfied the material and spiritual needs of all its members?

In the aftermath of victory, the prospects seemed magnificent – impressive enough, certainly, to quell the doubts of those who, up to the moment of the insurrection, had remained faint-hearted or sceptical. Yet the enterprise into which by power of will and intellect Lenin had pushed his fellow Bolsheviks was appallingly hazardous. For if this act of revolutionary boldness was not to culminate in disaster, no less than three major conditions had to be fulfilled. First, it had to be followed fairly quickly by the worldwide socialist revolution,whose imminence Lenin had trumpeted during the run-up to October. Without that, the creation of socialism in Russia was unimaginable; without that, the Bolshevik experiment would suffer the fate of a bud that opens in a false spring and is then killed off by the frost.

Second, Bolshevik power had to save the country from ruin and bring about that rapid economic transformation and increase in productive capacity which Lenin had so confidently predicted in *The State and Revolution*. The Bolsheviks had done much more than argue the general superiority of socialism to capitalism; their special claim, which marked them off from the Mensheviks and even the SRs, was that under their direction Russia would, despite its backwardness, be brought to socialism fairly soon. Their case now had to be proved, and the essence of the proof would lie in economic performance. They had taken power in a land of ruin; they had to turn it into a land of material abundance, and without economic transformation socialism would remain nothing more than a dream.

The third condition was closely linked to the first two and especially to the second. Beginning from a minority position, the Bolsheviks had to reach out to the masses of the country's inhabitants: beyond the workers, whom they could surely count upon, to the millions of peasants and non-Russians. They had to win them for socialism, win their hearts and minds for a project that in certain respects – by sweeping away the possessing class, for instance – corresponded to age-old popular desires but in others was alien to anything the peoples of Russia had ever known. Without the willing and enthusiastic support of the masses, socialism could not be built in Russia or anywhere else.

Lenin had never suggested otherwise. Now his belief in the power of ordinary people, once freed from capitalism and false consciousness, to build socialism for themselves was about to be put to the test.

In the opinion of the Bolsheviks' opponents, none of these conditions was remotely likely to be met. The socialist project would fail to get off the ground; sooner rather than later the Bolsheviks would be ousted; and the outcome of their doomed and irresponsible adventure would in all probability be a disastrous right-wing revanche. The Bolsheviks themselves, by contrast, were exhilarated by their easy capture of power. Dizzy with success, they assumed that the conditions would be met and that socialism and even communism would be built in Russia, and worldwide, fairly quickly. They had cleared the first hurdle – power. Now they would clear the second hurdle – socialism. What almost no one envisaged was that the conditions would fail to be fulfilled but that the Bolsheviks would nevertheless entrench themselves in power, that the dictatorship of the proletariat would become the long-term dictatorship of the Bolsheviks over people who had not chosen socialism but would have what passed as that imposed upon them.

3
The Realization, 1917–24

1

The October Revolution was a gamble, an enormous leap into the dark. Towards the end of his life, Lenin admitted that he had under-taken it in the spirit of Napoleon – *'On s'engage et puis ... on voit.'* It was a Marxist leap of course, yet a Marxist leap of a very peculiar kind; and in another remarkable admission Lenin would concede that the Bolsheviks had 'started from the opposite end to that prescribed by theory'.[1] The western path to socialism by way of capitalism and bourgeois democracy was not a path to be followed inflexibly, and Russian circumstances had required something different. Far from waiting for the socio-economic and cultural conditions necessary for socialism to ripen, the Bolsheviks had taken power with the aim of hastening the maturation process. The political revolution, which should have come as the culmination of the process of change leading to socialism, had thus occurred in advance of the conditions which should have created it. 'Things have turned out differently from what Marx and Engels expected, and we, the Russian working and exploited classes, have the honour of being the vanguard of the international socialist revolution ...'[2]

The reason for this inversion, or so Lenin argued, was that Russia's very backwardness had made the socialist revolution easier to accom-plish there than in the west. Yet it was important not to be deceived by the ease with which the revolution had been carried off. Backwardness might have facilitated the socialist revolution in Russia, but it would also, Lenin emphasized, make the actual creation of socialism there very much harder than elsewhere.[3]

The gamble had taken the Bolsheviks into territory that was almost entirely uncharted. For there had been no Marxist revolution before, still less an inverted Marxist revolution. Precedent and practical guidance were wholly lacking, and not even much theoretical help could be got from Marx and Engels. Committed to the creation of socialism, the Bolsheviks had very little idea, except in the most general terms, of what this socialism would amount to. Six months into the revolution, Lenin admitted: 'We cannot give a description of socialism; what socialism will be like when its completed forms are arrived at – this we do not know, we cannot tell.'[4] They had even less idea of the stages by which they would get there, and on the question of the timescale their ideas fluctuated wildly.

The problem was reflected in Lenin's use of the word 'socialism', which was remarkably sloppy for someone who was generally a stickler for rigour and contemptuous of loose thinking in others. Sometimes he applied the word to 'the first stage of the new society arising out of capitalism': that is, to the period of transition between capitalism and communism – a period in which characteristics of the old society would blend with and gradually be replaced by those of the new.[5] At other times he applied it instead to the fully transformed, that is, communist, society, in which the rule 'from each according to his ability, to each according to his work' would have been superseded by 'from each according to his ability, to each according to his need'. And there were still other times when it was not at all clear in which of the two senses he was using the word. The water was muddied further, moreover, by the widespread use of the adjective 'socialist'. Russia, its new rulers declared, had undergone a 'socialist' revolution, yet their pronouncements made it clear that socialism even in the transitional sense was still 'a long way off'.[6] 'Socialist' soon became the vaguest and most catch-all of terms, conveying little more than the party's approval for whatever it qualified.

Elusive yet the focus of everything, socialism was thus for the Bolsheviks like a crock of gold which lay at the end of a difficult march of unforeseeable duration. At each stage of the journey, as they stumbled and battled against the elements, they would invoke the noun or the adjective to justify the twists and turns they had taken. Socialism was the goal, but it was also – this was crucial for morale, yet a basic source of confusion – the journey towards the goal. It was there in the distance, but it was also here and now. It was everywhere in Bolshevik Russia, yet when you tried to describe or define or simply lay hands on it, it somehow escaped you.

2

Despite this lack of clarity in their intentions, the Bolsheviks set out with immense confidence, and this confidence rested upon certain key assumptions. They took it for granted, as we have seen, that their seizure of power would quickly be followed by socialist revolution in the advanced countries, beginning most probably with Germany. The victorious proletariat of the west would give them massive support by way of machines, manufactured goods and skilled helpers. This help would be vital; once it came it would 'solve all our difficulties'.[7] Yet the international revolutions marked time. Worse than that, the regime became locked for two years (1918–20) in a civil war in which its opponents, the 'Whites', were helped, directly and indirectly, by the capitalist powers. The Bolsheviks thus found themselves in the polar-opposite situation from the one they had expected. Far from being able to solve their problems with the help of friends abroad, they faced foreign enemies whose hostility made their task very much more difficult.

Another key assumption had been that the socialist economic system was intrinsically more rational and more productive than the capitalist one it would supplant. Bolshevik management of the economy would therefore lead to economic recovery – to a rapid increase in production and improvement in living standards. Here, too, however, the Bolsheviks' hopes were dashed, and here too they soon found themselves in the very opposite situation from the one they had anticipated. There was no smooth diversion of the economy to socialist purposes, no rapid increase in production or improvement in living standards. About half of all large factories closed during the first year of Bolshevik power; industrial production and the productivity of labour went into a steep and rapid decline; and by 1921 real wages were little more than one-third of what they had been in October 1917. The Bolsheviks had come to save the economy and create that material base without which socialism was unthinkable. Within a short time, however, they had brought about economic collapse and living conditions that were appalling even by the Russians' own wretchedly low standards.

The disproving of these key assumptions was bad enough. Yet there was a still more fundamental assumption upon which the Bolsheviks' confidence as builders of socialism had rested, and the confounding of that raised up a still greater obstacle to their ambition. For Lenin had persuaded himself, as we know, that there was a latent demand in

Russia for socialism, which once the Bolsheviks had power they would convert into active and enthusiastic support for socialist policies.

This belief that the Bolsheviks would quickly win and would then retain the overwhelming support of a population that was already semi-proletarian was, in turn, closely linked to another. Although the Bolsheviks would make a vital contribution as organizers and inspirers, socialism was not something they could create by their own efforts and then impose – socialism could only be made by the masses themselves. At one level this was the most obvious of truisms. How could so sweeping a transformation be brought about other than by the millions of ordinary people? How could the communist minority get things done except through the physical and mental exertions of the majority? Lenin's belief that socialism could only be created *by* the people did, however, go well beyond the obvious point that peasant hands were indispensable to the task. Only if the masses understood socialism, only if they entered into its spirit and worked voluntarily, eagerly and in full consciousness towards it – only then could it be achieved. An active, informed, and initiative-taking population was both the goal and a condition of getting to the goal. And the link between these two fundamental propositions on which Lenin's revolutionary gamble rested was clear enough. If the Bolsheviks could rapidly gain the enthusiastic support of the great majority, then these supporters could be turned into active collaborators whose energy and initiative would play a crucial part in creating socialism. On the other hand, were this initial 'if' to prove mistaken, were support for the Bolsheviks to fall well short of what Lenin had hoped and expected, then he would have little alternative but to de-emphasize popular initiative and instead highlight the *party* as the chief creator of socialism.

As of October, however, Lenin had no serious doubts. The urban proletariat was already on the Bolsheviks' side, and the bulk of rural proletarians would soon swing to them. The liberated masses would then throw themselves vigorously into the socialist project, learning the skills that were necessary for management of the economy and state administration. As people were drawn in their millions into the project, so the gulf between Bolshevik ideas and the wishes of ordinary citizens would narrow, and the result of this convergence would be a steadily decreasing role for the government.

The Bolsheviks' early pronouncements reflected their conviction that popular support lay within their grasp. Their priority was of course to demonstrate that they indeed were the party of the people, that they alone had the people's welfare at heart, and within days they had made a major gesture towards each section of the toiling population. The Decree on Peace offered soldiers the prospect of an imminent suspension of hostilities. The Decree on Land set aside the Bolsheviks' ideas of a large-scale, collective cultivation of the soil and instead endorsed what had largely been done already – the egalitarian dividing-up of landowners' estates among the peasants. The Draft Regulation on Workers' Control gave workers' representatives the right to oversee all aspects of production and distribution. The Declaration of the Rights of the Peoples of Russia confirmed the non-Russians' right of self-determination and hence of secession.

Not only did the government quickly give people what they seemed to be wanting. It invited them to take power into their own hands, to exercise it intelligently and energetically, and by their own initiative to build a new society from the bottom upwards. It was 'the oppressed masses', Lenin said on 25 October, who would create the new government. 'Comrades,' he told a meeting a few days later, 'remember that now *you yourselves* are at the helm of state.' People should 'unite and take into your hands all affairs of state'. And again: 'Get on with the job yourselves; begin right at the bottom, do not wait for anyone.' In much the same spirit, he urged that 'Every factory committee should concern itself not only with the affairs of its own factory, but should also be an organizational nucleus helping arrange the life of the state as a whole.' Plans were not what was essential: the new life had to be created 'from below, by the masses, through their experience'.[8] The Bolsheviks would thus arouse this hitherto inert people, would unleash its energy and initiative; and this creative outpouring, properly guided by the party, would bring about socialism.

Before long, however, signs appeared that the Bolsheviks might have misread the masses, that there might be a fundamental gulf between themselves and those on whom they depended. True, the Bolsheviks' aim of sweeping change which rid the country of all privilege and exploitation spoke to a deep bitterness and sense of injustice in the masses – no wonder that Petrograd was awash with red in the post-October days. Both sides wanted to destroy the old, both wanted to create something utterly new. The Bolsheviks undoubtedly tapped a vein of utopian expectation in the masses. Yet the two sides approached the tasks of destruction and creation very differently.

In these early months, the Bolsheviks needed the destructive passions of the masses and to some extent stirred them up. Violence against landowners, priests, bourgeois politicians and capitalist parasites could only help. Yet the violence had to be carefully controlled. Everything and everyone that might contribute to socialism had to be put to use. Art, science, technology and know-how had to be saved from the bonfire; so, too, had the artists, scientists, technicians and experts, bourgeois or otherwise. Without science, technology and enlightenment, socialism was inconceivable. The last thing the Bolsheviks wanted was a holocaust, mindless destruction, a descent into what they would soon be calling 'petty bourgeois anarchy'.

As for creating the new: in a country so backward and so ruined by war and revolution, socialism could not possibly be achieved without an immense sustained collective effort, without organization and discipline and unremitting labour centrally directed over a lengthy period. This the Bolshevik leaders had realized within a matter of weeks; ordinary people too would surely understand that there could be no socialism without hard work and discipline.

Yet here the gulf in mentality between the two sides was at its most unbridgeable. For the masses, 'socialism' and 'democracy' signified something utterly different from discipline and organization. These words were a summons, rather, to cast off all burdens and constraints imposed by the state. They seemed to offer people freedom to control their own lives, though freedom of a distinctively Russian kind: freedom exercised within a community, be it the village, the work-shop, or the factory, in which the members jointly made the decisions, shared the ensuing benefits and burdens, and were only minimally subject to outsiders. Within a few months, however, Lenin and his colleagues would be thinking along very different lines, and they would condemn such 'freedom' as petty bourgeois, anarchist, and alien to socialism.

3

A first warning of the trouble ahead came with the Constituent Assembly elections, in mid-November, when the Bolsheviks won only 23 percent of the votes and were roundly beaten by the SRs. The result came as a sore disappointment; its sequel was the dispersal of the assembly on 5 January 1918. By seizing power the Bolsheviks had already signalled their rejection of 'bourgeois constitutionalism'. Letting the Constituent Assembly elections go ahead had, therefore, been something of an anomaly; once the gamble had failed, they had little choice but to use force. Lenin himself would have preferred to postpone the elections, but he had not put the case very strongly and he must have later regretted having allowed himself, for once, to be talked around by his colleagues.

Yet although the Bolsheviks bungled badly with the Constituent Assembly, the election result was not really surprising and was by no means wholly discreditable to them. They at least had the support of a solid and highly committed minority. They dominated the major towns and industrial areas; they were also strongly supported in the army. And if they had gone down less well among the peasants, that was not unexpected: three weeks was hardly time enough for the impact of the new regime to reach out to the countryside. What the Bolsheviks needed, clearly, was to build on the solid support they already had and to extend the revolution from town to country.

The rural areas, where 80 per cent of the population still lived, were crucial. Without peasant support there could be no socialism. Lenin's unspoken premise, as we have seen, was that the peasant masses could be won, that they were already semi-proletarians. And the Bolsheviks had got off to a promising start with the peasants by giving them the Decree on Land. That was admittedly more in line with SR than with Bolshevik ideas, as Lenin candidly acknowledged, but the effect nevertheless was to make the peasants see the Bolsheviks as their benefactors.

The honeymoon between peasants and Bolsheviks did not, however, last long, and by the spring of 1918 a major shortfall in the delivery of grain to the towns had soured the relationship badly. Lenin put the grain crisis down to the peasant bourgeoisie, the kulaks – they had revolted against Soviet power and were trying to sabotage the revolution by withholding their grain. His response was uncompromising. Party militants from the towns were sent into the countryside to 'requisition' grain – i.e. to commandeer, at a fixed price, any which they considered surplus to the peasants' own requirements. Peasants who tried to resist these grain seizures were labelled 'enemies of the people' and threatened with imprisonment.

What was at stake was not just food but socialism. The militants who invaded the villages did not go simply to seize grain; they went to preach class war and socialist ideas and to stir up the peasant masses against the kulaks. The arithmetic of this rural class conflict, as Lenin calculated it, was very much in the Bolsheviks' favour. Out of 15 million peasant families, 2 million were kulaks and 3 million were middle peasants, leaving 10 million families in the 'poor peasant', semi-proletarian category.[9] These 'poor peasants' were the Bolsheviks' natural allies. The urban militants would link up with them, recruit them by explaining matters to them, and lead them into battle against their kulak exploiters under the slogan 'Representatives of the poor, unite!'[10] The class warfare would be coordinated on the spot by Committees of Poor Peasants, set up throughout the country in June 1918.

Had Lenin calculated rightly, then urban and rural proletarians would have fought shoulder-to-shoulder against the kulaks. The attempt to set peasant at war with peasant turned out, however, to be a fiasco. Differentiation in the countryside had not gone very far before the revolution, and the redistribution of landowners' land had since had an equalizing effect. The overwhelming majority were, in Lenin's terms, 'middle peasants', and they united against these urban invaders who not only seized grain but looked like overturning their entire way of life. The abolition of the Committees of Poor Peasants after six inglorious months was a belated victory for common sense over dogma. The attempt to take class warfare into the midst of the peasantry had failed. Its failure had, for the time being, killed off any hopes of replacing a small-scale, peasant ('petty bourgeois') agriculture by the only agriculture considered appropriate to socialism – a collectivized one.

The failure had serious implications for Lenin's whole socialist strategy, since this was based on the assumption that the peasant masses, being 'semi-proletarian', would link up with the urban proletariat and respond readily to socialism. By the end of 1918, any such belief lay in ruins. Most peasants, Lenin now reluctantly acknowledged, were not 'small' but 'middle'; most, it followed, were not likely to welcome socialism and collective farming. The brute reality, indeed, was that Lenin and his colleagues ruled over a population most of whose members, far from wanting socialism, fiercely opposed it.

If there was no peasant proletariat, then a gaping hole had been struck through the very heart of Lenin's revolutionary strategy. Where did the party go from here? One thing was certain: there could be no question of surrendering to the 'petty bourgeois masses' (as the peasants were now seen). Grain and other produce was still requisitioned from them; private trading continued to be banned. Come what might, the Bolsheviks would not be thwarted by the peasants. They would use the power they had won for socialist purposes. Yet unlike many of his colleagues, Lenin was careful not to adopt an attitude of blanket hostility towards the peasants. Stupid and greedy they might be, but somehow they had to be brought to a voluntary acceptance of socialist agriculture and of socialism itself. There could be no way forward without the peasants, and yet after the great disillusionment of 1918 it was by no means clear how or when a bridge between them and socialism could be built.

4

With the non-Russians, too, Lenin suffered an unexpected setback. His hope had been that most would choose to stay within the Soviet state and that those who did opt out would before long think better of it. His policy of killing off nationalism by kindness had, however, quickly run into difficulties. Civil war, the failure of revolution in the west, Russia's emergence as an isolated bastion of socialism surrounded by hostile powers – all of this worked against his idea of winning the non-Russians' voluntary adhesion. So too did the attitude of colleagues, including the commissar for nationalities, Joseph Stalin, who were against indulging the non-Russians and saw no alternative to forcing them into the socialist camp.

Lenin himself admitted that force might sometimes be unavoidable. No Marxist, he wrote in January 1918, 'can deny that the interests of socialism are higher than the interests of the right of nations to self-determination'. If the existence of a socialist republic was being imperilled, then naturally 'the preservation of the socialist republic has the higher claim'.[11] This justification for force had particular relevance to Ukraine. When the regime found itself with its back to the wall, armed intervention against its Ukraine-based opponents became irresistible; and after protracted and confused fighting Ukraine was brought firmly within the new state's fold. But self-defence was not the only reason for intervention across the new national borders. Did the Bolsheviks not owe help to the proletarians of the non-Russian areas? Should they not intervene on their side? '... we must probe with bayonets whether the social revolution of the proletariat' has yet ripened, Lenin and his colleagues decided with regard to Poland.[12] In this case, however, the attempt to help social revolution along by 'probing' with bayonets proved counter-productive. The revolution had by no means ripened in Poland; the Poles preferred their own kith and kin of whatever class to the invading Russian workers, and the Red Army suffered a disastrous defeat outside Warsaw.

Nor had the social revolution ripened in Finland or the Baltic states, the other areas that seemed most propitious for it. In Estonia the Bolsheviks had won 40 per cent of the vote in the Constituent

Assembly elections, and in Latvia they had won no less than 70 per cent. Yet here and elsewhere on the former empire's western fringe the Bolsheviks' attempts to export revolution failed badly, and they finished by having to accept the independence of the western borderlands under bourgeois and anti-Russian regimes. The national community, bonded by religion, language and cultural tradition, exercised a far stronger appeal than any notion of socialist internationalism and the brotherhood of workers. These people of the periphery reacted in fact to the Bolsheviks' intervention much as the Russian peasants had – they closed ranks against the outsider and rejected his class war slogans.

Despite these reverses, the Bolsheviks reconstituted much of the old multi-national state. By the spring of 1921, Ukraine, Belorussia, Transcaucasia and the broad expanses of central Asia had all been brought by conquest within the Soviet fold. Yet there was little in the achievement to satisfy Lenin, and on the nationalities issue he remained at odds with most of his colleagues. The Bolsheviks were in danger, he argued, of acting like tsarism's Great-Russian chauvinists. Chauvinism and oppression, he warned, had made the minority peoples hate the Russians, and the party's aims could never be achieved until this hatred was dispelled. It was vital to show utmost respect for the culture, language and traditions of the minority peoples. Moreover, tactful treatment was not enough – national distinctiveness had to be reflected in the structure of the state itself.

On this issue of the state structure Lenin had, as it happened, turned turtle. Till October, the Bolsheviks had fiercely resisted federalism. The revolutionary state would be centralized and unitary; each people of the former empire would have a choice between entering fully into it and opting for independence; no midway position would be allowed. In the wake of October, however, the advantages of a federal structure for the new state rapidly became apparent. Federalism had an obvious appeal to small nations fearful that the Russians might swamp them; as for the more dogmatic anti-federalists among the Bolsheviks, they were bought off by the assurance that federalism would not be extended to the party itself, which would remain a monolith and hence a bulwark against centrifugal tendencies. Federalism seemed as a result to offer something to everyone. It would assuage the tender feelings of the minorities, yet the semblance of independence offered them would not affect the essential control exercised by the party from Moscow.

The federal idea had not, in the event, averted the need for force, and Lenin had accepted that military methods were unavoidable. Yet he viewed these methods rather differently from most of his colleagues and field commanders. The use of force should, he believed, be discreet, minimal and linked directly to the party's socialist objectives. It should not, whatever happened, smack of Russian imperialism; on the contrary, the Red Army's interventions should appear a response to the wishes of the local population and the requests of local communists. What Lenin wanted, in short, was a skilfully veiled and minimal intervention which, far from inflaming national feeling and anti-Russianness, would promote socialist consciousness among the conquered and make them willing partners of the workers and peasants of Russia in a common federal state.

Lenin's attitude towards the non-Russians was thus very similar to his attitude towards the peasants. In both cases he accepted the need for coercion; in both he insisted that the coercion should be tactful and minimal; in both he wanted this discreet use of force to help bring about a state of mind in which its objects would happily accept the party's aims. To his less fastidious colleagues, however, Lenin was being absurdly finicky. Indeed, he was asking for the moon in wanting a conquest so stealthy and tactful that it would produce no negative reactions and even come over as a form of assistance. Yet Lenin refused to bow to his colleagues' *realpolitik*. And the question of whether there could be a distinctly Leninist way with the nationalities, a way that blended coercion and persuasion, was shortly set in relief by events in Georgia.

This small Caucasian republic would have attracted the Bolsheviks for economic and strategic reasons alone, but what made it stick out like a sore thumb for them was that it had a Menshevik government. Georgia's Mensheviks had carried off what their Petrograd counterparts had singularly failed to achieve – they had won overwhelming support, taking more than 80 per cent of the vote in the February 1919 elections, and had managed to remain popular. They had set up democratic institutions but also managed to keep the support of the peasant masses, without losing that of the workers, by putting through a major land reform. In the words of a recent historian, in its brief period of independence 'Georgia exemplified the social-democratic ideal – a working class deferring to its socialist intelligentsia, prepared to follow its lead in building a democratic nation-state, and willing to wait for the distant victory of socialism'.[13]

The episode was to be bathed in an especial poignancy by what would follow it, but the significance of the Mensheviks' achievement was by no means lost on observers at the time. A delegation of leading members of the Second International, including Lenin's one-time idol and now bête noire, Karl Kautsky, visited the country in September 1920; and Kautsky, who stayed on for several months, subsequently wrote a book about it in which he praised to the skies this attempt by 'a real socialist government' to maintain itself 'without dictatorship or terrorism, using the means and methods of democracy ...'[14] The achievements of this small republic were therefore more than a pinprick in the Bolsheviks' flank; they were a glaring ideological affront, a vindication of what the Petrograd Mensheviks had tried and failed to do and of that whole bourgeois-democratic socialist tradition which Lenin had written off with contempt.

All of this gave the Bolsheviks a powerful incentive to unleash the Red Army, which by the end of 1920 had already crushed the independence of the two other Transcaucasian republics, Azerbaijan and Armenia. From Lenin's point of view, however, there were countervailing arguments against any intervention. The Georgian government might be Menshevik, but it had overwhelming popular support. The Georgian Bolsheviks, by contrast, had very little following, even among the small working class. A Soviet take-over would be nothing other than a coup d'état and would be hard to pass off as anything else. Without the Red Army – without naked coercion – there could be no Soviet power in Georgia.

For a time Lenin resisted his pro-interventionist colleagues, including Stalin and the especially gung-ho Sergo Ordzhonikidze, the Bolshevik commander in Transcaucasia. He eventually yielded in February 1921, but only under great pressure and with evident misgivings; and within days of the fall of Tiflis he had sent Ordzhonikidze instructions that embodied his own distinctive approach to the nationalities question. First, a Georgian Red Army should be created – troops from elsewhere might have established Soviet power, but Georgian workers and peasants would maintain it. Second, there should be 'a special policy of concessions with regard to the Georgian intelligentsia and small merchants'. Intellectuals should be handled with kid gloves; and, unlike in Russia, private trading should be permitted. Third, 'it is of tremendous importance to devise an acceptable compromise for a bloc with Zhordania or similar Georgian Mensheviks ...' There was a clear suggestion here that the ousted Mensheviks should if possible be drawn into a coalition government. Finally, the Georgian communists should 'avoid any mechanical copying of the Russian pattern' and should 'work out their own flexible tactics, based on bigger concessions to all the petty-bourgeois elements'.[15]

By 'the Russian pattern' Lenin presumably had in mind anything that smacked of War Communism, which by now (2 March 1921) had outlived its usefulness even in Russia. But he also of course meant that the Georgian communists should have especial regard to the distinctive traditions of Georgia, that they should not automatically copy the Russian example and that they should do their utmost to avoid offending national feelings. Nor was this a passing whim. Six weeks later he urged communists in all three Transcaucasian republics 'to effect a slower, more cautious and more systematic transition to socialism' and 'to show more readiness to make concessions to the petty bourgeoisie, the intelligentsia, and particularly the peasantry' than had been done in Russia.[16]

These soft words could hardly disguise the fact that Soviet power in Georgia rested upon an act of blatant aggression. Lenin's approach would nevertheless have differed very significantly from the one actually adopted. The new regime would not have touched the Menshevik land settlement, which allowed the peasants full ownership of their land and left small areas to the nobles. It would have let private trading continue, treated intellectuals with sympathy and tried to build bridges with the Mensheviks. Above all, a Leninist approach would have implied acting in ways that that seemed to reflect the needs and wishes of ordinary Georgians and did not violate their immediate material interests or their national feelings. The new regime would in fact have made a determined attempt to create what the Bolsheviks so far signally lacked in Georgia – a social base among the intelligentsia, the working class and the peasantry.

Were such ideas pie in the sky on the part of an isolated dreamer in the Kremlin? Perhaps they were; but in the event they were never even put to the test. Not that Lenin's approach lacked sympathizers among the communists themselves. On the contrary, a majority of members of the Central Committee of the Communist Party of Georgia initially cleaved strongly to Lenin's line. Among the Leninists was Pilipe Makharadze, chairman of the Georgian Revolutionary Committee, who on the eve of the Red Army's invasion had met Lenin in Moscow to discuss the cautious tactics that were needed, and Budu Mdivani, his successor in the Revcom, who as centralizing pressures increased would defiantly invoke Lenin's name in support of the approach that was being flouted – 'If you find me guilty of nationalism, then you must also find Comrade Lenin and the Central Committeee of the RKP(b) guilty.'[17]

Even with Lenin's directives so clearly favouring them, however, such communists were unable to get the better of Ordzhonikidze, the apparatchiks in the Bolsheviks' Transcaucasian headquarters, and Stalin. These were implacably opposed to Georgian nationalism – which needed to be burned away 'with red-hot irons', declared Ordzhonikidze, quoting Stalin.[18] The priority of such people was to integrate Georgia with the other Trancaucasian republics and Transcaucasia as a whole with the Russian Federation (RSFSR). While paying lip-service to Lenin, they overrode the local communists and used strong-arm methods to achieve their purposes. And before long Georgia would become an emblem of all that separated Lenin from fellow Bolsheviks, especially Stalin, not only on the nationalities question but on the broader problem of building socialism.

5

Resistance from peasants and non-Russians was not wholly unexpected. But the Bolsheviks had counted upon the urban workers, and a falling-off in support from them came as a bitter blow. The problem was, in part, one of numbers. The Bolsheviks had confidently expected that economic upturn would lead to a rapid increase in the size of the proletariat. Economic collapse, however, produced quite the opposite effect, and the $2^{1}/_{2}$ million urban workers of 1917 had by the end of 1920 declined to little more than 1 million. The urban proletariat, which should have been the bedrock of Bolshevik support, which should indeed have formed the leading and ruling class, was melting away under the Bolsheviks' disbelieving gaze.

Numbers, however, were not the only issue. Doubts soon emerged as to whether the Russian proletariat was capable, as things stood, of the leadership role for which history had apparently predestined it. Did the workers indeed constitute a proletariat at all? In his pre-October thinking Lenin had seen the urban workers setting an example to the rural masses and making a decisive contribution to economic development and state administration. Within a few weeks, however, this romanticized view of the workforce had vanished; and evidence then steadily accumulated that the workers had neither the skills, the creative initiative nor the necessary self-discipline for the role which the Bolsheviks had expected them to play.

The problem began with the hallowed idea of workers' control, which had done much to win workers to the Bolsheviks' cause. Lenin's commitment to this was genuine enough, yet the two sides understood the term somewhat differently. By the eve of October, workers were demanding nothing less than the right to manage the factories themselves on an egalitarian and cooperative basis. By contrast, Lenin's notion of workers' control was one in which input from below would be balanced by input from above, in which employee creativity would be complemented by planning and centralization. The difference was glossed over at first, but within a short time worker anarchism (as Lenin came to regard it) and deepening economic crisis had driven the two sides far apart. By the spring of 1918, Lenin was interpreting workers' control as nothing more than the right of workers' representatives to monitor management. Worse still for the workers, he had entirely rejected any idea of industrial democracy. His emphasis from now on was on organization, centralization and discipline. There was no more talk of worker initiative; one-man management was instead the order of the day. Factory managers would in effect become dictators, since industry required compulsion and 'absolute and strict unity of will'. Before the end of the year, he had rejected workers' control altogether in favour of 'workers' industrial administration on a national scale'. Workers' control, he remarked, was bound to be 'chaotic, disorganized, primitive and incomplete'.[19] Thus was killed off what, for a time, had appeared to be one of Bolshevism's cardinal ideas.

If the workers were incapable of running the factories, still less could they run the state; and the death of industrial democracy implied the death of democracy in the public sphere as a whole. Here, too, Lenin suffered a bitter disillusionment. He had looked to a vigorous soviet movement which, at first in the towns but before long in the countryside as well, would draw millions of people into the task of everyday administration. Soon, however, he was lamenting the shortfall of talent among the workers, the lack of proletarians capable of taking a leading role.' 'The section of workers who are governing', he told the Eighth Party Congress, 'is inordinately, incredibly *small.*' This dearth of talent at the grass roots inevitably changed the nature of the soviets. Intended to be 'organs of government *by the working people*', they had, he admitted, instead become 'organs of government *for the working people* by the advanced section of the working people, but not by the working people as a whole'.[20] Far from gingering the population and making their own contribution to the building of socialism, the soviets had willy-nilly become administrative organs which carried out the party's orders. When a constitution for the new state was drawn up in 1918, this did, it is true, attribute supreme power to the soviets, but that simply described how things *should* have been; the reality was that the party decided everything in the soviets' name.

Not only were the workers incapable of running the country; many, it began to appear, did not even support the party which was carrying out the task on their behalf. Worse still, they seemed to lack any underlying commitment to socialism. At the Constituent Assembly elections, worker backing for the Bolsheviks had still been solid; but elections to soviets during the first half of 1918 showed a swing in the workers' sympathies towards the SRs and the Mensheviks. That was cut short by the simple expedient of excluding the SRs and Mensheviks from political life. Lenin's trust in the urban working class had, however, been destroyed and would never return.

Lenin had come to power believing that a rock-solid proletariat in the towns would draw a massive rural semi-proletariat along in its wake. But within a year he had been forced to a shatteringly different view of the social landscape. There was little or no proletariat in the countryside; as for the urban masses, most of them were petty bourgeois rather than proletarian. Far from the villages being won over by the militant socialism of the towns, there was a real danger that the flickering socialist consciousness in the towns would be extinguished and that the urban population would return, in spirit at least, to the peasantry from which it had so recently emerged.

6

This revelation had profound implications for the governance of the Soviet state. In *The State and Revolution* and other of his pre-October writings, Lenin had depicted the dictatorship of the proletariat as the rule of the immense majority over a small minority of exploiters. For the majority, this dictatorship would be an instrument of democracy and liberation; its coercive powers would be used solely against the minority, who would be repressed with relative ease. The discovery, however, that the masses were not proletarian and not even close to becoming that, risked putting the government on a par with run-of-the-mill dictatorships. Instead of facing a small minority of easily crushed opponents, it would have to struggle against the indifference if not hostility of the overwhelming majority. 'What dictatorship implies and means is a state of simmering war, a state of military struggle against the enemies of the proletariat.'[21] There would have in fact to be sustained repression of the majority ; and the best that could be done to justify that was to argue, as did Nikolai Bukharin and others, that it was only under the dictatorship of the proletariat – that is, a dictatorship exercised *on behalf of* the proletariat – that the proletariat could grow to maturity.

The dictatorship of the proletariat was thus the rule of the few who were genuinely proletarian, in attitude if not in background, over the many who had not yet been able to realize their proletarian vocation. The party ruled as a temporary substitute for the people, and it was in turn ruled, in practice, by the handful whom Lenin referred to as the 'Old Guard'. In conditions of civil war and economic collapse, the centralist tendency in the party had got the better of its flimsy democratism. Swift and firm decision-taking became essential. Party officials were increasingly appointed from above; elections, if they took place at all, became a formality. The tendency to concentrate unlimited power at the top was reinforced by massive expansion, which saw the party's numbers swell from 20 000 in early 1917 to 732 000 by March 1921. These newcomers who swamped the Old Bolsheviks (as pre-revolutionary members, especially those of intelligentsia background, came to be known) were nearly all workers or peasants radicalized by Red Army service. The educational and cultural level of most was little higher than that of the non-party masses. A party so composed needed, for practical and ideological reasons alike, to be ruled very firmly by the handful of initiates at its apex, and most of its members expected nothing else.

Lenin had little difficulty in justifying a government so different from the one he had envisaged in the run-up to October. There was not much difference, in principle, between the short-lived dictatorship he had anticipated and one forced by popular recalcitrance to prolong its existence. The situation of being a tiny island of enlightenment in a sea of darkness was, after all, familiar enough to any Bolshevik of Lenin's vintage. It was precisely with that perspective that Bolshevism had begun. The truths of socialism had not been devalued then by the fact that so few appreciated them; nor were they devalued now by the whims and fancies of those who were being unexpectedly laggardly in seeing the light. Until the masses acquired socialist consciousness, numbers remained an irrelevance. The Bolsheviks would have to continue acting for the people, even if this meant having to seem to act *against* them; and history would vindicate what they did.

Yet while the theoretical difficulties might be glossed over, the practical problems created by the Bolsheviks' minority situation were immense. They had seized power on the assumption that political revolution could rapidly be followed, with the support of the overwhelming majority, by socio-economic and cultural revolution. Instead, they found themselves high and dry, with almost no popular support. How, short of admitting their error and surrendering, could they get out of this absurd situation? The obvious solution was to bull-doze their way out, to force through changes that would bring the backward socio-economic and cultural 'base' into line with the advanced 'superstructure'. And the very fact that they had applied force so successfully in the political sphere simply encouraged them to think that forceful methods could be applied equally effectively else-where.

None of this implied any change in Lenin's basic thinking about socialism, but it did imply new thinking about methods, stages and timescale. What he was doing, without saying so, was to insert an entirely new developmental stage in what he admitted would be a long and difficult transition from capitalism to the new society.[22] Socialism, itself a transition stage in one of the two meanings Lenin attached to it, would have to be preceded by another, still more elementary transitional stage, a stage that would almost certainly be lacking in any characteristics of the completed socialism. During this transition-to-the-transition, the regime would force people to work towards ends they did not yet believe in. Compulsion and iron disci-pline would be the hallmarks; and the regime would even use naked terror in order to create the necessary foundations for further advance.

The make-or-break issue, apart from actual political survival, was economic. While they fought the Whites, the Bolsheviks began an economic transformation, spurred on by zealots who wanted to liqui-date all traces of capitalism, money included. In the summer of 1918 all of heavy industry was nationalized; two years later, small-scale enterprise was brought under state control as well. Private trade was banned; shops were closed; the very idea of a market in which indi-viduals and enterprises exchanged goods and services was declared unsocialist and therefore impermissible. Distribution would from now on be wholly organized by agencies of the state. All economic activity indeed would be controlled by the state through its Supreme Council of the National Economy and subordinate bodies, and a burgeoning officialdom would apply Marxist principles to economic decision-making.

These changes had a devastating effect upon everyday existence. Placing all economic activity under centralized state control led to the run-down and closure of factories, rampant inflation, a steep decline in real wages, and general chaos. Intended to strike a deadly blow at the bourgeois, the economic transformation in fact created misery for everyone. In order to mitigate its ravages, the Commissariat of Supply ordered that basic foodstuffs should be distributed free; rent, electricity, travel and other basic services likewise cost nothing. Bolshevik zealots exulted that the destruction of capitalism and virtual disappearance of money had brought communism close. But while the infrastructure of a socialist economy had been put in place, one basic ingredient for the new society was wholly missing. There was no material abundance, there was not even an upward curve of economic activity. On the contrary, two years of 'War Communism', as the radical policies of the period would become known, had created unprecedented material deprivation. The communists had promised plenty – they had brought destruction.

The outcome of War Communism was a crisis, which struck early in 1921. The Bolsheviks had won the war, but the country was ruined, starving and seething with discontent. Peasant hostility had so far been held in check by fear that victory for the Whites would make things even worse. The Bolsheviks' victory had, however, destroyed restraint, and in the winter of 1920–1 widespread peasant revolts broke out. There were signs, too, of serious discontent among what remained of the urban working class. There was even resistance to the leadership from within the party itself. Democratic Centralists campaigned for more power for the soviets, more say for the party rank-and-file, and genuine elections, while the Workers' Opposition denounced bureaucracy and stood up for the rights of the workers in what was meant, after all, to be a workers' party. But the thunderflash which lit up quite how terrible the situation was came at the end of February 1921, when the sailors and workers of Kronstadt, the naval base guarding Petrograd, broke into revolt.

This was no ordinary place. Kronstadt's sailors had much the role in Bolshevik mythology that the sansculottes who stormed the Bastille had in French revolutionary mythology. In October they had brought the cruiser *Aurora* to the mouth of the Neva and trained its guns on the Winter Palace. But the Kronstadters no longer saw the Bolsheviks as their representatives; they also refused to accept the Bolshevik path to socialism as the true one. Free speech, free elections to the soviets, freedom for trade unions, the release of all socialist political prisoners – these were the rebels' demands. This challenge to Bolshevik rule from people whose working-class and revolutionary credentials were impeccable could not have been more damaging.

At risk was not only Bolshevik power but Bolshevik morale. In the opinion of Zinoviev, the party's supporters were now down to no more than 1 per cent of the working class. Lenin's own conclusion was more chastening still: the proletariat, he told delegates to the Tenth Party Congress as the battle for Kronstadt went on, 'has been largely declassed'.[23] The workers had gone back to their peasant roots and become infected by 'petty bourgeois anarchism'. What his words implied was clear enough. The proletariat was not only under-sized, immature, and incapable of carrying out its mission unaided. This class on whose existence the October Revolution had been predicated had all but disappeared. A declassed proletariat was little different from a non-existent proletariat. The conclusion should have been devastating. Yet Lenin's attitude was one of total defiance. Numbers did not matter. The Kronstadt rebels did not matter. The Bolsheviks were right, and the Bolsheviks would win.

That said, the crisis of 1921 underlined how completely the Bolsheviks' plans had miscarried. By now, had their assumptions proved correct, they should have won the support of all but a few former exploiters. The masses should have become their partners in the day-to-day running of the country and the building of socialism. The economy should have been developing strongly; the machine of repression should have become largely redundant; the state itself might have begun shedding some of its functions. The country should in fact have moved into the stage of socialism in the transitional sense, even if full socialism or communism would still have lain well ahead.

But how the realities of 1921 mocked these naive expectations! For Bolshevik policies had not unleashed any 'latent socialism' among the masses. The base of strong minority support with which they began in October had not expanded but disintegrated. They were having to coerce not merely a minority of exploiters but the vast bulk of the toiling population, workers, peasants and non-Russians, the very people without whose voluntary and informed support they could never achieve socialism. They had indeed got to the situation, as Zinoviev pointed out, of having no significant support at all – apart from the power apparatus itself. Their regime had become an embattled fortress ruling over a hostile population, and in that respect at least it had an uncomfortable resemblance to tsarism. Such a position would have been unthinkable to any Bolshevik before October. In the long term it was clearly untenable. It was perhaps untenable in the short term as well.

7

The gravity of the situation led to the New Economic Policy (NEP), which, beginning as a concession to peasant demands, would develop into an entirely new strategy. From 1918 the party's leaders had acted as if the preconditions for socialism could be created by methods similar to those which had won power for them in October. That assumption was clearly mistaken. True, Lenin himself had succumbed to it rather less than most of his colleagues. He had continued to insist that socialism itself could only be created through the willing cooperation of the masses; it could not be implemented 'by a minority, by the Party', but only 'by tens of millions when they have learned to do it themselves'.[24] His emphasis, too, had nevertheless been on coercion rather than persuasion, on iron discipline, organization, and the mobilization of manpower. By February 1921, however, he, unlike many of his colleagues, had come to see that the policy was leading not to socialism but towards disaster. Politicians rarely admit to major policy blunders, but Lenin in effect now did so. In April 1921 he was talking of War Communism as a 'makeshift' which the party had been forced into by extreme circumstances. In October 1921 he declared outright that the attempt to implement an economic policy that would lead direct to full socialism had been a mistake, that it was impossible to introduce socialist economic principles 'by direct assault'.[25]

The sharp light of the crisis revealed quite how far the party had deviated from his original project. Pressured by adverse circumstances, it had tried to impose socialism upon an unwilling population. For the remaining two years of his political life, Lenin would try to retrieve this error and find a new way forward, without, however, admitting that the original revolutionary 'leap' had been mistaken.

Going back to his project in its previous form was of course impossible. For that had assumed that the Bolsheviks would be able to reorganize society with the willing cooperation of the masses. That assumption had now gone into history. For the time being, the party would have to rule for rather than with the masses and even against them. The organs of repression – the army and secret police – would have to remain on full alert; relaxation was out of the question. On the contrary, if the Bolsheviks' rule was to survive they would have to hold the country in a still tighter grip.

Lenin's response to the crisis was, therefore, double-edged. His belief in persuasion and peaceful evolution, which had fallen somewhat into abeyance since 1918, came back strongly. Yet towards anyone who publicly challenged the party he remained implacable. Not an inch would be yielded; each and every challenge would be crushed. The Kronstadt mutiny was bloodily suppressed; its demands were condemned as petty bourgeois and anarchist; none was conceded. The Menshevik and SR parties were finally liquidated; many leading intellectuals were expelled from the country. Little mercy was shown, either, to the party's internal critics. The task of the proletariat in a peasant country 'is so vast and difficult', Lenin told the Tenth Party Congress, 'that formal cohesion is far from enough'. With its back to the wall, the party could not afford the luxury of public bickering, still less of organized internal opposition. On this premise he won overwhelming support for a resolution banning factions within the party, and similar support for a resolution which condemned the Workers' Opposition as a syndicalist and anarchist deviation whose ideas represented 'a complete break with Marxism and communism'.[26]

'This', Lenin admitted, 'is an extreme measure that is being adopted specially in view of the dangerous situation.'[27] Later commentators would cite that and similar statements as proof that, once the emergency had passed, he would have had the ban on factions lifted. But whatever Lenin's intentions, the ban on factions stayed and was to have fateful consequences. What remained of the party's democratic tradition had been destroyed. At the apex a handful of people made all the major decisions; beneath them a second-tier elite of bureaucrats and troubleshooters, marshalled by the party's secretariat, fixed things on the leaders' behalf; and beneath them the massed ranks of ordinary party members acted as a 'transmission belt' (Lenin's term) between leadership and people.

The party, in short, had become again the creature of its leaders, who did their business in the Council of People's Commissars and a still smaller body, created in 1919, the party's Political Bureau or Politburo. There could be no free choice for the simple reason that the masses would vote the Bolsheviks out. The unlimited power of the Bolshevik party-state, and the repression of anyone who publicly challenged it, turned out to be the most fundamental precondition for socialism. Were that precondition to be given up, or even seriously diluted, the socialist cause in Russia would most probably be ruined for the foreseeable future. So at least the matter looked, even to Bolsheviks of principle, in the early 1920s.

And yet while Lenin took his stand on unlimited Bolshevik power, he insisted that this power should be used with far greater sensitivity to the wishes and feelings of the people. NEP began by abolishing the hated requisitioning of produce. Instead, there would be a tax in kind, set at a much lower level, and peasants would be given a limited freedom to trade their surpluses. What began as a retreat over the issues of requisitioning and free trade had, however, within a few months become a significantly different strategy. 'What is new for our revolution at the present time', Lenin wrote in November 1921, 'is the need for a "reformist", gradual, cautious and roundabout approach to the solution of the fundamental problems of economic development.'[28]

Progress, the new thinking had it, could not be other than slow. The party had to link up with the people. That could be done only by giving them the right to earn a living in familiar ways – even if this meant temporarily letting capitalism back in. 'The idea of building Communist society exclusively with the hands of the Communists is', Lenin observed, 'childish, absolutely childish.'[29] The Bolsheviks were a mere drop in the ocean.They could not lead unless their policies were acceptable to the masses and made conditions better for them. Socialism was, therefore, no longer on the immediate agenda. The party had so far done no more than complete the bourgeois-democratic stage of the revolution; a socialist economy still lay beyond reach. Making a direct assault on the goal had proved futile, indeed counterproductive. What was needed was a zigzag approach that would at first go backwards in order to ensure later success.

The main thing was 'to advance as an immeasurably wider and larger mass, and only together with the peasantry …'[30] But it was not enough simply to buy off hostility by making concessions. And near the end of his career, Lenin came to see that the way to ease the transition from a small-peasant to a socialist agriculture was via the cooperative system. For the peasants, cooperatives were 'the simplest, easiest and most acceptable' form of transition to the new system; they were a bridge over which the peasants would pass painlessly from private enterprise to socialism.[31] All that was needed was to get them to see the advantage of taking part in cooperative organizations.

That was 'all' – and yet what an enormous 'all'! The task of getting the peasants involved in cooperatives was, Lenin admitted, daunting. It would require 'a whole historical epoch' and 'a veritable revolution'. This revolution, on which at the end of his life Lenin set his hopes, would, however, be quite different from the October one. It would be gentle and gradual; there would be no crude propaganda and a minimum of philosophizing and 'acrobatics'. Haste was out of the question. The pace of the advance might well be a hundred times slower than the Bolsheviks had hoped for, yet what mattered was that 'it will be a million times more certain and more sure.'[32]

So at the end of his life Lenin made a fervent restatement of one of his cardinal pre-October beliefs. The party could not achieve socialism except through the willing and informed cooperation of the masses; the undertaking begun by a supreme assertion on the part of a few could only succeed if it grew into the common endeavour of all. With this he drew back from the one-sided emphasis on coercion and reshaping society to a blueprint which had marked him in 1918–20; from now on the two sides to his political character were brought back into something approaching a balance. Soviet society as he envisaged it at the end of his life would be held in a tight grip by the party, which would brook no challenge from any other organization or ideology. This all-powerful party would, however, do its utmost not to alienate people by imposing unfamiliar ideas or practices upon them; instead, it would bring them to socialism gradually by way of material induce-ments, the cooperative system, and education.

The NEP strategy etched by Lenin at the end of his life rested upon two largely unspoken assumptions, one economic and the other polit-ical. The economic assumption was that the concessions made to capitalism – to private enterprise and personal interest – would not be long-lasting and would help rather than hinder the transition to socialism. For a while, the Soviet republic would experience 'state capi-talism' and would have a mixed economy in which state and private enterprises existed side by side. The peasants would, however, come to see the superiority of the socialist economic system, thanks largely to their experience of the cooperatives, and this realization would help ensure the ultimate triumph of socialism over its rival.

That political power remained in the hands of the proletariat would make it doubly certain that capitalism could be controlled and in time eliminated. The party was the guarantor of that path of development which Lenin now saw as the only one by which this backward society could be brought to socialism. It would make sure that the capitalists served socialism's purposes; its unchallenged supremacy would be the safeguard of steady and undeviating progress towards the goal. The party could not of course create socialism by itself, but its guiding role, its fidelity to Marxism and to the NEP strategy, were vital for socialism's success.

All of this, however, placed an enormous burden of responsibility upon the party. That in turn created dangers. The party could only fulfil its function if it was all-powerful; any dissipating of its power would, in the short term, be fatal. But how to ensure that unlimited power did not lead to arrogance, corruption and other abuses? How to ensure that the party did not stray from the socialist path? The Bolsheviks had scored a magnificent victory; they had set up the first government ever dedicated to socialism; yet for the last two years of his active life Lenin would wrestle with the problem of how to stop that triumph turning sour.

8

The safeguards against abuse provided by liberal democracy – a parliament, an independent legal system, guaranteed civil liberties, a press open to all opinions – were of course out of the question. These were simply part of the chicanery by which the bourgeois hoodwinked the masses and utterly irrelevant to a society that had put the bourgeois phase behind it. The problem, however, was that the safeguards which should have superseded the bourgeois ones were not yet available. In a socialist society, the masses would participate directly in the process of government; the organs of repression – police, army and bureaucracy – would be abolished; state power itself would slowly dissolve as society became self-administering. The masses had, however, proved incapable. As a result, there was no likelihood whatever of Soviet state power dissolving in the near future. Instead of less government, there would be more and more government.

If the masses could not govern, they might at least have provided an effective check on those who governed for them. This belief had underpinned the Workers' and Peasants' Inspection, created in 1920 with the specific task of monitoring government activities and exposing and eliminating abuses. Lenin's intention had been that this should, as its name implied, draw ordinary citizens – even, he suggested, illiterates – into the task of rooting out abuses. There was certainly an urgent need for that: abuses that he had seen as intrinsic to tsarism – red tape, arbitrariness, corruption, gross incompetence – were, to his alarm, reappearing on a large scale in a Soviet guise. The experiment, however, proved a failure, and before the end of 1920 he had more or less written off the Workers' and Peasants' Inspection. While the masses remained uneducated and petty bourgeois in mentality, they were incapable of making a useful contribution.[33]

If the party could not be regulated, it would have to regulate itself. And the machinery of self-regulation and democratic accountability existed in the form of congresses, conferences, the election of office-holders, etc. The machinery had, however, always been something of a formality. What underlay this democratic tokenism was an unspoken assumption that the leaders knew best, that the rank and file could have absolute trust in them; and during War Communism the various democratic procedures had, as we have seen, become a dead letter. Party democracy had to be put on hold for much the same reason that general democracy had been put on hold. The newcomers who had swelled the party's ranks were useful as administrators, but they could hardly be admitted to decision-making. Indeed, this influx of ill-educated workers and peasants presented a potential threat. The party's purpose, after all, was to stand outside society, to act upon it and to turn it into something utterly different. But what if this horde of immature newcomers deflected it from its purpose? What if the party ceased to reshape society and was itself reshaped and deformed by the petty bourgeois mentality of the newcomers? The threat was so serious, Lenin decided, that surgery was essential. Almost half of the membership would have to be discarded. There would be a purge of the greedy, of those who had lost touch with the masses, of the 'puffed-up careerists' and the 'bureaucrats'. 'Out with the self-seekers who have crept into the Party, out with the thieves!' Lenin fulminated – only honest communists should be allowed to stay.[34]

Such surgery was, however, only part of the remedy; the other and more positive part was to consolidate the power of those at the party's apex. The way forward was in fact the very opposite of the one Lenin had fondly imagined up to 1918. Authority could not be devolved to the masses or even to the party's own rank and file; instead, it would have to be concentrated more completely at the top. The 'Old Guard' would save the party from degeneration. They would have to be its bulwark against the self-seeking and the dishonest; they alone could ward off the petty bourgeois miasma and preserve the party's integrity, its mission, its proletarian character.

However, during 1921–2 Lenin's faith in the ability of this small group to guide the party successfully and save it from degeneration became seriously undermined. First, doubt emerged about his own ability to continue as leader. Till now it was he who had had the decisive voice in all questions of strategy. Moreover, he had become the party's conscience and its court of appeal; it was he who set and who upheld the standard of socialist virtue. In the eyes of many, and perhaps even of himself, he had become indispensable. But towards the end of 1921 his health began to fail. In May 1922 he suffered a stroke, which put him out of action for several months. He returned to work in the autumn, but he never regained his former vigour; and a further stroke in March 1923 finally brought his career to an end.

Lenin might have faced the prospect of his own removal with more equanimity had he had an obvious successor. But despite men of obvious talent, such as Trotsky and Stalin, the inner circle had no one capable of taking over as helmsman – that at least was Lenin's own opinion. To make matters worse, evidence reached him that the rot affected not only the lower and middle echelons of the party: it had penetrated to the very top. The evidence came from Georgia.

Resuming work in September 1922 after a prolonged absence, Lenin soon became caught up once more in Georgian affairs. Stalin had devised a plan to regularize the relationship between the various Soviet republics by incorporating the smaller ones within the Russian Federation with the status of 'autonomous republics', and he won approval for the plan despite opposition from the Georgian communists. Lenin, however, reacted strongly against the 'autonomization' idea and insisted instead on the creation of a federal union of independent republics. To the Georgians' delight, his intervention proved decisive and Stalin gave way. Lenin was not yet, as it happened, wholly committed to the Georgians' defence, and on the further issue of whether Georgia should join the Union as a separate entity or as part of the Transcaucasian Federation he, like Stalin, came down in favour of the second. By early December 1922, however, Lenin's attitude towards Georgia and towards Stalin had changed dramatically; he had become an impassioned protector of the Georgian communists and from now on he would defend them as vigorously as the ups and downs of his health allowed against what he saw as persecution by Stalin and Ordzhonikidze.

At the end of December he gave full vent to his feelings in a memorandum on the national question which began with an admission of his guilt for not having taken the issue sufficiently seriously before. The non-Russians were being treated in a manner that was basically tsarist and simply given a Soviet gloss. Their right of free secession was mere 'empty verbiage' and incapable of protecting them from 'that truly Russian person, the Great-Russian chauvinist, in essence a rogue and a thug, like the typical Russian bureaucrat'.[35] And the butt of his attack, ironically enough, was the Georgians Stalin and Ordzhonikidze, who had acted like 'Great-Russian chauvinists' and 'true Russian ruffians'. The non-Russians would have to be protected against such people and such behaviour by a policy of positive discrimination. Their languages would have to be safeguarded. And it might even be necessary, he suggested, to rethink the structure of the federation, giving Moscow control only of foreign affairs and defence and leaving all other matters to the individual republics.[36]

Not only did Lenin reject Stalin's stance on the nationalities question; he now rejected Stalin altogether. This was a striking volte-face, since till very recently he had regarded Stalin as an invaluable lieutenant, a trouble-shooter who could be relied upon in any crisis. Precisely for that reason he had early in the year approved Stalin's appointment to the new position of general secretary of the party. By the end of 1922, however, Lenin had developed grave doubts as to whether Stalin would use his 'boundless power' with 'sufficient caution'. A few days later he went much further. Stalin's appointment as general secretary had, he in effect admitted, been a mistake: 'Stalin is too rude and this failing ... is intolerable in a General Secretary'. He should be dismissed from the post and replaced by someone 'more tolerant, more loyal, more polite, and more considerate to the comrades, less capricious, etc.'[37]

The misdemeanours of Stalin and his henchmen highlighted the danger that the party might get out of control, that it might spawn a ruling class as arrogant, self-seeking and unaccountable as the old one. They also drove home the message that the inner circle of leaders could no longer be relied upon as a bulwark against degeneration. All of Lenin's most prominent colleagues had significant failings, as he pointed out in a schoolmasterly review of them. A piecemeal approach to the problem of abuse would therefore be useless: nothing less than a major restructuring would do. And in his 'Letter to the Congress' (the impending Twelfth Party Congress) of late December 1922 he proposed that between 50 and 100 new members should be recruited to the party's Central Committee, the Politburo's nominal master. The new members should attend not only Central Committee but also Politburo meetings; they should read all documents and receive help from specialist advisers; and they should be rank-and-file workers and peasants with no previous experience as Soviet officials.[38]

These ideas were amplified in further writings of late January and early March 1923, in which Lenin argued that the Workers' and Peasants' Inspection and the Central Control Commission, which exercised nominal supervision over the activities of government and party respectively, should be rejuvenated and turned into effective instruments of control over the executive. The Workers' and Peasants' Inspection, slimmed down to 300–400 members, should be made an exemplary state institution; as for the Central Control Commission, nobody, not even the general secretary, should prevent its members 'from putting questions, verifying documents, and, in general, from keeping themselves fully informed of all things and from exercising the strictest control over the proper conduct of affairs'.[39] The two institutions should, moreover, to some degree be merged to create an elite watchdog body which would monitor the work of all government and party agencies and officials, from the lowest to the highest.

The power at present concentrated in the hands of a few people of less than guaranteed reliability would thus be dispersed among several hundred enlightened and incorruptible party members – workers and peasants untainted by the spirit of bureaucracy – who would check one another and spread the highest standards of conduct throughout the whole administration. They would act on behalf of the masses of workers and peasants who had not yet fully achieved socialist consciousness; and they would guide the country slowly but surely, without upheavals and with a minimum of coercion, towards socialism.

Lenin warned, however, that socialism would not be attained until people were ready for it and willed it. Education was vital. The country still lacked civilization and needed to be lifted out of its 'semi-Asiatic ignorance'. Teachers would have a crucial role in instilling the new mentality, though they would not be effective unless they avoided crude propaganda.[40] Education was in fact indispensable to the success of the cooperative movement, which Lenin now saw as the bridge by which the peasants would be brought to socialism. If all the peasants had been taking part in cooperatives, he wrote early in January 1923 in his landmark essay 'On Cooperation', 'we would by now have been standing with both feet on the soil of socialism'. A cooperative peasantry could not be achieved without a cultural revolution; that in itself, however, would be enough 'to make our country a purely socialist country'.[41]

In the same essay Lenin wrote: 'We have to admit that there has been a radical modification in our whole outlook on socialism.' Before, the main emphasis had been 'on the political struggle, on revolution'; now the emphasis had shifted to 'peaceful, organizational, "cultural" work'. The revolution in Russia, he reflected, 'started from the opposite end to that prescribed by theory … because in our country the political and social revolution preceded the cultural revolution, that very cultural revolution which nevertheless now confronts us'. He was not, however, apologising, not confessing that October had been a mistake, not in the least conceding to the 'pedantic Marxism' of the

Mensheviks. 'You say', he addressed these imagined opponents a few days later, 'that civilization is necessary for the building of socialism. Very good. But why could we not first create such prerequisites of socialism in our country as the expulsion of the landowners and the Russian capitalists and then start moving towards socialism?'[42] Those necessary preliminaries were now behind, however, and the tasks as he saw them in early 1923 were wholly different from those that had faced the regime at the outset.

Such were Lenin's thoughts when his second stroke, on 10 March 1923, left him mute and half-paralysed and removed him from the political scene forever. These short, highly compressed writings in which the ailing and marginalized leader ranged across the whole Soviet experience and tried to indicate the direction the country should take when he was no longer there to guide it would go down as his 'political testament'.[43] Part suppressed under Stalin, and never given much prominence until the perestroika period, the 'testament' would enter into myth: it would become the staple of the alternative faith, of the belief in a 'good socialism' of which the country had been cheated by Lenin's successors. Here was the true voice of the founder; here was the socialist way that Russia would have followed had death not prematurely removed him. In the long perspective of Soviet history, the short writings of the 'testament' resonate very power-fully.[44]

These final thoughts were crystallized, as we have seen, by Lenin's anger about the injustice done to the Georgians and the non-Russians in general. The precipitant was, however, something particular and absolutely specific: a physical assault by Ordzhonikidze on a Georgian communist, Akaky Kabikhidze, which seems, once his indignation cooled, to have focused Lenin's mind with extraordinary clarity on the Soviet predicament.

News of Ordzhonikidze's fisticuffs reached Lenin in early December, and his immediate reaction was incandescent anger. On the face of it, this was a surprising and disproportionate response. He, after all, had cold-bloodedly sanctioned acts of real violence, by comparison with which Ordzhonikidze's outburst paled into insignificance. The incident in Tiflis had nevertheless touched him on the quick, and he read – and would continue to read – a profound meaning into it. If matters had come to such a pass, he wrote more than a fortnight after first hearing the news, 'one can imagine what kind of quagmire we have got ourselves into'.[45] Two months later, determinedly pursuing the Georgian affair, he laid down these guidelines for those he had personally commissioned to investigate it: '(i) it is impermissible to fight; (ii) concessions are indispensable; (iii) one cannot compare a large state with a small one.'[46]

The blow was thus more than a piece of random hotheadedness; in Lenin's mind it had become linked with the problems of Georgia and beyond that with the wider Soviet predicament. For some time he had known that the country was in a mess, a quagmire (*boloto*); now he knew more exactly what was wrong and what needed to be done. Ordzhonikidze had not only struck a blow against a fellow communist (which was bad enough in itself); he had also struck a blow against Lenin's long-standing conviction as to the only way by which a socialist society could be built, the only approach that would lead to socialism.

Lenin's belief in the need to win people's willing support had always been tempered by his realization that coercion was unavoidable in the early stages of the transition. His insistence in the 'testament' that only a non-coercive approach could bring the country to socialism originated in his revulsion against events in Georgia, which showed how easily the instrumental use of violence could get out of hand. To discuss the 'testament' without referring to his stance on the national question and the associated issue of violence, as Malia and Walicki both do, is to miss the crux of the matter.[47] The violence that Lenin accepted as a temporary necessity was calculated, minimal, clearly end-related and for the short term only. What he was witnessing, however, was a perversion in which violence seemed to be entering into the very culture, the pith and marrow, of Bolshevism. He rejected that perversion, and in the few months that remained to him he would struggle desperately against it.

Nor was this the overreaction of an invalid who was losing his grip on both power and the rough realities of politics. The roots of Lenin's position on the Georgian affair go back to the beginning of his serious engagement with the nationalities. Take, for instance, the following exchange he had had before the war – in December 1913 – with a Bolshevik who wanted to impose Russian on the non-Russians as the language of the socialist state.

Russian would indeed help the non-Russians, Lenin admitted, 'but don't you see that it would have still more progressive significance if there were no coercion? That "state language" means the big stick, which *repels* people from the Russian language??' And he continued:

Why don't you want to understand the *psychology* which is so important in the national question and which, if the least coercion is applied, defiles, ruins and nullifies the undoubtedly progressive significance of centralization, large states and a uniform language?[48]

'Psychology' and coercion were not mutually exclusive; coercion had an indispensable preliminary role. But psychology alone could bring the peoples of this backward country to socialism. And if Lenin's belief in the psychological approach had lapsed somewhat between 1918 and 1921, it had returned since the spring of 1921: fitfully with NEP, but then in full force as a result of the piercing beam shone on the Soviet situation by events in Georgia.

9

These final efforts of Lenin's proved, however, to be almost entirely in vain. Nothing was done to make good the injury suffered by the Georgians or to benefit the small nations as a whole at the Russians' expense. Even as Lenin was writing on the nationalities question, a new state, the USSR, in which all essential power was concentrated in Moscow, was emerging. Trotsky's half-hearted and Bukharin's much more determined attempts on behalf of the Georgians came up against a wall of hostility. Majority opinion in the party was strongly centralist, if not Russian-chauvinist, had accepted the federal principle with reluctance, and was unwilling to make a reality of it, except in the area of language and culture.

Just as Stalin's *realpolitik* got the better of Lenin's dream of a free union of peoples, so Stalin himself survived Lenin's attempt to get rid of him – though only due to the fact that Lenin's illness turned out to be terminal. The letter in which Lenin urged Stalin's dismissal was read out to the Central Committee shortly after his death. Kamenev and Zinoviev, however, insisted that the letter be hushed up rather than publicized to the forthcoming Thirteenth Party Congress – and the first congress to be told of it would be the Twentieth in 1956. As a result, Stalin continued in post as the party's general secretary. His colleagues had rallied to his defence because it was the charismatic Trotsky rather, they sensed, than the dour Georgian who posed a real threat to themselves. It was a misjudgement they would soon regret.

Stalin's survival in office would have mattered less if Lenin's plan for transforming the political system and creating a much broader governing elite had succeeded ; but it came to nothing. The plan went against the tradition of a party which had throughout been ruled by a tiny oligarchy. It also challenged the existing power structure; and not surprisingly the proposed counterweights soon became converted into instruments of the very body they had been meant to control. By rejecting both democracy in general and party democracy in particular Lenin had already ruled out the only means by which an effective restraint might have been imposed upon the Politburo. All that remained to keep his Politburo colleagues in line was his own influence, and that disappeared in early 1923, never to return.

These problems of policy, personnel and political structure were problems, as it were, of the lower slopes. Beyond them rose the mountain of socialism itself. Whoever governed and by whatever means, one thing was clear: if socialism was to be achieved, there had to be a tremendous improvement in economic performance and in the country's level of material wellbeing. The situation was getting better, thanks to NEP – trade was flowing between town and country and the miseries of War Communism were being put behind. While the immediate benefits of NEP were undeniable, some in the party nevertheless doubted whether the current pace of economic development was fast enough. Industry and technology lagged far behind their counterparts in the west; nothing less than an intensive development programme could bring them up to the level required for socialism. And yet the pressures such a programme created might destroy the goodwill of the peasants, which Lenin for one now saw as crucially important to the achieving of socialism.

The need to juggle these conflicting considerations arose from the Bolsheviks' inversion of the 'normal' Marxist order and their capture of power in order to speed the modernizing process. The Soviet state had to equip itself with a modern, productive, high-tech economy; equally importantly, it needed a population that was well-educated, self-motivating and willingly implemented the party's programme. Both were indispensable. Yet it would be hard to achieve the first without coercion, discipline and ruthless organization, without *making* people do things, whereas the second implied winning hearts and minds and going forward with the masses' eager cooperation.

Lenin saw these two approaches as complementary rather than contradictory and never admitted any need to choose between them, even though the relative weighting he gave to them fluctuated from period to period. During his final years he had turned away from 'the political struggle' and 'revolution' and emphasized instead the need for persuasion and conciliation. Yet he did not in the least renounce his belief in discipline, suppression of any flicker of opposition and control by the regime of virtually all aspects of life. His conviction that the Bolsheviks' vision was the sole valid one and that they had an absolute right to impose it remained unwavering. No less fervently, however, he wanted to stir the initiative and self-activity of the masses, to make them active participants in society's transformation.

These two apparently incompatible facets to his political character were reconciled by Lenin's belief that the masses were potential socialists and potential partners in the Bolshevik enterprise, which before long they would voluntarily and eagerly implement. That belief – that leap of faith – had admittedly suffered a serious blow in the aftermath of October, when it had appeared that the masses were not proletarian at all. With NEP, however, the belief had come back in a modified form: the masses might not be socialist yet but they would be soon, and they and the party would then work together to create a fully socialist society.

This fundamental belief, which bridged the two sides of Lenin's political personality, rested in turn from 1921 on two more specific prescriptions, one cultural and the other economic. A mixture of education, sympathetic treatment and the material benefits of Bolshevik rule would give the masses a socialist outlook and make them ready to reconstruct their lives on socialist lines; and a limited permissiveness towards capitalist enterprise and the widespread creation of cooperatives among the peasantry would bring about a slow but steady transition to a socialist economic system.

Thus Lenin at the end of his life reconciled his contradictions and sketched out a future in which an authoritarian but benign state would guide Soviet society by peaceful methods towards socialism with increasing popular support. Whether the non-coercive society he envisaged in the 'testament' had much in common with the democratic socialism which would be pursued in his name during the late 1980s is a moot point. Andrzej Walicki for one has challenged attempts to put a liberal gloss upon the late Lenin. In particular, Walicki has rejected the view that Lenin became genuinely converted to the idea of persuading people, arguing that 'genuine persuasion assumes free dialogue, while Lenin's conception laid the foundation for a program of organized and unscrupulous indoctrination ...'[49] The point is well made: even at his most liberal, Lenin never accepted the pluralist assumptions of liberal democracy. To portray him as being en route to a liberal-democratic position is absurd. The freedom Lenin envisaged was strictly within a Marxist frame, the freedom of those whose lives would be based upon universally accepted values and assumptions, all of them lying beyond the bounds of possible questioning.

However, it would be equally absurd to pretend that Lenin's attitude remained what it had been during War Communism, and still more so to think that in respect of persuasion and coercion his attitude was indistinguishable from the Stalinist one. 'Psychology' – the belief in minimal and camouflaged coercion, in concessions, and in a determined attempt to win hearts and minds – implied an approach that was neither Stalinist nor liberal-democratic. This approach accepted coercion but regarded it as a short-term expedient towards ends that could only be attained by willing consent. It viewed the inhabitants of socialist society not as passive objects to be manipulated and imposed upon but as active agents in a common endeavour, without which there could be no socialism. The realization of Marx's vision would result from an upsurge of socialist consciousness among workers and peasants, who would say to the communist minority: 'You have achieved splendid results, after which no intelligent person will ever dream of returning to the old.'[50]

All of this may have been the make-believe of a doctrinaire who had lost touch with reality. In any event, Lenin's attempt to find a non-coercive path to socialism came to nothing, and the spring of NEP soon turned into the winter of Stalinism. The 'testament' had reflected values that mattered deeply to him but not to all of his colleagues and still less to party members at lower levels. NEP rested, moreover, upon highly questionable economic and cultural assumptions. It may be, in addition, that there was a contradiction built into the very idea of achieving a Marxist-socialist society without the sustained use of force. Lenin's example was nevertheless important; his belief that only by willing hands and informed minds could socialism be created had been planted in the party, would lie there dormant and apparently forgotten, and would one day be remembered.

4
After Lenin, 1924–9

1

Lenin's death, on 21 January 1924, mattered little in the sense that for quite some time he had taken no part in politics. To say that his death ended an era would nevertheless be an understatement. Lenin had founded, shaped and guided the Bolshevik party, had played a decisive part in the creation and development of the Soviet state, and had made a vast contribution to the content, style and implementation of Soviet policy. Had he lived on, he might have prevented the leadership from splintering; he might even, just possibly, have managed to modify NEP without sacrificing its essence. His premature death, at the age of 53, deprived the party of a leader of unmatched practical and theoretical skills. It also marked the beginning of the end of a distinctive culture within the party.

This intellectual of upper-middle-class background had launched Russia on a social experiment of unprecedented magnitude which had scythed through the possessing class, destroyed much of the intelligentsia, and turned the country away from the civilization of the west. Yet despite the proletarian identity he had taken on, Lenin had steadfastly remained an Old Bolshevik paternalist with a high-minded, almost Victorian attitude towards the masses. He and his core associates had loathed ignorance, inertia and irrationality and had wanted to raise up the inchoate human material they now ruled over to the highest cultural and moral standards. The members of the future socialist society would be educated and genuinely cultured, would have cast off the sloth, stupidity, egoism and other petty bourgeois vices of their forebears, and would have learned to act responsibly, intelligently and in the interests of the whole community. Meanwhile, the few who already embodied these values of the future society had the duty of defending and promoting them indefatigably. The Old Bolsheviks' defence of the 'proletarian' character of the party on behalf of proletarians too immature or declassed to defend it themselves was thus shot through with the high-minded assumptions of the most enlightened section of the bourgeoisie. After Lenin, however, this style of cultured-bourgeois paternalism would go into eclipse. The cultural gap between leadership and rank and file would indeed be narrowed, but by a process of levelling down rather than levelling up; and a vigorous recruitment campaign, carried out in Lenin's name, would bring into the party a mass of proletarians who fell well short of his standards but would nevertheless form the pool from which the new generation of party leaders would be drawn.

Lenin had gone, then, much that was distinctively Leninist would go with him – and yet Lenin lived on. He would live on, in the longer term, because the problems and contradictions the Soviet state would grapple with had been created by, or derived indirectly from, his headstrong bid for socialism in a country that was wholly unprepared for it. But he also continued to live in the immediate aftermath of his death because the regime needed him and somehow or other had to keep him in the foreground. For 'Ilich' – the reverential name by which he was often henceforth known – was the only charismatic figure this unpopular clutch of rulers had. The working class at least had developed a real affection for him and felt orphaned by his loss. Lenin had in fact begun to fulfil the role of a traditional Russian ruler, that of father to his people, even though he had not seen himself in such a role and had not sought any formal acknowledgement of his own pre-eminence. Now that he had gone, however, any inhibitions the leadership might have had about putting him on a pedestal were swept aside. 'Lenin lives!', the billboards proclaimed; and a vigorous campaign was launched to create a cult of him, to turn the dead Leader into an absent yet eternally living Leader.

It was not simply that his praises were sung incessantly, that busts, portraits and statues of him sprouted everywhere, that the remotest village soon had its 'Lenin corner', that a Lenin Institute was set up and that the former capital was renamed in his honour. The decision was taken that his body should be preserved, rather than buried, and placed on display in a mausoleum in Red Square; and before long streams of people from all over the country would come 'on pilgrimage', as Stalin put it, to gaze with reverence at the embalmed body of the Leader, rather as Russians in distant times had gone on pilgrimage to the remains of a prince who had come to be regarded as a saint.

That the cult of Lenin had nothing to do with Bolshevism – was utterly unBolshevik – hardly needs to be said. The Bolsheviks stood for collective leadership, as their democratic principles required; they had not fought against tsarism in order to replace it by a regime that was equally leader-fixated. The Bolsheviks were, moreover, rationalists as well as democrats, and the religious overtones of the Lenin cult, the scarcely veiled sanctification of the dead leader, were wholly contrary to the Bolshevik ethos and to the party's basic beliefs. Lenin had objected strongly to any attempts to adulate him, and he would certainly have regarded the posthumous deification of himself as scandalous. A number of Old Bolsheviks were indeed worried by the wildfire growth of the cult. Trotsky, Bukharin, Kamenev and Lenin's own wife were among those who were perturbed in particular by the decision to preserve the Leader's body and make it an object of reverence. The cult nevertheless went ahead in this overblown form because Lenin's death had unleashed a huge outpouring of grief, and because many in the leadership, Stalin among them, scoffed at these Old Bolshevik scruples and were determined to extract maximum benefit for the party from the Lenin effect.

The decision about what to do with the dead Leader foreshadowed the nemesis that would in time come upon the party. Lenin and his associates had set out to Bolshevize and civilize their country, to bring a backward people towards socialism by raising it up to their own enlightened worldview. The cult which developed spontaneously in the wake of the Leader's death and was then vigorously promoted by the party suggested, however, that the relationship between the Bolsheviks and their country would by no means be a one-way one. Russia would be Bolshevized, but Bolshevism would be unable to resist russification. That in turn set a question mark against Lenin's idea of reversing the normal order and having the chosen few make the socialist revolution in a country not yet ready for socialism on the assumption that they could then take the masses with them in the necessary direction. The conquering few, the burgeoning cult suggested, might in the end be overwhelmed by the culture of those they believed they had conquered.

But while some in the party glimpsed possible dangers in the cult, none denied that the party had somehow or other to prolong Lenin's charismatic effect. And for that, fulsome commemoration of what he had done was not enough; it was necessary to endow his life and thought with especial significance, to turn them into a benchmark against which all future policy and conduct would be judged. Zinoviev made the point: if policy could no longer be made 'according to Lenin', it would instead have to be made 'according to Leninism'.[1] Lenin might be dead, but his spirit and his teaching would continue to guide the country. All political activity, all thought, all education, would from now on have to be 'saturated' with Leninism.

Putting 'Leninism' in place of Lenin would not, however, be easy. The living Lenin had made his own decisions as to what was Leninist, and had been quite prepared to contradict himself and strike out in an entirely new direction. But if his successors were to decide the Leninist stance on any particular issue, they could only do that by first deciding what was fundamental in Lenin's teaching; particular opinions, in other words, could only be inferred from a clearly defined body of general principles. Lenin had, however, written so much and had so often contradicted himself that defining an essential core of Leninism would be difficult, and what made the task still harder was that those engaged in it would approach it with different aims and from different standpoints. The task was nevertheless crucial. No statement or policy could carry conviction from now on unless it could be credibly presented as Leninist.

True, one leading Bolshevik – Leon Trotsky – objected to the very idea of establishing a Leninist credo and making it binding. Lenin, Trotsky protested, had been wholly opposed to dogmatic rigidity; he had been innovative and open-minded and quite prepared, if the circumstances required it, to flout current orthodoxy and set out in a new direction. But Trotsky's suggestion that Lenin should provide a framework and an inspiration rather than Mosaic tablets whose injunctions had to be followed to the letter made little impression, so determined were most in the party to turn the dead leader into an oracle. Moreover, the fact that Lenin had written so much and often so inaccessibly created a crying need for a clear and concise statement of the essence of his thinking. The ordinary party member, overawed by all those pages, badly needed guidance. He would get it from the party leader whom, at the end, Lenin had condemned and seemed to regard as utterly unLeninist – Joseph Stalin.

Even before the funeral, Stalin had set the new tone of ritualistic exaltation of Lenin. 'Departing from us, Comrade Lenin enjoined us to hold high and guard the purity of the great title of member of the party. We vow to you, Comrade Lenin, that we shall fulfil your behest with honour!'[2] Again: 'Departing from us, Comrade Lenin enjoined us to guard the unity of our Party as the apple of our eye. We vow to you, Comrade Lenin, that this behest, too, we shall fulfil with honour!' And so Stalin went on, in a liturgical incantation which would have scandalized Lenin himself, making vow after vow to fulfil what he presented as Lenin's commandments. In a further eulogy two days later, he depicted the Leader as 'the mountain eagle' and 'the genius of revolution', who was nevertheless utterly modest and had a profound faith in the creative power of the masses.[3] During the next few years, Stalin would build up the image of Lenin as a biblical authority, an infallible guide, an absolute touchstone of right and wrong. A few lines from Lenin were enough to decide any issue; and, using skills that he must have learnt as a seminary student, Stalin became adept at excavating from this infallible source quotations that reinforced his own arguments and discredited his opponents'.

If Lenin's authority was to be absolutely binding (and Lenin, it should be remembered, had neither possessed nor claimed such authority), then anyone who aspired to lead the party had to get himself accepted as Lenin's heir. Stalin did his utmost to win that position by portraying himself as Lenin's most faithful follower, by raking up alleged sins committed against the Leader by Trotsky and others of his leadership rivals, and by depicting Lenin's character and outlook in such a way that they strongly resembled the image he projected of himself. This principled and indomitable, yet humble, Lenin, this man who combined 'Russian revolutionary sweep' with efficiency and practicality, was nothing other than Stalin writ large. Stalin was already doing, in fact, what Soviet leaders would do for the next sixty years: shaping Leninism in such a way as to strengthen and legitimize his own authority. Faithfully following the Lenin line as he defined it was not, however, enough to win him the succession. The issue would be decided by battles over the economy and the NEP road to socialism.

2

NEP had from the outset been bitterly resented by many in the party; indeed, it had needed all Lenin's skill and authority to get the policy through against fierce opposition. For it seemed to postpone socialism until the distant future, and it made major concessions to the class enemy, the peasants, at the workers' expense. From 1923, aspects of the policy came under fundamental attack from critics on the left. The Left Opposition, led by Trotsky and Preobrazhensky, and later joined by Kamenev and Zinoviev, made two essential points. First, the policy gave too little emphasis to industrialization. A faster rate of industrial development was necessary. This could only be financed by the peasants, who would have to pay what Preobrazhensky called 'tribute' in the form of the difference between the low prices they received for their produce and the high prices they paid for industrial goods. Second, the current policy would create serious problems in the countryside, impoverishing the mass of the peasants and raising up a rural bourgeoisie in the shape of the kulaks, who would then present a major obstacle to socialism.

NEP's chief defender was Nikolai Bukharin, who underlined the need to keep good relations between countryside and town and made much of Lenin's belief that the worker–peasant alliance was a precondition of successful advance to socialism. The peasants had to be given incentives; should incentives be replaced by punitive fiscal policies, as the left proposed, then the peasants would simply withhold their grain and thus make industrialization impossible. Industrial growth was of course vital, but it had to be slow and steady and the way to finance it was through the increased buying power of a peasantry that was encouraged to prosper.

The cornerstone of Bukharin's case, however, was a defence of the short-term benefits of private enterprise: far from being a threat, that would help bring the peasants to socialism and would then self-destruct. 'As it turns out, we will arrive at socialism through market relations themselves. One can say that these market relations will be destroyed as a result of their own development.'[4] The socialist and capitalist economic systems would exist side by side, and their coexistence would convince the peasants, as no amount of propaganda would, of socialism's superiority. As for the left's scaremongering about the kulaks, this ignored the cooperatives, whose role in the transition to socialism Lenin had seen as a vital. The masses of the poor and middle peasants would be brought together in marketing cooperatives, which the state would subsidize and support; and these would successfully fight off the private enterprise challenge presented by the kulaks.

Before the end of 1927, the left had been routed as a political force, yet paradoxically its criticisms of NEP had by then been largely vindicated. Industrialization, it was now generally agreed in the party, had to go ahead much faster. An overall economic plan was indispensable; drafts of a five-year one were being drawn up. Getting back to the country's 1913 industrial level no longer seemed adequate. The advances in western industry and technology posed a threat both to the regime's security and to its socialist objective. Only an intensive growth programme could narrow the gap – that, however, would require investment on an immense scale.

But it was not only in this respect that the left had shown up NEP's shortcomings: its criticisms of policy towards the peasants were also being borne out. Differentiation in the countryside was growing, yet there were few if any signs that private enterprise was taking the peasantry in a socialist direction. The contradictions of the policy should have been resolved by the cooperatives, and the cooperative movement was certainly flourishing – by 1927 almost 50 per cent of peasants were enrolled in agricultural cooperatives. Yet the cooperatives were not emerging as crucibles of socialism. It was not the poor and middle peasants who dominated them, nor were they effectively resisting the private-enterprise activities of the kulaks. On the contrary, the cooperatives were dominated by kulaks, who were using them to further their own, private-enterprise, interests. The growth of cooperation, Lenin had written in 1923, 'is identical with the growth of socialism'.[5] Four years later, that seemed a highly dubious proposition.

Yet while the left's analysis had to a considerable extent been borne out, Bukharin had in one respect at least been vindicated. Rapid industrialization, he had insisted, was incompatible with the worker–peasant alliance. The peasants needed incentives; forced to pay 'tribute', they would simply hold back their grain. And when the government tilted its pricing policy against the peasants, they reacted precisely as Bukharin had predicted. The peasants' action in turn threatened the whole industrialization project. There had to be a reliable and ample grain supply if the urban population was to expand; moreover, it was grain exports, above all, that would have to pay for the much-needed foreign machinery and technology. The formula appeared in fact to be as Bukharin had stated it: no contented peasantry, no industrialization, no socialism.

The ideal solution to the dilemma would have been for a victorious western proletariat to alleviate the burden on the peasantry by helping Russia to industrialize.The left indeed saw a revolution in the west as vital if the socialist project in Russia was to be completed. But such a revolution had not yet happened and showed no sign of happening. Worse still, the capitalist threat to the Soviet Union was again on the rise, and that made industrial development seem all the more urgent. Bukharin's reaction to the absence of revolution in the west had been to argue that a backward country such as Russia could, if the worst came to the worst, achieve socialism on its own. But for this to happen the government had to keep the goodwill of the peasantry. That over-riding need in turn dictated that the advance could only be 'at a tortoise pace'. By the late 1920s, however, moving towards socialism that slowly seemed as impossible to many in the party as trying to ride a bicycle at a crawl. The country either got to socialism quickly or it would not in the foreseeable future get there at all. What was needed, it appeared, was a policy which combined Bukharin's 'Socialism in One Country' approach with a fast rate of industrial growth. But where would such a policy leave NEP?

NEP was now in fact in serious trouble. It had assumed that socialism could be achieved by a process of gradual change which won the peas-ants' willing approval; that the cooperative system, assisted by education, would over a period of time instil socialist consciousness into the rural population; that the conflict between socialism and capi-talism in the countryside would be resolved decisively in socialism's favour. All these assumptions were now looking implausible. Bukharin had no alternative but to give ground. He accepted the need for faster industrialization and a five-year plan; he was prepared to have some curbs placed on the kulaks. Yet he still clung to NEP and, back to the wall, he made a defence of its essence.

There was more here than fidelity to Lenin – the Lenin who, in his final years, had had an almost father-and-son relationship with him. Bukharin had not only filled out the sketchy ideas left behind by Lenin; he had taken the reformist, evolutionary emphasis of Lenin's final thoughts and worked it up into a philosophy of his own. At the heart of 'Bukharinism' was boundless confidence in the prospects for socialism. As an economic system, it would outdo capitalism; in the sphere of culture and ideas, it would overcome the challenge of rival ideologies. For all his optimism, Bukharin was not, however, suggesting that the Bolsheviks should relax their grip. The dictatorship of the proletariat and the one-party state were for the time being indis-pensable; the party could allow no political opposition, nor should it slacken its all-out effort to convert people to socialism.'Yes, we will put our stamp on the members of the intelligentsia, we will fashion them as in a factory.'[6] Yet while Bukharin endorsed the party's monopoly, he was becoming increasingly worried by the monopoly's ill effects. What he wanted was a state that was all-powerful, yet used its power gently and wisely, and he was alarmed by signs of the emergence of a corrupt new ruling class. Lenin had sensed the same problem, but Bukharin's solution to it was more radical than his. If an enlightened few at the top could not safeguard the party, then they would have to be assisted by whistle-blowers at the bottom. Bukharin believed in the spread of grass-roots, non-party organizations; he even argued for relatively free elections to local soviets and happily contemplated the election of non-party members. Criticism and a flow of ideas from below could only benefit the party. The state, he seemed to be saying, should not be regarded as a god; its decisions were not infallible and its activities should be kept to a necessary minimum. Lenin's aim, he reminded his colleagues, had been a 'commune-state' in which the masses largely governed themselves. That was still far distant, but it was important not to forget the commune-state or socialism's ideal of an altogether stateless society.

All of this was impeccable Marxism and Leninism, yet in the late 1920s it left Bukharin in an isolated and exposed position in a party that was bracing itself for further battles with the peasantry. How faster industrialization could be achieved without antagonizing the peasantry Bukharin did not know, and the minor adjustments he had made to his ideas hardly provided a solution. But while Bukharin did not know what was necessary, he knew very well what he did not want, what indeed would be disastrous. What would be disastrous was a solution that discarded NEP altogether – and that was the very solution that Stalin now came up with.

3

During the battles between left and right Stalin had kept a middle position, though one that was closer to Bukharin's than the left's. He was not a 'superindustrializer', yet his pro-peasant line was lukewarm, and he had castigated Zinoviev for suggesting that the essence of Leninism lay in Lenin's view of the peasants (rather than, as Stalin insisted, his advocacy of the dictatorship of the proletariat).[7] On the face of it, Bukharin and he made a most unlikely partnership. Bukharin was a refined Moscow intellectual, a bourgeois, a visionary, and an embodiment of Old Bolshevism; Stalin, by contrast, was a roughhewn provincial who projected himself as a man of the people and had a strong rapport with the rawest elements among the party's recent recruits. However, they needed one another. While Bukharin needed Stalin's political and organizational skills, his clout, his rank-and-file following, Stalin needed Bukharin's theoretical prowess, his credentials as a Leninist, the affection he inspired; and Bukharinism, which was less to his taste, he for the time being put up with. Most of all, Stalin needed Bukharin as an ally against his enemies on the left, especially against his formidable and long-standing adversary, Leon Trotsky. And it was hostility to Trotsky which lay behind Stalin's best-known policy stance up to 1927: his fervent advocacy of what became known as 'Socialism in One Country'.

The Bolsheviks had all taken it for granted that socialism could not be achieved in Russia without a socialist revolution in the west; but it was Trotsky's 'Permanent Revolution' which had provided the classic exposition of this belief. The continuing absence of revolution in the west had, however, by the mid-1920s made the belief an embarrassment and something of an anomaly. Soviet theory had by now got badly out of step with Soviet practice. Had Ilich himself not said that this was a socialist society? Was a socialist society not one that was creating socialism? What made 'Socialism in One Country' so attractive was that it seemed to close the yawning gap between theory and practice. But it did more than that: it gave Stalin a stick with which to beat Trotsky.

He attacked 'Permanent Revolution' mercilessly on various scores. It was unrealistic: for several years the Soviet government had been laying the foundations of socialism without foreign aid, indeed in the teeth of foreign hostility. It was ideologically unsound – 'a variety of Menshevism'. And it was defeatist since it left the revolution 'either to rot away or to degenerate into a bourgeois state'. Permanent revolution, Stalin taunted his opponent, was in effect 'permanent gloom' and 'permanent hopelessness'. But not only was Trotsky a defeatist. By implication, Stalin charged him with a still greater crime – that he was not a patriot, did not believe in Russia, its people and its mission. 'Lack of faith in the strength and capacities of our revolution, lack of faith in the strength and capacities of the Russian proletariat – that is what lies at the root of the theory of "permanent revolution".'[8]

Socialism in One Country was thus a heady cocktail in which a spirit of revolutionary defiance and heroism combined with a strong implied nationalism. It touched Trotsky where he was most vulnerable – as a westernized intellectual and a Jew. And it suggested a Bolshevism that was close to the instincts and emotions of everyday Russians. Till now the Bolsheviks had come across as determined internationalists who would sooner or later eliminate most that was distinctively Russian and merge the country in an international socialist community. Russia, for instance, had been excluded altogether from the state's new title – the Union of Soviet Socialist Republics. Socialism in One Country, however, did something to redress the balance. It spoke to the proletarian militancy of the party's new recruits, but also to their nationalism, their refusal to be patronized by westerners and westernized Russians. Russia, the new doctrine suggested, was not dependent on the countries of the west, did not have to follow them to socialism. On the contrary, it could lead the others and get there largely by its own exertions. For a century, Russian thinkers had been searching for a path that was distinctively the country's own yet did not by that very fact condemn it to backwardness. Now Stalin seemed to have found a solution to the problem: the country would strike out on a distinctive path along which, sooner or later, the so-called civilized world would have to follow it.

With Bukharin's help, Stalin got Socialism in One Country accepted as official party doctrine in April 1925. The resolution which set out the new doctrine made the proviso that the 'final' victory of socialism could not be achieved in one country alone. All that meant, however, as Stalin soon made clear, was that socialism in any one country could not be considered secure until the socialist revolution had triumphed generally. There was no limit upon the extent to which a particular country could develop a socialist economy and a socialist social structure; the proviso simply underlined the dangers from capitalist encirclement and the need for ceaseless vigilance against capitalism's agents. It in no way detracted from the 'indisputable truth', as Stalin put it, that 'we have all that is necessary for building a complete socialist society.'[9]

Stalin and Bukharin had fought shoulder-to-shoulder on the Socialism in One Country issue, yet the two viewed the doctrine somewhat differently. While Bukharin was a fervent believer in NEP whose support for Socialism in One Country was secondary to his NEP commitment, Stalin's order of priorities was the other way round: for him, NEP offered what looked, for the time being, like the most expedient route to socialism in Russia. While Bukharin emphasized slowness, caution, and kid-glove treatment of the peasantry, Stalin's message was that drive and determination, properly guided by the party, were capable of overcoming all obstacles to socialism. While Bukharin said 'Yes, we can create socialism in one country, but only if we go slowly,' Stalin's message was 'Yes, we can create socialism in one country, but only if we strain every muscle.' And it was not far from that to an attitude that was the very opposite of Bukharin's: 'Yes, we can create socialism in Russia, but only if we industrialize fast and brook no opposition from the peasantry.'

In 1926 Stalin went over to a belief in fast-track industrialization. It was not until the following year, however, that a clear breach emerged between him and Bukharin. Two factors lay behind the breach. First, during 1927 the left was defeated, crushed, and removed from the political scene altogether. Trotsky, Kamenev and Zinoviev were expelled from the party, as were many so-called 'Trotskyites'; Trotsky himself was exiled to Alma-Ata, near the Chinese border, early in 1928, and expelled from the Soviet Union altogether in 1929. With his rivals out of the way, Stalin no longer needed Bukharin. Now he could map out his own route to socialism in Russia.

The second precipitating factor was renewed problems with the grain supply. Not that there had been a poor harvest in 1927: the peasants were simply withholding their surpluses, and they did this so effectively that in January 1928 the leadership declared a grain crisis. Stalin's response to the peasants' action was swift and uncompromising. Far from backing down, he urged the need for massive industrial investment – which, he claimed, could come only from the peasants' resources. He insisted, moreover, that the underlying problem was not economic but political. The kulaks had grown so strong that they were now using grain as a weapon against the regime. That being so, conciliating them was out of the question. Any resistance by the peasants to what was necessary for socialist construction would be crushed. Peasants could no longer exercise a veto over government policy, nor would the rural economy remain a semi-autonomous sector under kulak control; and early in 1928 grain began to be taken from the peasants by strong-arm methods which recalled those of War Communism.

Stalin had thus 'solved', after his own fashion, a problem that had perplexed left and right alike – how to reconcile rapid industrialization with keeping the peasants' goodwill. The left had accepted the dangers of pressing the peasantry too hard but had failed to find any solution to a situation in which the peasants reacted to unfavourable prices by withholding their grain. The right had accepted the need for faster industrialization but been unable to find any way of achieving this that would not jeopardize the worker–peasant alliance. Stalin, however, cut the Gordian knot by eliminating one of the elements to the contradiction. Faster, indeed breakneck, industrialization would go ahead, and force would be used against any peasants who resisted the consequences.

In November 1928 the Central Committee endorsed a forced industrialization programme which emphasized the need to catch up and surpass the capitalist countries. Stalin even invoked the name of that ruthless modernizing autocrat, Peter the Great – so much had NEP gradualism fallen out of favour. A month earlier, the first five-year plan had begun with targets for industrial growth that the 'superindustrializers' of the defeated left would have regarded as wildly unrealistic. The targets were nevertheless subsequently revised upwards several times; and in 1930 Stalin would tighten the ratchet still further by demanding that the targets be attained in four years rather than five.

Strong-arm methods solved the immediate problem, but were clearly no more than a stop-gap. The permanent solution, Stalin suggested, was 'socialization of agriculture' – that is, collectivization, a long-standing aim of the party's which had been quietly shelved during NEP. But how to collectivize? And over what timescale? It had always been assumed that the conversion to collectivized agriculture would have to be voluntary and that it would take a long time. Stalin appeared at first to accept both assumptions, but then swung against them. A long-drawn-out and voluntary collectivization would by no means do what he now saw as vital – give the state enough control over production to ensure the grain necessary for rapid industrialization. Moreover, a voluntary scheme would leave the class enemy – the kulaks – untouched, since they would certainly choose to stay outside it. And in the early winter of 1929 the policy was radicalized. There would be an all-out collectivization as part of a decisive socialist offensive. As for the kulaks, it was no longer enough to denounce them or restrict their activities. Nor could they be allowed to join the collectives. The collective-farm movement, Stalin declared in December 1929, was assuming 'the character of a mighty and growing *anti-kulak* avalanche, is sweeping the resistance of the kulaks from its path, is shattering the kulak class and paving the way for extensive socialist construction'. What was now required, therefore, was a 'policy of *eliminating the kulaks as a class'*.[10]

Nothing could have been further from Lenin's NEP approach than 'dekulakization', as the policy became called. Stalin had, however, already devised a Marxist–Leninist justification for it – the intensification of the class struggle.[11] Bukharin and his allies were mistaken in claiming that the kulaks would grow peacefully into socialism. They would not. As the country progressed towards socialism, the class struggle would not peter out, Stalin declared, but would instead become more intense. The weaker the capitalists were, the more desperately they would fight; intensification of the struggle as socialism continued its victorious course was therefore inevitable. 'The fact is that we are living according to Lenin's formula: "Who will beat whom?" Will we overpower them, the capitalists ... or will they overpower us?'[12]

That Lenin had in his later years abandoned the 'who will beat whom?' approach was an inconvenient fact that could be side-stepped; so too could his belief that the peasants as a whole would grow into socialism. After all, there was ample Leninist justification elsewhere for such confrontational thinking. What was happening in the countryside emerged, in the light of Stalin's new theory, as a desperate rearguard action by a doomed exploiting minority against the interests of the toiling masses. When the issue was presented in such 'them' and 'us' terms, what could any honest Bolshevik do but plunge determinedly into the struggle?

So in effect, though not in name, NEP was abandoned. It was replaced by what Stalin called 'the Great Breakthrough' – and a revolution which would be as great an earthquake as the October one. Bukharin and his allies in what was now dubbed 'the right deviation' did their best to resist this new revolution. Bukharin, who had done much to bring about the Left Opposition's downfall, now even made a desperate overture to Kamenev. Confronted by Stalin's violence, he saw how much left and right had in common. Both shared the same Old Bolshevik culture; neither would have used violence against the peasantry. But the leftists had little chance and little incentive to come to the aid of someone so obviously doomed, and the overture only blackened Bukharin further in Stalin's eyes.

Down but not yet out, Bukharin made a spirited defence of his beliefs in the autumn of 1928 in 'Notes of an Economist'. He could not of course criticize the Stalin line directly. Instead, he turned his fire on the 'Trotskyites'; and under this cover he justified the principles of NEP, attacked an exaggerated emphasis on planning and the elimination of spontaneity, criticized those who 'do not understand that the development of industry depends upon the development of agriculture', and warned of the dangers presented by a hypercentralized state run by an unaccountable bureaucracy whose members showed 'complete indifference to the interests of the masses'. 'We have', he argued, 'overcentralized everything to an excessive degree. We should ask whether we ought not to take some steps in the direction of Lenin's commune-state.' The country was, moreover, reverting to 'Russian provincialism', when it needed 'to follow each development of scientific and technical thought in Europe and America ...'[13] Moderate, pro-peasant, anti-statist and pro-western opinions were no longer, however, in vogue, and by now Bukharin had the look of yesterday's man.

In January 1929 he made a last stand. Using the one weapon that still remained to him, the writings of the dead leader, he gave a lecture on 'The Political Testament of Lenin' in which in effect he challenged Stalin's claim to be the heir and interpreter. The essence of Lenin, Bukharin argued, lay in the five last articles, which were 'organic parts of a single large whole, of a single large plan comprising Lenin's strategy and tactics'. Here in fact was 'a great, forward-looking plan for all our communist work'.[14] Lenin as he presented him on the basis of these final articles warned against haste, deplored excesses of coercion and centralization, saw state power as at best a necessary evil, encouraged personal initiative, rejected anything that would jeopardize the goodwill of the peasantry, and advocated a gradual approach to socialism through policies that appealed not to class animosity or to a spirit of self-sacrifice but rather to the self-interest and the good sense of the peasant masses.

This emollient and patient teacher was, however, by no means the Lenin of Stalin and the dominant element in the party. The Stalinists' Lenin was a militant activist who urged people to strain every muscle and to make major sacrifices in a wholehearted collective effort to drag the country out of backwardness and achieve the transformation indispensable to socialism. Their Lenin preached the inevitable intensification of the class struggle. He looked ceaselessly for enemies, even within the party's own ranks, and was merciless when he found them. 'We love Bukharin,' Stalin remarked as he denounced him to the Central Committee in April 1929, ' but we love truth, the Party and the Comintern even more.'[15] That, his followers no doubt concluded, was the view Ilich would have taken.

The Central Committee meeting ended with the complete rout of Bukharin and his allies. Vilified as a factionalist, an opportunist, a deviationist and, worst of all, an anti-Leninist, Bukharin was expelled from the Politburo in November of the same year. He then rounded off his own humiliation by making a formal recantation of his errors. The victory of Stalin, the man now lauded as Lenin's 'most faithful pupil', was complete. But why had Bukharin and his version of Leninism been defeated? How had Stalin made himself 'the Lenin of today'?

4

Stalin had won, in the first place, because he was an abler politician than his rivals, and he had exploited the difficulties of NEP with consummate skill. Yet he had not of course created the difficulties, even if his policies had aggravated them. The friction between peasantry and proletariat was not simply something contrived by a wily politician who wanted to finish NEP off. Relations between town and country, and between urban militants and the peasantry in particular, had been bad when NEP began and had steadily worsened. Hopes that an equilibrium could somehow be established between the two sides, that their collaboration could pave the way to socialism, had come to nothing. The grain crisis reflected the broader and wholly unresolved problem of the relationship between party and people, between red islands and the great peasant sea which lapped and threatened to submerge them; and what in turn loomed behind that was the question of whether and how the few could drag the many – assuming that they were unable to *persuade* them – in the direction of a society that was recognizably socialist.

A decade after October, the cumulative effect of the miscalculations made then had caught up with the party. Lenin had believed, as we know, that the revolution would rapidly win both overwhelming domestic support and the support of victorious revolutions in the west. Having been proved wrong on both scores, he had fallen back on a policy of coercion and terror, but then had given up what seemed an unequal battle with the peasantry. NEP in its turn assumed that socialism could still be achieved, if much more slowly, by policies that conciliated the peasants and appealed to their self-interest. By the late 1920s, that assumption too appeared mistaken. Where could the regime go from here? The right by now had no more constructive ideas to offer. Surrender was, however, unthinkable – power, after all, was still firmly within the party's grip. What, then, could the regime do but go back to force, to the 'voluntarism' which had served it so well already? In 1918–20 it had used force against outright opponents, both domestic and foreign, but had balked at taking on the peasantry. A decade later the regime was better placed for an assault on this last bastion of capitalism. It had a leader who had escaped the control of his more moderate colleagues, and behind him party rank-and-filers who were determined on a showdown. The solution the leader now came up with had immense appeal to the militants. It was energetic, uncompromising, and likely to be effective; it would safeguard socialism, protecting the country against both foreign predators and their domestic hirelings; and it would strengthen the hand of the new ruling class and any who aspired to join it. Moreover, after several years of wishy-washiness the party was again speaking with the voice of true Leninism.

Once prompted by Stalin, many members responded to the grain crisis as their predecessors had responded in 1918. Aggressive feelings towards the peasantry that had been bottled up since 1921 came bursting out. The collectivization campaign took the form of an armed crusade against the rural enemies of socialism – here was a reprise of the 1918 crusade, but this time there would be no turning back. There was a surge of support, too, for the attacks on 'bourgeois specialists' and intellectuals. The changes in the party's composition had of course made Stalin's task easier, since they had brought in people far more attuned to his crude brand of radicalism than to Old Bolshevism. Part of Stalin's appeal to the new membership was, however, that his populist radicalism went together with deep traditionalism. He called for violence against opponents of socialism, aliens, members of social or cultural elites, against anyone in fact who might be passed off as an enemy of the people; at the same time, he presented the building of socialism as something that required a charismatic leader using the powers of the state to the utmost. Violence, xenophobia, and hatred of the bourgeois, the better-off and the non-conforming, on the one hand; a cult of the ruler and a hyper-statist traditionalism, on the other. All of this made for a potent, indeed a lethal, mixture.

Outmanoeuvred and isolated within the party, Bukharin hardly stood a chance. Those who tried to resist the leadership were inevitably tainted as 'factionalists' and 'deviationists'; the clear implication was that they had either to submit and recant or else be expelled. Unity around what was now known as the 'general line' was indispensable. A party that claimed to stand for uncontestable truths in a country where most people failed to accept those truths either spoke with a single voice or perished. The case for silencing opposition within the party had been set out clearly enough by Lenin, who had given Stalin all the justification he needed for crushing Bukharin.

Could the clash of policies have been put to a popular vote, then the outcome would almost certainly have been different. But Lenin, with Bukharin's willing assent, had long before ruled out any appeal to the masses: the party, the elite within the party, and the dominant element within the elite decided for everyone else. The party was always right, and the party was the leadership. Bukharin, who had accepted both propositions, was hoist in the end by a petard of Lenin's, and his own, making. Admittedly, diversity of opinion had not been so thoroughly purged under Lenin as it would be under Stalin. But the leap from Lenin's Russia to Stalin's, from a tightly controlled and repressed society to one that required positive affirmation of the party line from every citizen, would be a change of quantity rather than quality.

5

Imagine, however, that Lenin had lived on and that he had witnessed, as a fully aware bystander, the battles of the late 1920s. Whose side would he have taken? Would he have endorsed Bukharin's version of Leninism or would he have gone instead for Stalin's? Or might he perhaps have accepted neither version? Such questions would be debated furiously sixty years later, as we shall see, and the majority opinion then would be that Lenin would have supported Bukharin or at least would not have supported Stalin.

What can be said certainly enough is that Lenin would have loathed the more grotesque and extravagant consequences of the revolution that began in the late 1920s. He would have loathed its irrationality, its reckless squandering of human life, its counterproductive overkill. That Lenin could be ruthless and that he did not shrink from violence and terror hardly needs to be said, but he used these weapons in the manner of Machiavelli – in a cold-blooded, economical way and for ends that were strictly political.[16] He had not pursued glory for himself or set out to avenge personal grievances; he had acted, rather, like a surgeon who cuts deep where necessary but takes no pleasure in the pain he has to inflict.

The grotesque consequences of the new revolution – in a word, Stalinism – still lay ahead, however, and they could not have been easily foreseen. At least until the second half of 1929, Lenin might well have backed Stalin's confrontational and revolutionary course. True, that would have meant rejecting his own NEP. But Lenin had never been afraid of admitting mistakes, indeed had prided himself on being flexible enough to change his views in accordance with changing circumstances. That the circumstances of 1927–8 were very different from those of 1921–3 was undeniable. Bukharin had responded by modifying his views somewhat, yet he had failed to come up with a revision of NEP that looked likely to safeguard socialism against bourgeois and petty bourgeois revanche. Worse still, there was a germ of something alien to Bolshevism in Bukharin's thinking about state–society relations, something which – were it allowed to develop – might weaken the power of the proletarian dictatorship and in the end undermine it altogether. And so, perplexed by the dashing of the hopes he had invested in NEP, shaken by the gravity of the current crisis and unimpressed by Bukharin's response to it, Lenin might well have accepted that there was no alternative to a second round of revolution.

He and the leadership had, after all, assumed back in October that the modernizing of the socio-economic and cultural base could not be left to natural processes but had to be pushed ahead by an enlightened few who took control of the state and used its coercive and directing powers to the full. The second revolution could be seen as reincarnating the spirit of that militant Bolshevism of 1917; it was both a necessary and a logical follow-up to the original 'push'. Any other approach, including Bukharin's current one, was inadequate and looked likely to put the socialist cause in jeopardy. Heavy industry had to be developed rapidly, in view especially of the threatening international situation; coercive measures would have to be applied to the peasants or at least to the kulaks; collectivization had rightly been put back on the agenda; and in these circumstances the imposition of iron discipline upon the party had become a necessity.

Before the end of 1929, however, Lenin would most probably have seen the far-reaching implications of what was happening and changed his mind. The cult of Stalin, which began in full force with his fiftieth birthday in December 1929, would have scandalized him. He could no longer have overlooked the treatment of his former colleagues Kamenev, Zinoviev, Bukharin and, most of all, Trotsky. He was all for purges, indeed one of his major complaints against the leadership might well have been that it had purged too little since 1924 and had let in too many of the unqualified and the unworthy: but to purge a man who, whatever his past errors, was a brilliant theoretician, a dedicated Marxist, a magnificent fighter for socialism – to purge Leon Trotsky! As for collectivization, he had always stood for it in principle; but equally he had always insisted that the change-over to collectivized agriculture had to be voluntary and gradual, and even during War Communism he had held back from pressing the matter. While he had said bitter things about the kulaks, he wholly opposed any suggestion of liquidating them as a class. Moreover, he could no longer turn a blind eye to the campaign against 'bourgeois specialists' and bourgeois culture in general. What made this emergent 'Stalinism' all the more abhorrent was that it was being buttresed by countless quotations from himself, while it was being driven by a barrack-room notion of socialism which he had never subscribed to; and where it would lead to was not socialism at all but the very thing that Trotsky and Rosa Luxemburg had long ago, to his indignation, accused *him* of wittingly or otherwise promoting – a semi-Asiatic despotism. These critics of his were in a sense being proved right, though with the proviso that they had wrongly aimed their arrows at him and should have aimed them instead at someone whom no one would then have taken seriously as a future leader of the Russian communists.

What this reconstruction suggests is that Lenin might have swung either way in the Stalin–Bukharin standoff and that most probably he would have swung both ways. The uncertainty underlines his dualism, his fundamental ambivalence. There were two very different political selves within him, and after his death two very different 'Lenins' would be carved out of this contradictory material – two mythological figures with sharply contrasting faces. Bukharin and Stalin each claimed to have captured the real Lenin; but each had taken only a part of him and had created a totem of his own by extrapolating from it.

This monomaniac whose every energy had been devoted to creating a Marxist-socialist society happened also to believe that only if the masses properly understood socialist ideas and internalized them enough to become self-motivating 'builders of socialism' would the goal be achievable. Between his desire that people should be imbued with Marxism and his desire that they should accept and act upon Marxist ideas as their own there was an obvious potential conflict. The point of the psychological approach, in which coercion was camouflaged, crude propaganda avoided and major concessions were made to popular sensitivities, was that it appeared to head off this conflict. The approach was seen most clearly in the 'testament', but something of it had come through also in NEP: here was a strategy that combined continuing authoritarianism and intolerance towards opponents with gentle treatment of the peasantry and emphasis on the need for gradual economic and cultural change. By 1929, however, there was a widespread feeling in the party that the relatively painless path to socialism that NEP had seemed to offer was an illusion. Historians would later debate – and the debate continues – whether NEP died a natural death or was killed off unnecessarily by Stalin. But what can hardly be denied is the general *perception* at the time that NEP was failing, that the country had come to a crossroads and that a difficult choice would have to be made. Put at its starkest, the choice lay between an all-out drive for socialism, an 'offensive', with as a result an immense increase in coercion, and a slower, more relaxed and even, within limits, pluralist path which, however, ran the risk that it might not get the country to the socialist destination at all.

Lenin, had he lived until the late 1920s, would not have welcomed having to make such a choice. The one route risked creating a caricatural socialism under a semi-Asiatic despotism, the other raised the spectre of a degeneration towards capitalism and the bourgeois state. But what other options were there? Was the country's current plight not the inevitable result of that mixture of falsehood and make-believe, of necessary untruths used in the service of utopian expectations, with which he had pushed the party into the original October gamble? The gamble had paid off in the sense that power had been seized and held on to; but as he looked back he would have seen a series of shattered illusions, of beliefs – or hopes that passed as beliefs – which had been unable to withstand reality. The failure of the masses to respond to the socialist 'choice' the Bolsheviks had made for them. The failure of the proletariats of the west to rise up and fulfil their socialist mission. The failure of NEP to carry rural Russia peacefully towards socialism. The failure of 'psychology' to remove or even to paper over the contradictions inherent in trying to create a Marxist-socialist society in this backward country. Broken hopes behind; and ahead – uncertainty, danger, and little chance that amidst this disaster-strewn landscape the socialist cause could be retrieved. As he approached his sixtieth birthday, Lenin would have been on a painful learning curve. It was lucky for him, and perhaps lucky for his reputation, that death had saved him from the dilemmas of the late 1920s.

5
Stalin's Socialism, 1929–53

1

Enormous changes came over the Soviet Union during the Stalin period and in particular during the 1930s. Till 1929, the Bolsheviks had ruled a mainly peasant society with a small-scale, private agriculture. During the 1930s, however, Soviet society would be turned into something more suited to its rulers' aspirations. Small peasant farms were replaced by a collectivized agriculture, heavy industry expanded massively, the urban population grew by leaps and bounds, while remaining areas of independent activity were wiped out as the state took control of society in all its aspects. This transformation amounted, in the regime's own view, to a revolution, and it cut so deep, or so the official line maintained, that it was 'equivalent in its consequences to the revolution of October 1917'.[1] Lenin might have begun the endeavour, but it was Stalin who had completed the first phase of the task, Stalin who had directed and even devised the strategy which had led to the building of socialism.

The 'Stalin revolution', as historians would come to know it, began with an assault on the peasants by communist militants, backed up by the Red Army and the secret police. The collectivizing of agriculture caused far more of an upheaval than those two other landmark events in recent peasant history: the 1861 emancipation from serfdom and the October Revolution. Through them, the agricultural system and the rural way of life had remained essentially unchanged. Now everything changed as the peasants' world collapsed beneath the onslaught. One and a half million of them, dubbed kulaks, were dispossessed and many sent into internal exile. The remainder had the new system of socialist agriculture imposed upon them. A small number worked in state farms or sovkhozes, which ran on factory lines and treated the peasants as wage labourers. The great majority, however, had their holdings merged into a collective farm or kolkhoz, where the worker was paid from the residue of grain and cash once other obligations had been fulfilled.

What was left over was, however, far too little. Up to 40 per cent of the produce went to the state – a much higher percentage than had been marketed before ; in addition, payments in money and kind had to be made to the machine tractor stations (MTSs), which provided the kolkhoz with tractors and combines but also acted as political fortresses in a hostile countryside. Yet if the peasant suffered materially, the loss of his independence was perhaps a still greater blow. Now he was simply a cog in a huge enterprise, labouring in a brigade and doing what he was ordered to by urban militants turned kolkhoz bosses. All that made life bearable was that he was allowed to keep a private plot of not more than an acre and a small number of livestock. These plots not only helped the peasant household to survive – they would provide much of the nation's food. Could the plots have been larger, how much more peasants and urban consumers would have benefited. Enlarging them was, however, out of the question: the private plots were unsocialist and no more than a temporary concession to the petty bourgeois mentality.

The peasants had lost almost everything that mattered to them: the commune (abolished 1930), the church, their independent way of life. A second serfdom had been imposed on them, or so it seemed to many, and a serfdom more crushing and exploitative than the old one. The kulaks put up a fierce resistance, as did many peasants in the non-Russian areas, especially Ukraine; but their cause was hopeless. The more talented and ambitious simply got out and moved to the industrializing towns. Those they left behind accepted their fate in the submissive spirit that Russian peasants had shown over the centuries. Bukharin had predicted that violent action against the peasantry might prove disastrous for the regime, but his prediction had been wrong. The peasants bowed to this new 'military-feudal exploitation'; and within a few years many of them would go into battle shouting 'For Stalin! For country!'

Stalin had done what Lenin had never contemplated – he had challenged the peasants on the issue of private landholding and made them submit. Agriculture was now wholly under state control. The peasantry would have to feed the towns. Resources could be pumped out of the countryside into the urban economy. Stalin's flouting of

Bukharin's warning had been vindicated. An end was now in sight to the anomaly of a Marxist government ruling over a largely petty bourgeois and agrarian country. Yet Stalin had won his war with the peasantry at a price. The peasants had been left apathetic and demoralized; the Soviet countryside had been turned into a place of desolation. A collectivized agriculture with very little incentive for the worker would prove grossly unproductive, and in time it would develop into a brake on the whole Soviet economy.

2

Collectivization was in a sense a preliminary, even if a vital one: an independent peasantry was an obstacle in the way of what had to be done. And what had to be done – the central theme of the Stalin revolution – was to create an urban, industrial and technological society wholly directed by the state. Creating that, Stalin judged, was tantamount to creating socialism.

Planning was of the essence. Scientific planning, based on Marxism, would enable the Soviet Union to outstrip the capitalist nations, mired as they were in the anarchy of the market. Planning would harness all the country's energies and resources, directing them unerringly to socialist construction. Heavy industry was the immediate priority, and iron and steel became the symbol of a transformation presided over by someone whose very name suggested 'man of steel'. The campaign to industrialize took the form of a military offensive – 'There are no fortresses', Stalin proclaimed, 'that Bolsheviks cannot capture.'[2] Tempos and targets could not be high enough. The wildly ambitious first five-year plan, and its rather less ambitious successor, generated a mood of exhilaration. If some achievements were the result of forced labour, many were the work of zealots who believed that by erecting giant plants in the wilderness they were helping to create a new heaven and a new earth. Size of plant and quantity of output were what mattered; quality was a secondary consideration, while the immense sacrifices demanded of the workforce were disregarded. Yet the loyalty of the working class held. Trotsky predicted that sooner or later the workers would revolt against this Soviet state which had usurped their rights and was coercing them in the interests of a new ruling class, but no such revolution came then – or later.[3] By the end of the 1930s, enthusiasm and coercion, in combination, had transformed the USSR into a mighty industrial power. These huge plants, crude and polluting, would later stand out as unwanted dinosaurs; but when new they seemed to many an emblem of the country's unstoppable march towards a fully realized socialism.

Great plants on the steppe were not, however, enough. Socialism could not be achieved without a workforce that was educated, had technical skills and was utterly committed to the state's objectives. The 'bourgeois specialists' satisfied on the first two counts but fell down, it appeared, on the third. Not only were they not committed to socialism; they were, or so Stalin suggested as he radicalized policy in the late 1920s, potential if not actual wreckers and saboteurs. They could no more be trusted than those other class enemies, the kulaks. Only proletarians could be trusted. As a result, a massive programme was launched to give higher and especially technical education to talented and ambitious young men of worker or peasant background. The cultural revolution was in its way as drastic as collectivization or forced industrialization. By the end of the 1930s, the upheaval had produced an intelligentsia of a quite new kind, consisting largely of workers or peasants who had mastered technical skills but had little or nothing in the way of humane education. This new intelligentsia had no links with Old Bolshevism or pre-revolutionary liberalism; its members were untainted by the independent-mindedness and café-society mentality of the former intelligentsia.The country, Stalin told the Eighteenth Party Congress in 1939, now had 'an intelligentsia of the people', an intelligentsia 'intimately bound up with the people and, for the most part, ready to serve it faithfully and loyally'.[4] He might have added that this new, technically trained, plebeian intelligentsia would be uncritically loyal towards himself.

These transformations in agriculture, industry, culture and social structure underlay Stalin's claim that socialism had been achieved in the Soviet Union. But what did he mean by socialism?

3

Lenin had, as we know, used the word inconsistently, slipping from the 'transitional' to the 'end' meaning, perhaps because, for him, there was no very sharp difference between them. Stalin, however,was more rigorous. He drew a clear-cut distinction between socialism and communism, and he applied 'socialism' exclusively to the transitional phase. He then divided the transition into three parts: a ground-clearing preliminary which had led on to the period in which the country now was – 'the period of direct and sweeping socialist construction on all fronts', which in turn would lead on to socialism proper.[5] With the second, the country had, however, already entered 'the period of socialism'; what lay immediately ahead was to complete the building of a socialist society. It was on this task that Stalin concentrated, rarely raising his eyes to the further goal of communism.

Stalin's talk gave the impression that the task was largely organizational. And the language he applied to it from the late 1920s was above all military: an 'offensive' had to be waged, 'battles' fought, 'enemies' put to flight. What was crucial was to create a fully socialist economy, by which he meant an economy controlled entirely by the state in the interests of socialism and having an advanced, technological, heavy-industrial base. This in turn meant crushing or expropriating those whom he regarded as remnants of the exploiting classes – kulaks, bourgeois specialists, former industrial capitalists. It also meant harnessing the whole of society bar these potential or actual wreckers to the task of modernization and overtaking the capitalist countries. The distinction between the necessary conditions for socialism and socialism itself, which Lenin had hung on to, if only just, disappeared. Creating the institutions and social structures necessary for socialism had become identical to creating socialism itself. Socialism was thus the sum of the institutional and structural changes which the state was pushing through. Stalin was doing the very thing which in the summer of 1917 Lenin had warned against – he was 'introducing socialism'.

The mainspring of progress would not, therefore, be a largely self-motivating and self-directing proletariat; the drive would come, rather, from a state committed to 'revolution from above' – to propelling its citizens towards the socialist goal. Once his dominant position within the party had been secured, Stalin's pronouncements about socialism were above all about the state as the indispensable means of achieving and maintaining it. Only 'a strong and powerful dictatorship of the proletariat' could 'scatter to the winds the last remnants of the dying classes'. But it was not simply that the dictatorship would have to continue for the time being; Stalin went much further. 'The state will wither away', he declared, 'not as a result of weakening the state power, but as a result of strengthening it to the utmost ...'[6] That would have seemed strange indeed to anyone who assumed that a withering away of the state was to be one of socialism's features. In 1919, only fourteen years before Stalin's pronouncement, Bukharin and Preobrazhensky had stated in their *The ABC of Communism* that after 'two or three generations' the need for 'laws and punishments' would have passed.[7] But those who still dared to hint at such a view were roundly condemned. 'They are', Stalin said, 'either degenerates or double-dealers and must be driven out of the Party.'[8] To deny the need for a strong and still stronger state was to espouse 'the counter-revolutionary theory of the extinction of the class struggle'. It was also to ignore the 'capitalist encirclement' and the looming threat of nazism. And those who tried to resist the juggernaut of the Soviet state on socialist or any other grounds were duly crushed.

By the mid-1930s, the state's immediate aims had been achieved. Collectivization was more or less complete, the country was acquiring a strong heavy-industrial base, a new and distinctively Soviet intelligentsia was in the making. Crucially, the remnants of the exploiting classes had been wiped out. This enabled Stalin to claim that Soviet society no longer contained 'antagonistic classes': its inhabitants consisted, rather, of two 'friendly classes', the workers and peasants, plus a non-class stratum, the intelligentsia. These changes provided the background to his historic announcement of 25 November 1936: 'Our Soviet society has already, in the main, succeeded in achieving socialism ; it has created a socialist system, i.e. it has brought about what Marxists in other words call the first, or lower, phase of communism.'[9]

Curiously, the announcement was tucked away in a lengthy speech devoted not to socialism but to the new constitution. Loud fanfares and much triumphalism might have been expected; instead, the event was reported almost casually, as something that had happened *already*, and there was no suggestion that a Rubicon of epochal significance had been crossed. Not only did completion of the first phase get low-key treatment; the announcement was not followed by any upbeat appraisal of what still had to be done or by exhortations – in this most hortatory of societies – to get on and finish the job. Quite the contrary: Stalin's comments on communism were terse and negative. Soviet society, he pointed out, 'has not yet reached the higher phase of communism'. The constitution should not be based on communism since that did not yet exist. He even ruled out making any reference in the constitution to 'the ultimate goal'.[10] As far as communism was concerned, this breakneck collectivizer and industrializer was evidently determined to drag his feet.

Communism in fact presented Stalin with a dilemma. Once the victory of socialism had been proclaimed, basic doctrine made it impossible to deny that communism was Soviet society's next destination. Yet communism as it had been defined until now was the negation of Stalinist civilization – and would have the same effect on its driving force, the all-powerful state, that sun would have on an iceberg. It was no wonder that Stalin very rarely referred to communism or to the features usually associated with it. Only one aspect of communism appeared to arouse his enthusiasm: the extinction of national consciousness and the merging of cultures into 'one common culture with one common language'.[11] That, he left no doubt, was much to be desired. Otherwise, he paid mere lip-service to communist ideals – understandably enough, given that under his guidance Soviet society was tending *away* from rather than towards them. It was becoming less and less egalitarian; within this society supposedly free of antagonistic classes, a new privileged elite was taking shape. And it was of course being subjected to an unbridled state. These developments did not necessarily rule out a long-term communist outcome. But they implied that the path to communism would be a complex and 'dialectical' one; and they suggested a sharp discontinuity between the phases rather than a smooth and natural transition from lower to higher.

Justifying an ever more vigilant state did not require much ingenuity. Antagonistic classes might have disappeared, but mentalities were in danger of lagging behind the new social reality. Soviet citizens could still be led astray by anti-socialist propaganda, should the state be remiss enough to let it through. 'Enemies of the people' had, moreover, by no means given up their struggle. Proof of that was conjured up by the show trials of 1936–8, in which leading Bolsheviks one after another confessed to having betrayed socialism and the Soviet fatherland. Further, if less publicized, proof of the danger was provided by the massive purge of high- and middle-ranking officials during the same period. Since enemies were everywhere, vigilance by ordinary citizens and the intelligence services alike was indispensable. And if the domestic enemies were largely fictive, the foreign ones were by the late 1930s all too genuine.

Not, however, until the Eighteenth Party Congress in March 1939 did Stalin deal head-on with the central problem: that Soviet society's next destination, communism, appeared inseparable from statelessness. Marx and Engels had given that impression unambiguously. So, too, had Lenin. *The State and Revolution* had been nothing if not a sustained attack on the state, and it had suggested that under Soviet power there would from the outset be no more than a 'semi-state'.

Marx and Engels, however, were easily disposed of. They could not be expected, Stalin informed the congress, to have foreseen 'each and every zigzag of history in the distant future in every separate country'. Their tenets concerning the state were only of a general and abstract character. Moreover, 'certain of the general tenets of the Marxist doctrine of the state were incompletely elaborated and were inadequate'[12] – which came close to saying that they were mistaken. Lenin could not of course be treated so cavalierly. *The State and Revolution* was a potential embarrassment. However, with some adroitness Stalin sidestepped the problem by suggesting that Lenin had intended to write a second volume of his work in which he would have further developed 'the theory of the state on the basis of the experience gained during the existence of Soviet power in our country'.[13] That was a way of saying that, had he lived, Lenin would have admitted the need for a full-blooded socialist state. Death having forestalled him, the task of working out a theory of the socialist state had been left instead to his disciples. (At this point loud applause interrupted the discourse.) That Stalin then set about doing. And after a few minutes he outlined to the delegates an idea which, had it been floated a decade or so earlier, would have been condemned as a grotesque violation of orthodoxy.

'Will our state remain', he asked,' in the period of communism also?'

'Yes, it will', he answered his own question, 'if the capitalist encirclement is not liquidated ...'[14]

And so he solved his problem, though only by conjuring up something that would have seemed preposterous to Marx, Engels and even Lenin: a state that continued to exist during the higher stage, a *communist* state.

On the face of it, this was a doctrinal innovation of the first order. Yet in reality Stalin was merely making a logical extension of the case he had already made so forcefully on behalf of the state under socialism. The real breach with the founding fathers had occurred already. By demolishing the Marxist doctrine of the state and substituting his own, he extricated himself from the position of having to suggest that an extreme of statification would come immediately before the statelessness of communism. Now the prospect of abrupt discontinuity and a dialectical leap was banished – except of course in the unlikely event that socialism surged to victory in the west. Stalinist socialism would in all probability pass smoothly into Stalinist communism, and the Stalinist state would continue to be a mighty fortress guarding over the landscape it had shaped to the master's satisfaction.

4

The way of life created under Stalin's direction in the Soviet Union of the 1930s was accepted by the great majority as properly socialist and as a universally valid model of socialist construction, which would sooner or later be copied throughout the world. Socialism, people had it drummed into them, was a way of life that was the polar opposite of life in the west. Under capitalism, the means of production were owned by and used for the benefit of a tiny minority; under socialism, they were owned by the state and used for the good of all. Capitalist society suffered from recurring economic crises and the scourge of unemployment; socialist society enjoyed economic stability, full employment and an impressive upward curve in living standards. Under capitalism, the charade of parliamentarism with its constant wrangling cloaked the reality of state power exercised by and for the bourgeoisie alone; under socialism, a nation no longer riven by class conflicts worked single-mindedly for the common good, its members all pulling together in the direction indicated by the Leader. The contrast was so stark and unnuanced that no Soviet citizen in his senses could have the slightest doubt as to which was the superior system; and not until the late 1980s did Stalin's claim that under his direction socialism had been achieved in the Soviet Union come in for serious public questioning.

But was this socialism? If it is enough that the state should own all the means of production, control the whole economy in accordance with an all-encompassing plan, attach an overwhelming priority to the needs of heavy industry and mobilize all social activity towards ends prescribed by the leadership, without regard to the hardships thus inflicted – if these are the tests of socialism, then this was undoubtedly a socialist society. By Stalin's own criteria, the Soviet Union had by the mid-1930s passed the test with flying colours. Yet his chosen criteria ignored certain principles which had always been seen as intrinsic to socialism. Had the changes introduced by Stalin done much for equality? Had they led to any significant improvement in living conditions? Was society becoming more self-managing? Was it achieving real advances in personal freedom? And was the union of peoples based upon a deepening voluntary commitment to socialist internationalism? The answer in each case is 'no' – that hardly needs to be said. It is nevertheless worth examining how far and why Stalinist socialism deviated from those principles without which, as most non-Stalinist socialists believed, socialism was unthinkable.

Equality was arguably the basic socialist principle, yet the Bolsheviks had been careful not to commit themselves to any immediate equalization of material conditions. As long as 'bourgeois right' prevailed, there would have to be inequality of rewards; and with some embarrassment Lenin had defended paying higher salaries to bourgeois specialists. Similarly, there would have to be inequalities of power and status this side of communism. Policy in the early Soviet years nevertheless had a strong egalitarian emphasis – symbolized, for instance, by the 'party maximum' rule, under which no party member was allowed to earn more than a skilled worker. The levelling tendency was reflected, too, in a reaction against hierarchalism. The badges of power were democratized (thus 'minister' became 'commissar'), undue deference towards office-holders was discouraged, and unequal status was to some degree camouflaged by the common designation of 'comrade'.

Once firmly in the saddle, Stalin, however, took a very different attitude towards equality. The state's equalizing mission had for the time being, in his view, been accomplished by the elimination of antagonistic classes and the creation of a society in which workers and peasants collaborated harmoniously. It was no part of the state's current mission to level material conditions: quite the contrary. Far from taking Lenin's apologetic attitude towards wage differentiation, Stalin advocated it wholeheartedly: 'We cannot tolerate a situation in which a locomotive driver earns only as much as a copying clerk ... even under socialism "wages" must be paid according to work performed and not according to needs.' Wage differences would in fact have to be increased in order to reward those with skills and to encourage others to acquire them. And he fiercely attacked 'leftists' who defended wage equalization – 'a reactionary petty bourgeois absurdity' which had nothing in common with Marxism and which Marx and Engels had explicitly condemned.[15] Having thus bulldozed possible doctrinal objections, Stalin pressed ahead with wage differentiation. Lenin's 'party maximum' was abolished and high rewards were heaped upon production workers who exceeded their norms, while qualified engineers were soon getting eight times the pay of unskilled workers. Indeed, it has been reckoned that the gap between the best-paid and the worst-paid had by the end of the 1930s become greater in the USSR than in the USA.

Pay was by no means, however, the end of the matter. Since Stalinist society had an endemic shortage of goods and services, the deserving could be additionally rewarded by being given privileged access to whatever was scarce. In large factories, canteens were usually allocated according to rank – those for the higher ranks served meat, the others not. High-ranking party and state officials could be given chauffeur-driven cars, larger and better flats, dachas in the countryside, holiday homes in the mountains and by the sea. They could also have access to stores in which they could buy goods never seen on the open market and to special clinics which provided unusually good health care.

These benefits – some of them open, others carefully concealed – were the reward of a new class of privileged functionaries, which burgeoned rapidly during the 1930s. To the outcast Trotsky, these people – about half a million strong, by his calculation – were nothing less than a new ruling class.[16] On the face of it, that was overstating the case somewhat. For these people who attracted Trotsky's ire did not share power with the chief executive but were bound in absolute obedience to him, and many would be pitilessly scythed down during the Great Purge of 1936–8. Moreover, they did not constitute a class in the usual sense, since all production resources belonged to the state; none was in private ownership. And in stark contrast to the old ruling class, the members of this group were almost all of proletarian or peasant origin, and in speech and general culture they remained indistinguishable from the masses. Yet if these people were not rulers, they did exercise enormous, arbitrary and unaccountable power on behalf of the real ruler – and in that respect had an uncanny resemblance to the old ruling class, the tsar's satraps. And while production resources did indeed belong in name to the nation, unlimited control of the nation's assets and hence disproportionate access to them put the new elite in a position that in essence differed little from that of people with rights of private ownership. Moreover, however humble the group's origins, its members soon lost touch with the factory floor, and once the ordeal of the Great Purge was behind they and their families settled into a comfortable 'bourgeois' lifestyle with a standard of living far higher than that of ordinary citizens. Two decades later, Milovan Djilas would point out how, behind the rhetoric of socialism, members of this 'new class' pursued their own interests and pillaged the nation's resources.[17] Stalin no doubt took the view that such an elite was essential and that its privileges had to be shielded from public scrutiny. He may well have reasoned that, just as the state had to grow still stronger before it could wither away, so too an elite of privileged functionaries had to burgeon before the conditions for genuine equality could be created. But if the first was sayable, the second was not; such an admission would indeed have been unthinkable.

5

Material wellbeing for all was of course one of the basic promises of the Bolsheviks: without abundance there could be no communism. NEP had been Lenin's attempt to redeem the promise; but the modest advances of the 1920s were then wiped out by collectivization and the industrialization drive. Stalin nevertheless put the best possible gloss upon living conditions, and his efforts in this respect were helped by a piece of good luck – that economic catastrophe struck the west at the very time when the Soviet Union was undergoing its revolution from above. Against the background of the Great Depression, of spiralling unemployment and collapsing production, the case for Soviet socialism looked extremely plausible. What was happening in the west seemed to bear out all that Marxists had said about the evils of capitalism; only the manifestly superior socialist economic system could safeguard against them.

'The abolition of exploitation, the abolition of unemployment in the towns, and the abolition of poverty in the countryside' – these were among the achievements Stalin announced to the Seventeenth Party Congress in 1934. The national income had increased from 35 000 million roubles in 1930 to 50 000 million roubles in 1934; by 1939, official figures put it as high as 105 000 million roubles.[18] Not only had there been a threefold increase in the national income during the 1930s. Workers and peasants were now their own masters, or so they were told, and exploiters had been eliminated. As a result, working people took a much larger share of the national income than in capitalist countries, where they were deprived by the exploiters of a full 50 per cent of it. Already by 1930, on Stalin's calculation, real wages had reached 167 per cent of their 1913 level. From then on, the graph of wellbeing devised by the regime pointed steadily upwards. If Soviet people worked well, it was partly because they lived well. Or so Stalin suggested in 1935: 'Life has improved, comrades. Life has become more joyous. And when life is joyous, work goes well.'[19]

Official statistics, however, told at best part of the story. A tremendous rate of economic growth was achieved during the 1930s, but this was growth from a very low level – on Stalin's own estimate, in the early 1930s the country was still 'fifty or a hundred years behind the advanced countries'.[20] The catching-up, moreover, was almost exclusively in the area of heavy industry; and the price of the achievement was an actual lowering in living standards. The vaunted statistics of national income obscured this, since they failed to reveal how the income was apportioned between state and citizens; what they glossed over was the enormous sacrifice being exacted from people for the sake of industrial expansion. Real wages, having risen under NEP, went into a steep decline during the first five-year plan (1928–32). 1933, in the opinion of Alec Nove, was 'the culmination of the most precipitous decline in living standards known in recorded history'.[21] The slide was stopped in 1934, but it began again in 1936 as additional resources were switched to defence; and the level of 1925 would not be regained until the late 1950s.

Industrialization and the miseries of life in the countryside led to massive migration into the towns. In 1928 there had been fewer than 7 million industrial workers; by 1940 the number had topped 20 million.These were the shock troops of the new civilization and the creators of what was deemed socialism, yet they lived in dreadful conditions. Slums, Stalin boasted in 1934, had been replaced by 'blocks of bright and well-built workers' houses'.[22] But the blocks were in reality shoddily built, and since there were far too few of them a family was lucky if it could get even one room to itself. Food also was in desperately short supply. From 1929 to 1935, bread, meat and other important foodstuffs were rationed; in Leningrad, consumption of meat, milk and fruit fell by two-thirds during the period of the first five-year plan. Hardship at home went together with hardship at work. Tough discipline was imposed upon this new industrial workforce, with bosses acting like replica Stalins. Those who infringed the labour code risked losing not only their jobs but their housing and their food rations; from 1940, absence without good reason from work became a criminal offence. Yet morale among these bullied and deprived workers remained relatively high. They at least could feel that they were achieving something. That could not be said of those left behind in the countryside.

Collectivization, the official line declared, had rescued the peasant from 'kulak bondage' and from 'want'; in reality, it had turned the countryside into a disaster zone. So intense was the squeeze on the peasants that it led in 1932–3 to widespread famine. That had been a recurring feature of Russian life; but this particular famine, which came when the country was close to achieving 'socialism', proved more terrible than any before. In places people were reduced to eating the bark of trees, cats and dogs, even other human beings. No relief measures were undertaken; on the contrary, procurement quotas continued to be exacted from the stricken areas, and throughout the crisis a steady flow of grain exports helped finance the industrialization drive. Moreover, those caught 'pilfering' kolkhoz property – for example, taking grain – were liable to imprisonment or even execution. Across Ukraine, the north Caucasus and the lower Volga region perhaps seven million people died as a result of the 1932–3 famine. But from Stalin's point of view, the famine had served its purpose: it had broken whatever remained of the peasants' will to resist socialism.

Nothing of this got into the press, and the famine remained shrouded in the deepest secrecy. Anything that might contradict Stalin's picture of general wellbeing was taboo, anyone who dared question it an enemy. The thesis that socialism was being built could hardly have survived an admission that the revolution from above had created widespread misery and destitution. Soviet power, the regime on the contrary claimed, had brought the people both material well-being and freedom.[23] The second claim was no more true than the first.

6

Freedom, like equality, was a fundamental value of socialism. Prior to Stalin, few socialists would have imagined a socialist society that did not foster the full development of the human personality. The Bolsheviks had admittedly curbed civil liberties and destroyed democracy. Yet they had done this with the clear intention of putting freedom on an unshakeable foundation and making it available in the near future to all those previously so crushed by toil and poverty that any real possibility of free development had been denied them.

Though Leninist doctrine justified the destruction of 'bourgeois democracy', the Bolsheviks had been anxious from the outset to demonstrate that they had the support of the overwhelming majority. When it transpired that the very opposite was the case, they had fallen back upon the next best thing: they would make it *look* as if they had popular support. In the long term, however, nothing less than genuine support would do, and they were confident that the combined effect of education, propaganda and the benefits of Soviet rule would give them that. By 1921, this somewhat remote prospect had no longer seemed enough. They would have to conciliate their subjects straight away by giving them something at least of what they craved for. As a result, they hoped, grudging acceptance would soon turn into a real commitment to the party and to socialism.

Stalin and his followers had, however, jettisoned this approach – instead, they would storm their way to socialism. They had a highly effective machine for mobilizing and repressing; they also had the support of a core of proletarian militants, who were eager for a final showdown with the bourgeois and the peasants. It was War Communism all over again; and in Stalin's mind there seem to have been echoes, too, of the deeper Russian past – of Peter the Great and even Ivan the Terrible. The state would impose its revolution; the masses would willy-nilly accept the sacrifices and the upheaval inflicted upon them. This time, however, the means of coercion included the Gulag system, under which millions would work as slave labourers in camps in the most inhospitable areas of the country. And this time the offensive was not targeted at the masses alone. They had been conquered and subdued by the mid-1930s; there now erupted an offensive against the party's own, against some of its greatest names but also against many of its faithful middle-ranking functionaries.

The effectiveness of these methods vindicated Stalin's unspoken thesis – that the building of socialism did not require a willing and informed populace but could, and in Soviet circumstances *had* to, be carried through by the state in the face of popular resistance. That had not been Lenin's view; but it was a natural, and perhaps an inevitable, development from much that he had said and done.

The use of physical and mental coercion on an unprecedented scale did not of course make it any less necessary to demonstrate over-whelming popular approval for what was being done. The state had to be seen as an instrument of the will of the toiling masses. No one more piously incanted Bolshevik platitudes and the pseudo-democratic rhetoric of Lenin than Stalin, in this respect a true disciple of the founder, though with a tone of unctuousness that was peculiarly his own. He was nothing more than a humble servant of the people, dependent upon them and helping them to achieve what they willed. The masses were the Bolsheviks' 'mother', or so it was claimed in a purple passage which may well have come from his own pen; as mother, they 'gave birth to them, suckled them and reared them'.[24]

But it was not simply a matter of purple passages. For good reason, Stalin outdid Lenin in his democratic pretensions. The Bolsheviks had, after all, explained their initial violations of democratic practice by reference to the extreme circumstances in which they found them-selves. They could hardly give the vote to everyone when class enemies of Soviet power abounded. Yet by the mid-1930s, conditions were very different. Enemies of the people might still present a problem, but the exploiting classes had nevertheless been eliminated. This was a society in which friendly classes worked in collaboration, a society which had achieved socialism, and these changes needed to be reflected in the political system. The result was the 1936 constitution, which extended the vote to all adults, established a secret ballot, and set up a new, two-chamber legislature, the Supreme Soviet, which would be elected without the previous bias in favour of urban voters. All of this suggested a democratizing tendency; so, too, did another innovation – the sizeable section in the constitution devoted to 'fundamental rights'. Among the rights guaranteed were freedom of assembly, freedom of the press and freedom to demonstrate; the citizen's person, home and correspondence were, in addition, declared inviolate. 'No one', Stalin was moved to comment, 'will deny that our constitution is the most democratic in the world ...'[25] And he was indeed right: no one would.

But if constitutional forms had become more democratic since the 1920s, constitutional realities had gone in the opposite direction. During the 1920s, the dictatorship had at least been oligarchic, and the presence of rival leaders and factions had made for a certain degree of pluralism. By the mid-1930s, however, Stalin had converted his leadership of the party into a personal dictatorship backed up by all the resources of the police state. He controlled the party just as the party controlled the country. His word had become law; beneath him in the chain of command, a series of replica Stalins acted in the same autocratic fashion. All aspects of social activity were now subject to rigorous control: this had become, in T.H. Rigby's phrase, a 'mono-organizational society'.[26] The most striking case of centralization taken to extremes was the 'command economy', brought into being in the early 1930s. Nationalized industry was now complemented by a collectivized agriculture. All industrial production and all capital construction were centrally planned. Planning directives and constant pressure to fulfil targets turned managers and workers alike into cogs in a gigantic machine. But it was not only economic activity that was subject to Moscow's monopolistic control. In art and scholarship as well, the party now strictly imposed its line – artists and scholars were scarcely less regimented than peasants, workers and factory managers. Almost nowhere in fact could the citizen find refuge from the state. To suspend judgement, to adopt an attitude of benevolent neutrality, was no longer a tenable position. Anyone who did not show a clear commitment to the party-state and its concept of socialism was taken to be against it, and being against it spelled doom.

In these circumstances, the rights guaranteed by the new constitution were purely fanciful – this was constitutional gloss over a totalitarian reality. There was some talk of having multi-candidate elections, but by the time citizens went to the polls, in December 1937, the suggestion had been dropped. The electors would have no choice of candidate, let alone of party. And the Supreme Soviet, once elected,

would be no more than a legislative rubber-stamp, despite some orna-
mental provisions for what should happen if its two chambers fell out.
97 per cent of the eligible nevertheless performed their 'civic duty' and
voted; only 630 000 of these – less than 1 per cent – were brave or foolhardy enough not to endorse the offered candidate. The results, as the
party history would in due course declare, were 'a brilliant confirma-
tion of the moral and political unity of the Soviet people'.[27]

The elections were of course a puppet-show in which Stalin pulled
the strings. The police state could deliver whatever result the Leader
wanted. Yet this does not mean that the masses voted with reluctance,
still less that Stalin was willing to make do with mere formal and
external obedience. On the contrary, he wanted real and enthusiastic
support, and as time went on he got more and more of it. This was
support for the party and its objectives, but it was also endorsement of
himself as embodying all the aspirations of party and people.

The cult of the person of Joseph Stalin can be dated to 21 December
1929, his fiftieth birthday, when *Pravda* devoted most of its pages to
his praise. The cult firmed up support for the regime by presenting it
in human rather than abstract ideological form; it also built loyalty to
him and put him beyond the reach of envious rivals. His image was of
a stern yet just father, a man of iron will and supreme intelligence who
worked ceaselessly for the general good and had unlimited concern for
all who loyally served the party's aims. In his own eyes, he may well
have been a successor not only to Lenin but also to Peter the Great and
Ivan the Terrible, performing mighty deeds and putting enemies down
with the support of an adoring multitude.[28] And the novelist Anatoly
Rybakov has plausibly suggested that Stalin prided himself on 'understanding' the Russians and was privately critical of Lenin because 'he
did not know Russia well enough'.[29] The essence of this 'understanding' seems to have been that the Russians were natural
collectivists who needed a charismatic ruler to protect and guide them,
maintain group solidarity, hold the bosses on a tight leash, and keep
everyone equally prostrate before him. By turning Lenin into the
Leader, he had given them someone to worship. The dead Leader,
however, needed a living complement; and Stalin was just that – 'the
Lenin of our days' and 'the Great Successor'.

But if Stalin was to be a 'father' protecting his 'children', then there
had to be perils for him to protect them against. That was where the
Great Purge, the show trials and the terror came in. Accusations
against purge victims were widely believed, and the fact that those on
trial confessed to the most heinous intentions made belief all the

easier. The overthrow of the 'archfiends' provoked public rejoicing. Mass meetings – stage-managed no doubt, yet providing an outlet for very real passions – demanded 'the extermination of the fascist vermin'. In January 1937 some 200 000 people gathered in sub-zero temperatures in Red Square to demand immediate execution for those convicted in the recent show trial. These 'double-dealers', 'fascist hirelings', 'Judases', 'dregs of humanity' and 'assassins, spies and wreckers' seemed to be everywhere. No one could be trusted. Not even Yezhov, head of the NKVD until exposed as an enemy in December 1938. Not even Kamenev and Zinoviev, who had passed themselves off as Lenin's closest counsellors. Not even Nikolai Bukharin, ideologue of the alternative Bolshevik path, whose apparent acceptance of his guilt before the party must have been especially sweet to Stalin. If treachery was, as it seemed, almost universal among the leaders, to whom could people look? Only to Him. By turning the world upside down, Stalin had created the very conditions in which the cult of his own person could flourish. People needed certainty and stability; they needed someone radiantly good and unflinchingly strong, who could console and protect them, make sense of the turmoil and give them hope for the future. These needs were met by the fabrication of a Leader who, like God, was on the one hand all-powerful, yet on the other was in no way responsible for everyday misfortunes, indeed led the struggle against them.

In presenting himself as the friend and protector of ordinary people against their legions of enemies, Stalin was taking advantage of age-old resentments and insecurities. He made much in particular of the deep-seated resentment against the educated and westernized, and his exploitation of this could be seen in the treatment of political prisoners. In tsarist times, the 'politicals' had been treated with some leniency: they came, after all, by and large from the same class as those who sentenced them, whereas common criminals were seen as riff-raff. Under Stalin, however, it was the other way around: thieves and murderers were a 'socially friendly' element, whereas the politicals were 'socially hostile'. 'Even though you're a bandit and a murderer', the reasoning went, 'you are not a traitor to the Motherland, *you are one of our own people*'.[30] There was even a policy of encouraging the common criminals to rob and plunder the politicals. As far back as 1901, according to Alexander Solzhenitsyn, Stalin was accused by party colleagues of using common criminals against his enemies. By the 1930s, no one could stop him. Evgenia Ginzburg, incarcerated with other women politicals in a ship's hold, was attacked by 'murderers' and 'sadists', a 'half-naked, tattooed, ape-like horde' of women criminals who invaded the hold and 'set about terrorizing and bullying the "ladies"'.[31] Politicals were not real 'ladies' and 'gentlemen', but their education and free-thinking were enough to stamp them as such. And these dregs of the underworld, spurred on by the authorities, were acting out a desire to punish them which went deep in popular culture. Such attitudes had nothing of course to do with Bolshevik enlightenment. But then Stalin had never been a Bolshevik enlightener. He had attracted the rawest elements in the party, those who after Lenin's death had swamped the Old Bolsheviks. He and they had rid Bolshevism of whatever democratic, cosmopolitan and enlightenment characteristics it still had; they had made it into something that spoke to the archaic world of peasant and peasant-proletarian Russia, even if its idiom was Marxist-Leninist and its aim modernizing. And by stirring up fears, hatreds and fantasies, by re-opening wounds in the collective psyche, he had made himself all the more indispensable and his position as Leader more or less impregnable.

The great leap forward was thus at the same time a leap backwards. The modernizing thrust which produced enormous economic and technological advance went together with a marked retrogression in political culture, as the mass of the population slipped back into attitudes from which pre-revolutionary Russia had been beginning to climb out. The 1917 revolutions, remember, had in rapid succession ousted both tsar and God, those age-old supports and foci of devotion. In more favourable circumstances, a culture of democracy in which people took responsibility for their own lives might have gradually made good the loss. Unpopularity had, however, quickly killed off Bolshevism's democratic potential, and the Soviet regime had been left with neither democratic legitimacy nor the power of a charismatic personality to sustain it. But one or other of these was indispensable; and since democratization would have been tantamount, for the Bolsheviks, to suicide, the regime under Stalin took the unBolshevik but deeply Russian course of restoring the charismatic element. So successfully did Stalin do this that by the late 1930s much of the population had become abjectly dependent upon him. Lenin's aim of genuine mass support and a real bonding between people and rulers was thus achieved, yet it was achieved by means that had nothing whatever to do with socialism or the Bolsheviks' original ambitions. Stalin boasted that the Soviet Union was the most democratic country in the world; but instead of leading the Soviet people forward to

democracy, he had led them back, amidst conditions of utter insecurity, to a culture in which childlike dependency mingled with a fierc
rejection of anyone and anything alien – to a culture which th
Bolsheviks themselves, as democrats and enlighteners, had onc
intended to liquidate.

7

It was ironic that this Georgian should turn out to be a hammer of the
non-Russians. Yet there are grounds for thinking that very early in his
career Stalin had spurned his Georgian identity in favour of a Russian
one, and the very Russianness of the Bolsheviks may well have been
one thing that made him prefer them to the more cosmopolitan
Mensheviks.[32] Certainly, once the Bolsheviks were in power he had
taken a consistently harder line towards the non-Russians than Lenin.
He had of course been defeated on the issue of federalism and accepted
a federal structure for the Soviet state. Had he lived to witness the 1991
collapse, however, he would no doubt have insisted that events had
justified his original rejection of a nationality-based federalism: for
under the rulers who followed him, the federal structure turned out to
be an incubator of nationalism.

The non-Russians' right of self-determination was purely nominal,
yet their cultural freedom was real enough, and use of their own
languages was not only allowed but encouraged. This permissive attitude was summed up in the formula that socialism would lead to a
'*flowering* of national cultures that are *socialist* in content and national
in form'.[33] Thanks to the 'socialist in content and national in form'
approach, the 1920s saw a tremendous growth of non-Russian
languages, many of which appeared in written form for the first time.
Local languages were used in administration, and their use became
widespread in schools. In the case of Ukrainian, the most important
minority language, no schoolchildren had been taught in it before
1917; but by 1927 more than 90 per cent of Ukrainian schoolchildren
were learning in it.

Behind such developments lay the Bolsheviks' belief that the
national 'form' would not impede but would, on the contrary, help
the growth of a socialist 'content' and in particular of socialist
consciousness, which would in time make the 'form' redundant.
Economic development, the expansion of the working class (which, it
was assumed, was by nature internationalist), the material benefits of
Soviet rule: all would point in the same direction. As class solidarity

among the peoples of the Union grew, so national self-consciousness would lessen; and the different nations would eventually merge into a single nation speaking a single language – which would not, it was emphasized, be Russian.

Bolshevik hopes that the national 'form' would be undermined by a rapidly developing socialist 'content' proved, however, to be bookishly unrealistic. As national languages flourished, so too did consciousness of national history, literature and customs. Educated non-Russians became fascinated by whatever distinguished them from Russians; and this was especially true of the Ukrainians, who in the post-revolutionary years experienced a veritable cultural rebirth. The national 'form' thus began to create a national, if not nationalist, 'content'; the result was increasing friction between the non-Russian republics and the centre. Bolsheviks tried to explain these problems away by blaming them on 'Great Russian chauvinists' – expatriate Russians who refused to learn the local language and treated the local culture with contempt. In 1933, however, Stalin changed tack and placed the blame squarely on the non-Russians themselves: bourgeois forces, he announced, were fomenting nationalism in an attempt to undermine the Soviet system and restore capitalism. This announcement heralded what, in effect, was a reversal of the previous permissive policy towards national distinctiveness. The aim from now on was not to promote national cultures but to russify and to assimilate them.

The especial target of Stalin's wrath was Ukraine, whose 40 million people made it the second most important Soviet republic. It was in Ukraine, as it happened, that peasants had most stubbornly resisted collectivization. At the very time when their resistance was being crushed by famine, exile and execution, Stalin launched a campaign against Ukrainian nationalism. Party officials were purged on a large scale and replaced in many cases by Russians; and the Commissar for Education, Mikola Skrypnik, was condemned as a 'nationalist degenerate' for crimes that included wanting to separate Ukrainian from 'the fraternal Russian tongue'. The 1933 purge was, however, no more than a foretaste of what was to come. In 1937–8 the whole governing elite was swept away and Ukraine placed under the rule of one of Stalin's most zealous henchmen, Nikita Khrushchev.

After the 1933 reversal, there was heavy emphasis throughout the Union on the Russian language, Russian culture and Russian history. A Soviet patriotism began to be taught that glorified the achievements of the 'Soviet fatherland' and its Bolshevik leaders and presented the great figures of the Russian past as their precursors. Yet despite this russifying tendency, local languages continued to be promoted. Novelists, for instance, were encouraged to write in their own languages, provided they took the socialist-realist approach and chose Soviet or socialist subjects rather than 'bourgeois-nationalist' ones. And Stalin himself came forward as a determined proponent of the federal system he had conceded so reluctantly in the early 1920s.

The number of Union republics, originally only 4, was raised in 1936 to 11, and the rights of the republics were expanded in certain areas. One of the two chambers of the newly-established Supreme Soviet was a Soviet of Nationalities, which non-Russians dominated very heavily. In the somewhat artificial debate which preceded the new constitution, Stalin defended the creation of such a chamber; and he still more strongly defended retaining the right of secession from the Union. That said, however, he made it clear that the right was a purely nominal one. 'It is, of course, true', he pointed out, 'that there is not a single Republic that would want to secede from the USSR.'[34] Stalin's methods had indeed solved the nationalities problem, at least to his own satisfaction. 'The experiment of forming a multi-national state based on socialism has been completely successful', he observed. Mutual distrust among the peoples of the USSR had been replaced by mutual friendship; the outcome was a state 'whose stability might well be envied by any national state in any part of the world'.[35] The Bolsheviks' aim of a culture that was national in form and socialist in content thus appeared to be well on the way to being achieved, and fears that the form might subvert the content now seemed to be groundless. Socialism, spread through national cultures, was bonding the peoples in an indissoluble union. The reality, however, was that socialism had had and would have very little part in the bonding of the non-Russians to the Soviet state.

8

The ordeal of the Second World War gave the regime a new layer of legitimation. This was not, Stalin was at pains to point out, a war to save the party or socialism: it was a war to save everything that was sacred to the Soviet and especially the Russian people. This was in fact a war in defence of the 'motherland' – a term rejected by the Bolsheviks which had come back into vogue in the 1930s. And in summoning his 'brothers and sisters' to fight back against the Germans, Stalin invoked the heroic warrior-figures of the Russian past. This explicit identification of the regime with the great-power traditions of Russia ran a risk, of course, of offending the former subject-peoples. Some, in the event, welcomed the nazi invasion, while many more might have, had the invaders treated them less callously. But for Russians at least, the regime had now become a complete embodiment of the national will; and for them the effect of the struggle – of unspeakable shared suffering – was to anoint the regime with a patriotic chrism and to make Stalin still more unquestioned and godlike.

Victory when it came was presented as an achievement of the Soviet and especially the Russian people. It was also a victory for socialism and for the Leader. The industrial successes of the 1930s, which underpinned the eventual triumph, had been complemented during the war by the rapid creation of military-industrial plants in areas beyond the Germans' reach. And in this, as in the war strategy itself, the Leader's role was portrayed as decisive.

Russians had good reason for satisfaction at the end of the war. The Soviet Union, more than any other power, had brought about Hitler's defeat. Its boundaries now reached further west than at any time in the history of the Russian state. It was in the process of acquiring a buffer of satellite states beyond its western border. And with Germany destroyed and Britain and France exhausted, the Soviet Union now emerged on to the international stage as one of the two superpowers.

Yet the heroic wartime achievements of the Soviet people did not bring any rewards. There was no relaxation of controls; on the contrary, various concessions granted during the war were withdrawn and the repressive atmosphere of the 1930s returned. With fascism defeated, Stalin discovered a new bogy – his erstwhile allies. During the war, Soviet citizens had been exposed as never before to western influence. That was now rigidly excluded; ideological conformity was imposed; and a fierce campaign against westernizing tendencies put intellectuals, Jews, Leningraders and anyone suspected of being 'cosmopolitan' in especial jeopardy.

The despot's death, in March 1953, did not, however, provoke rejoicing or even any widespread feeling of relief. Some intellectuals and some prisoners may have rejoiced privately; but the reaction of most people seems to have been grief, a sense of personal bereavement, and alarm at the prospect of a Stalinless future. How, one person wondered, could life possibly go on without him – 'hadn't God died, without whom nothing was supposed to take place?'.[36] People who would later fight against everything Stalin had stood for were engulfed by the general desolation. Andrei Sakharov, the future eminent dissident, was 'overcome by the great man's death'; only years later would he understand 'the degree to which deceit, exploitation and outright fraud were inherent in the whole Stalinist system'.[37] Dmitri Volkogonov, son of a purge victim, who in time would publish a damning study of the Leader, believed on hearing of his death that 'the sky had fallen in' and was quite unable to see the link between his family's tragedy and Stalin.[38] If men as intelligent as these had fallen under Stalin's spell, it was hardly surprising that more ordinary citizens should succumb to him. The nation as a whole had accepted Stalin at face value. Here was a great and good Leader, under whose guidance the Soviet people had, first of all mankind, attained socialism. The achievement had recently been extended to eastern Europe and China; before long, life in the advanced countries as well would be reshaped in accordance with the scheme that had been devised by Lenin but turned into reality by his great successor.

9

The view of Stalin as the successor who implemented Lenin's vision would be bitterly disputed by perestroika ideologists of the 1980s, yet it is hard to deny that Stalinism was the outgrowth, however unintended, of Lenin's work. For the way to Stalinist socialism had been cleared by two theoretical improvizations of Lenin's, each an adaptation of Marxism to the Bolsheviks' peculiarly difficult circumstances but at the same time an attempt to justify Bolshevik practice within a broad Marxist frame. First, there was his insistence that, in the special situation of Russia, the socialist revolution could, indeed had to, come in advance of the socio-economic and cultural changes that were necessary for socialism. The effect of this was to separate the socialist revolution from socialism itself and to create a betwixt-and-between phase during which the proletarian dictatorship (that is, the party leadership) would, with broad popular support, take decisive actions that would put the missing conditions in place. The absence of the expected support and the presence instead of widespread opposition had then forced Lenin into a second improvization: if the population was not yet proletarian, that is, not yet mature enough to realize where its own best interests lay, then it was the duty of the state to act on the people's behalf and to use its powers singlemindedly in order to lay the economic and other foundations of socialism.

These were fundamental improvizations, yet they implied a clear distinction between foundations or preconditions and socialism itself.

There would be a pre-socialist transition, a transition to the transition, during which the state would push through measures that were socialist in aspiration but were not, and could not yet be, socialist in nature. The distinction was important for Lenin, since it set bounds upon his deviation, limiting it to certain ground-clearing preliminaries, and promised a return to a purely Marxist understanding of socialism as a phase already marked by the popular commitment and popular self-management that would emerge in their fullest form under communism. True, during War Communism the distinction was to all intents and purposes wiped out – and that flashed a warning of things to come. During NEP, however, Lenin reasserted the distinction strongly, and he did not hesitate to say that socialism was still a remote prospect in Russia. His improvizations were thus once more firmly placed within the frame of Marxist beliefs that had guided him since his twenties. But keeping Bolshevik practice within that frame would require a constant struggle; and the continuing conflict between theory and practical imperatives was what lay behind the policy zigzags and the internal agonizings which were such a feature of his final years.

Part of the problem was that many in the leadership had come to see the very attempt to reconcile Bolshevik practice with western-inspired notions of socialism as a popular creation as irrelevant and even harmful. What mattered above all to them was to deliver on the party's promise of socialism, if only because that alone justified its power. Broad popular support and victorious revolution in the west might be desirable but, as things had turned out, they were far from necessary. The Bolsheviks held power in a firm grip and had already shown that they could use it to good effect. Everything needed for socialism could in fact be put in place by skilled and vigorous use of the one undeniable asset they possessed: a state that had massive powers of mobilization and repression, that could, it seemed, go anywhere and do anything. As for Lenin's insistence on the difficulty of achieving socialism and on the need to distinguish preconditions from socialism itself, that had minimal significance for the intensely practical men who surrounded him. They could hardly be blamed in fact if they regarded it as somewhat formal and hair-splitting. It was Lenin, after all, who had taught them to justify whatever the Bolshevik state did as necessary for socialism and as having the people's willing approval. That double argument had entered into the pith and marrow of their thinking. How easy it then was for them to slip into the further assumption that measures which contributed to socialism and had popular approval were socialist in themselves, and to gloss over a distinction which no longer made any sense in terms of practical realities.

Stalin was simply the toughest, wiliest and most determined of those in the leadership who thought like this. Their thinking corresponded, moreover, to the expectations of those semi-peasant workers and proletarianized peasants who now made up the party's backbone. The eventual triumph of this group, and Stalin's domination within it, can be largely explained by the natural understanding between him and the rank-and-filers and the skill with which he articulated their wishes. They, like he, had climbed out of the peasant world; they, like he, knew very little of the west and socialism as it was understood there; they, like he, would turn savagely against the peasantry, yet remained indelibly marked by its mindset, by its fears, hatreds and insecurities. For him, as for them, socialism would be achieved by force or not at all – by vigorous assault against enemies of every stripe, be they the petty capitalists of the countryside or wreckers from the old bourgeoisie. The state would from now on move in a straight line and with irresistible force towards its objective: there would be no more zigzags, no more concessions, no more attempts to reconcile what had to be done with bourgeois notions of socialism. The moorings that had tied Bolshevism to western socialism had become badly frayed even during Lenin's lifetime; now they were cut altogether. Lenin had seen the Bolshevik party-state as necessary to create the preconditions of socialism; under Stalin, the party-state was elevated from this instrumental role into being the creator, guardian and arbiter of socialism itself. Thus the statist improvization by which Lenin adapted Marxism to Russia's circumstances was turned by Stalin into a self-contained system of thought and practice whose connection with Marxism was little more than formal.

That Lenin would have fiercely rejected this outcome has been suggested before and deserves to be said again. The Stalinist denouement was nevertheless the natural consequence of his work in the sense that, for many party members, it offered the only possible solution to the problems created by the party's original seizure of power. Nothing less would cut the Gordian knot. Moreover, the sword that lay to hand, the sword with which Stalin cut the knot, had been forged, in effect, by Lenin. It was he who had sanctioned the destruction of freedom both outside the party and within it; it was he who had justified what in effect was dictatorship by the party elite; it was he who had drilled into his colleagues that their right to power and their whole *raison d'être* rested upon the promise that the party – it alone – could deliver socialism. In the situation of the late 1920s, Stalin had little difficulty in winning most members to the view that this promise could be redeemed, and the party itself saved from destruction, only by a decisive drive which struck socialism's enemies out of its path. That was the message distilled, rightly or wrongly, out of Lenin's contortions. People will continue to debate what Lenin intended and how much responsibility he bore for the Soviet tragedy. Yet history in the person of Stalin gave its own unambiguous reply to the question, 'Which was the real Lenin and what did he stand for?'

6
Onward to Communism, 1953–64

1

Stalin had turned the Soviet Union into a mighty industrial and military power; he had imposed state control over all areas of life and called the achievement socialism; he had entrenched a highly privileged ruling class with unlimited authority, under himself, to carry out whatever policies he deemed necessary. Yet communism remained remote. To many foreign observers at least, it seemed that the socialist project in Russia had gone wildly and perhaps irreversibly off course. Material abundance was a far cry: living standards were lower than in the 1920s, and the plight of the peasantry was especially pitiable. There had been little progress towards the creation of a 'new person' living and working in a communist way. In terms of equality of conditions, there had actually been retrogression since the 1920s. As for Lenin's vision of a participatory society, a society of mass initiative: nothing could have been further removed from that than the repressed, terrified and abjectly passive society of Stalin's later years.

Stalin's death, however, made change inevitable – the autocracy had died with the autocrat. Dictatorship would continue, but it was likely to be the dictatorship of a group rather than of a single, all-powerful individual. Two factors, moreover, would probably incline the new rulers towards change. The very success of Stalin's programme had made gross centralization and repressiveness unnecessary. The Stalinist state had been created to drag a backward country into modernity; it had also been justified by the alleged threat of internal and external enemies. The Soviet Union of the 1950s, however, was by no means a primitive, peasant-dominated society, nor was the regime under any conceivable threat. Harshness was no longer necessary, and it would hardly be in the new rulers' own interests. For these figures who now came out of the shadows were wholly lacking in Stalin's charisma – grey men who could neither dazzle nor terrify. If they were to maintain their authority, they would have to make some concessions to their appallingly deprived and repressed subjects.

Yet there was scant prospect of major change. The regime was impregnable; any challenge from without the power structure seemed unthinkable. And the new rulers themselves would neither want nor be able to change things fundamentally. These were Stalin's heirs and former associates. All had risen within his regime; all had contributed to its achievements and its crimes. Extricating themselves from its assumptions – de-Stalinizing themselves – would be well-nigh impossible. There were also tactical constraints on them. Any sharp break with the past might jeopardize their inheritance. They needed to preserve all the power of Stalin's regime intact, even if the power would from now on be wielded by a collective leadership and with more regard to the subjects' needs.

The best hope for reform among the successors seemed to lie with Georgy Malenkov, Stalin's apparently intended heir, who on the dictator's death took over as head of government. This cultured, charming, rather bourgeois man in his early fifties had a commitment to consumer industries and to peaceful coexistence with the west. Here, it seemed, was the coming face of the Soviet Union. Yet Malenkov could not compare for political skill or force of character with an older, less prepossessing and overtly more traditionalist rival, who steadily got the better of him in the struggle for dominant position. Within weeks he had been forced out as party secretary; in 1955 he was ousted from the premiership; and when in 1957 he, together with Molotov and Kaganovich, was ejected from the leadership altogether, the triumph of Nikita Khrushchev was complete.

Born in 1894, Khrushchev was a peasant-proletarian whose family moved when he was young from the countryside to a coal-mining area of Ukraine. Very much a second-generation rather than an Old Bolshevik, he was one of many raw recruits drawn to the party in October's aftermath, and what education he had was largely picked up in party institutions during his twenties and thirties. As it turned out, he was a gifted as well as a tough administrator; he was also, unsurprisingly, a devoted follower of Stalin during the factional struggles of the 1920s. By luck or judgement – perhaps because of his readiness to play the peasant clown at Stalin's court – he managed to avoid being purged or even falling into disfavour, and he stayed in high positions from the mid-1930s right through until the Leader's death.

Yet this apparently wholehearted Stalinist used the supremacy he had won to launch a devastating attack on Stalin; and he followed the attack up by setting the country on a fast track towards communism. Khrushchev's programme had three main objectives, all of them essential to the creation of a communist society, all of them badly neglected by Stalin. The first was economic growth whose benefits reached the whole community – the material abundance without which communism was unthinkable. Economic advance could do no more, however, than provide communism's 'material-technical basis'. Khrushchev's second objective was the creation of a 'new person' and a new way of life. That required moral engineering of a high order – freeing people of undesirable character traits, as well as eliminating the remaining economic, social and cultural divisions among them. But the transformation necessary for communism could not be brought about, he made it clear, by an all-powerful state imposing its will upon a passive society and treating its members like so many pawns. The state and in particular the party would for the time being continue to have a major role, but communist society could only be built by people who wanted it, understood it, and worked eagerly, intelligently and creatively towards it. Khrushchev's third objective, in short, was to turn socialist democracy, which so far existed only on paper, into a reality.

Thus Khrushchev restored Lenin's long-neglected vision of the road to communism. But he did more than that. He committed the party to the ambitious – perhaps foolhardy – task of getting the Soviet Union to the threshold of communism by 1980.

2

The campaign began in the early hours of 25 February 1956. Delegates to the Twentieth Party Congress, which had just concluded, were summoned back then to an unheralded and closed session in which for more than four hours Khrushchev railed against Stalin. The 'secret speech' was, above all, a denunciation of Stalin's misdeeds. Stalin, Khrushchev told the delegates, had 'committed grave abuses of power'. He had 'ignored the norms of Party life and trampled on the Leninist principles of collective party leadership'. He was guilty in fact of 'a whole series of exceedingly grave and serious perversions of Party principles, of Party democracy, of proletarian legality'.[1] Khrushchev did not limit himself, moreover, to generalities. He shocked the delegates by giving statistics of Central Committee members and congress delegates – their own very predecessors – who had been arrested and executed during the 1930s. He raised a question-mark, too, against Stalin's leadership qualities, and set about demolishing the image of him as a great war leader. Stalin had impeded rather than helped the war effort; he deserved very little credit for the eventual victory. 'Not Stalin, but the Party as a whole, the Soviet government, our heroic army, its talented leaders and brave soldiers, the whole Soviet nation – these are the ones who assured the victory in the Great Patriotic War.'[2]

Stalin, then, was brutal, capricious and at times incompetent. He was also inordinately vain, and his vanity had required that Lenin be effectively downgraded. Khrushchev underlined the contrast between the two: between 'the genius of the revolution' and his vain and brutal successor. Modest, patient and principled, Lenin had 'mercilessly stigmatized any manifestation of the cult of the individual'. He had always believed in 'the role of the people as the creator of history'. But Khrushchev's most effective blow against Stalin's projection of himself as the ever-faithful Leninist was to reveal the conflict between the two in 1922 and Lenin's attempt to oust Stalin from the general secretaryship. By reading the relevant correspondence to the no doubt astounded delegates, he tore the veil from an episode that had been entirely suppressed. These 'negative characteristics' seen in Stalin by Lenin had in time, he commented, 'caused untold harm to our Party'.[3]

Yet Khrushchev stopped short of condemning all of Stalin's work. The essence of his case was that, while implementing Lenin's plans for socialism, Stalin had in vital respects disregarded Lenin's methods and his principles. He had violated or ignored important aspects of Marxism-Leninism; worst of all, he had marginalized the party and the masses of the people. What was necessary now was to unleash the creative potential of the latter and to restore the guiding role of the former. Provided this was done, communism's victory remained assured. Khrushchev did not, however, put his case quite so baldly. Congress delegates might warm to the theme of Stalin's crimes against the party; Stalin's flouting of democracy, on the other hand, was a more delicate issue. One thing, however, emerged clearly enough from Khrushchev's speech. While he led the party, return to Lenin and Leninism would be its motif.

The speech would be much criticized abroad and later in Russia for the shallowness of its attack. Khrushchev had concentrated, critics claimed, upon Stalin's personal characteristics and explained the tragedies of the period almost wholly in terms of them. This was an indictment of Stalin rather than of Stalinism; it focused upon symptoms rather than causes and provided no analysis of the underlying factors. Moreover, the praise for Stalin's 'services' which had here and there punctuated Khrushchev's denunciations had been far from perfunctory. For Khrushchev had actually endorsed Stalin's achievements up to 1934, including the destruction of the right, collectivization and breakneck industrialization. Only from 1934, if Khrushchev was to be believed, had Stalin gone astray; for a full decade after Lenin's death he had, or so it appeared, remained a faithful Leninist.

Yet the wonder is that Khrushchev's speech was made at all and that it cut as deep as it did. His colleagues in the Presidium (the former Politburo) were wholly against him raising the Stalin question and let him go ahead with the greatest reluctance. Lifting the veil on what had happened might endanger their careers, might even jeopardize the regime itself. The effects of an attack on Stalin were in fact unpredictable. It might provoke pro-Stalin outbursts; it might, on the other hand, unleash a movement against the party and the whole revolutionary inheritance. That was why the issue had to be kept strictly within the party itself.

Khrushchev may well have seen advantages for himself in taking the initiative on this ultra-sensitive issue. Some of his rivals had been closer to Stalin than he had; they were more likely, therefore, to be tainted by association with his crimes than he was. Yet whatever the tactical pros and cons, Khrushchev was bound in essence by the same internal constraints as his colleagues. He too had been a pith-and-marrow Stalinist. So much so, he would reveal in his memoirs, that 'I was a hundred per cent faithful to Stalin as our leader and our guide. I believed that everything Stalin said in the name of the Party was inspired by genius ...' The spell remained unbroken till the end – 'I wept sincerely over Stalin's death' – and indeed well after it: 'We did everything we could to shield Stalin, not yet realizing that we were harbouring a criminal, an assassin, a mass murderer.'[4] Within a couple of years, however, Khrushchev had begun to break free from the Leader's thrall – prompted, it seems, by the work of a party commission investigating the purges, whose revelations astounded him. Escaping from this person who had dominated his whole political life would nevertheless be a slow process, and in February 1956 the process had only just begun. His vehement attack on Stalin's character may well have been a diversion from systematic questioning of Stalinism, for which he was by no means ready. Yet if Stalinism was not analysed or attacked by name, the whole thrust of Khrushchev's speech carried an implicit, if not fully thought through, criticism of it. Criticism was implicit in the recurrent contrasting of Stalin with Lenin and Leninist principles. It was implicit in the suggestion that Stalin, while implementing Lenin's plan, had flouted Lenin's methods. It was implicit in the emphasis on socialist democracy and the people as the 'creator of history'. Had the collectivization been in accordance with Lenin's methods? Had the campaign against the right observed the principles of socialist democracy? In his 'secret speech' Khrushchev said, and probably still believed, that such actions had been justified. By the time he came to write his memoirs, he would have thought his way through to different conclusions.

3

Party members who had not been at the congress had the speech read out to them at closed meetings by local party secretaries. But all the general public gleaned was a terse congress resolution, in which the party undertook 'to put an end to the cult of personality, which is alien to Marxism-Leninism, to liquidate its consequences in all spheres of party, state and ideological work, and to ensure the strict maintenance of the standards of party life and the principles of collective party leadership worked out by the great Lenin'.[5] A *Pravda* article in July then revealed a little of what Khrushchev had actually said. The idol would be chipped away at – but toppling it was out of the question. Not until October 1961, at the Twenty-Second Party Congress, would Khrushchev put the Stalin question directly before the general public.

Between the two congresses, the atmosphere in the country had been transformed. Stalinism had flourished upon 'enemies' – encircling capitalist enemies abroad, 'enemies of the people' at home. Khrushchev adopted a new attitude to the capitalist world: peaceful coexistence. The capitalists were rivals rather than enemies; they would be beaten not by war but by peaceful competition, by the intrinsic merits of socialism. At home, the term 'enemies of the people' disappeared; so, too, did the notion that as Soviet society advanced, its internal enemies would fight back still harder. Whereas Stalin's state had been unremittingly suspicious, Khrushchev's acted as if it trusted its citizens and took their loyalty for granted. Prisoners streamed home from the camps; artists and intellectuals enjoyed a freedom unknown since the 1920s. Rather as at the revolution's outset, the authorities seemed to want ordinary people to participate actively and eagerly in the building of the new society.

Yet in the wake of the speech the party had become deeply divided on the Stalin question. Stalin lay in fact at the symbolic heart of the emerging struggle between reformers and conservatives. Those who welcomed Khrushchev's initiative and wanted a thoroughgoing de-Stalinization were confronted by a powerful phalanx of conservatives, who admitted that Stalin had committed 'excesses' but stoutly defended his achievement as a whole and rejected any attempt to belittle the 'heroic' 1930s or Stalin's war leadership. The muted response to the speech within the Soviet Union itself (apart from some rioting in Georgia) did something to disarm Khrushchev's critics. He was, however, damaged by the reaction in eastern Europe: the speech provoked upheaval in Poland and outright revolution in Hungary, which could only be dealt with by the Stalinist method of sending in tanks. This emboldened his opponents, and in June 1957 Malenkov allied with the veteran Stalinists Molotov and Kaganovich in an attempt to oust him. Khrushchev, however, beat the attempt off, thanks largely to strong support within the Central Committee from regional and younger party leaders; and the 'anti-party group', as his opponents became known, was then disposed of by the relatively gentle means of demoting its members to minor posts and sending them away from Moscow.

Victory gave an added impetus to Khrushchev's reforming zeal, but his increasing departure from the norms of life under Stalin only strengthened resistance to him within the party and government elite. The Stalin question became as a result inextricably meshed with the struggle over the reform programme. That was why at the Twenty-Second Party Congress Khrushchev took the question out of the closed circle of the elite, where opinion was hardening against him, and put it before the public. His report to the congress endorsed the 'correct decision' taken in 1956 to tell the truth about Stalin's abuse of power. The report held up Lenin as the source of the party's principles, extolled his goal of a participatory society which would 'enlist all citizens without exception in the task of governing the state', and denounced the 'anti-party group' for having wanted to return to the 'pernicious methods' of the past. Elevation of Lenin and attacks on the neo-Stalinists were accompanied by a symbolic toppling of the former idol. An elderly woman delegate astounded the audience by speaking of Lenin's unhappiness at having to share the Mausoleum with someone who had brought the party such misfortune. That night Stalin's body was removed from the Mausoleum and buried under a granite slab near the Kremlin wall. From then on until the end of the

Soviet period (and indeed beyond it), Lenin would lie in solitary state in the Mausoleum, the one and only object of devotion, the one and only source of authority, a unique embodiment of sacred power and revolutionary virtue.

Once the dead Leader had been ejected from the temple, all symbols of his cult were banished. Stalingrad became Volgograd, while busts, statues, portraits and so on rapidly disappeared from public places. Many intellectuals reacted with joy to the overthrow of the despot; for some, however, joy was tinged with apprehension that the Stalinists might yet make a comeback. These fears were well justified. A wide swathe of the ruling class resented Khrushchev's iconoclasm, his destruction of the pieties which for three decades had underpinned Soviet life. Yet Khrushchev was no saboteur, no capitalist in communist clothing, no proponent of a 'value-free' democracy. Quite the contrary: he was a dyed-in-the-wool Bolshevik, someone whose faith in the party and its mission was unbounded. And if he was knocking down Stalinism, he was putting something in its place. For what was wrong with the Stalin system, he had come to believe, was that it got in the way of the essential – creating communism.

4

Lenin had made the revolution and pointed the way ahead; Stalin had built socialism, if by somewhat dubious methods; now Khrushchev would lead the Soviet Union forward by a very different path to communism. When an extraordinary party congress met in 1959, it became known as the 'Congress of the Builders of Communism'. The country, Khrushchev told its delegates, 'now has the opportunity of entering a new and most important period of its development – the period of large-scale building of communist society'.[6] This was a dramatic change of perspective: till then communism had seemed something distant and unreal. The next year there appeared a mass-circulation textbook, *Fundamentals of Marxism-Leninism*, which justified the new perspective and brought the idea of communism down to earth.[7] Marx and Lenin had etched life under communism in the broadest outlines; now something was revealed of the everyday reality of this seemingly imminent new life.

The pace quickened in 1961 with a new Communist Party Programme, the first since 1919 – 'a programme for the building of communist society'. The Twenty-Second Party Congress, that same year, made communism a central theme. Not only had communism come close; Khrushchev now put a date upon it – the necessary 'material and technical basis' would be in place by 1980. By that date, the Programme claimed, 'a communist society will in the main be built in the USSR'. The qualification was important; Khrushchev's readiness to commit himself to a date was nevertheless startling. 'The triumph of communism', he told the congress, 'has always been the cherished ultimate aim of the Leninist Party. This dream of communism is now becoming a reality. Not only our descendants, comrades, but we as well, our generation of Soviet people, shall live under communism.'[8]

Khrushchev was thus staking his and the party's authority on the rapid creation of communism to timetable. Why was he being so audacious? Part of the explanation lay in the Soviet Union's situation within the international communist movement. The movement's successes had made the introversion and defensiveness of 'Socialism in One Country' things of the past. The capitalist and socialist world-systems existed side by side, and all the signs were that the latter was gaining ground on the former. Communism's very success had, however, created problems for Moscow in the countries outside its immediate control. On the movement's right flank, the Yugoslavs were making Leninist claims for a path to communism which in Soviet eyes was manifestly anti-Leninist; on its left, the Chinese were adopting a Stalinist posture yet promising to take a short-cut of their own to communism. It was vital in this situation that the Soviet Union resume its role as the standard-bearer of the world Marxist-Leninist movement – and how better than by striking out boldly towards communism? Domestic considerations pointed in the same direction. Khrushchev's opponents clung to Stalin's slow-track approach to communism, with its pessimistic view of society's maturity and its insistence on tight controls. That can only have made him more eager to take an optimistic view of society's capabilities. And the very fact that he stood for rapid development – for relaxation of controls and a marked improvement in living standards – inevitably made communism a high-priority issue for him.

Yet the revival of the communist project cannot be explained by such factors alone. Khrushchev was a lifelong true believer whose moment seemed in the late 1950s to have come. He believed in a world completely remade, his belief blending Marxism-Leninism with peasant utopianism, radicalism and earthiness. This faith of his had somehow survived the killing frosts of Stalin's cynicism; now, in the autumn of his life, it enjoyed a brief but brilliant efflorescence. These millennial tenets after all provided the foundation and justification of the whole Soviet endeavour. Yet never before had communism been described to Soviet citizens in detail, never before had it been presented as an imminent and almost palpable reality – and never again would the vision be put across to the public so vividly and with such conviction.

Khrushchev could not, however, have made his bid for communism had the circumstances of the late 1950s not been peculiarly favourable to it. By the end of the decade, one-third of the world's population belonged to the socialist camp, and there was good reason to think that before long most of mankind would live under socialist auspices. China had been a gain of incalculable importance. The fall of Cuba in 1959 to Fidel Castro represented a much smaller prize, yet it raised hopes of a domino effect which might soon place socialist regimes throughout Latin America, leaving the USA as a beleaguered bastion of capitalism. Developments at home, too, created a mood of optimism and suggested that the years of sacrifice were at last paying off. In 1957 the Soviet Union had astounded the world by launching the first earth satellite ever, the Sputnik. The landing of a rocket on the moon in 1959, and the first manned spaceflight ever in 1961, confirmed that in space technology Soviet scientists led the world. Here at last was proof that socialism could take mankind into a new era; here at last the Americans were being shown up as also-rans.

What mattered most, however, was to beat the Americans *economically* – the battle between the two world-systems would be decided in the end by which proved the more productive and which provided its people with the higher living standard. At the end of the 1950s, the USA was still far ahead in both respects. Soviet industrial production was only half that of American, Soviet agricultural production was a quarter less, and Soviet living standards were very considerably lower. The economic trajectory of the two countries, however, suggested a rapid narrowing of the gap. During the years 1952–8, industrial output in the USSR grew by 11.4 per cent, while in the USA it grew by only 1.6 per cent.[9] Were this differential to be maintained, then the economic victory of the Soviet Union would be assured. It was not Soviet leaders alone, moreover, who were now counting upon victory for their system; some seasoned western observers, among them the UK prime minister Harold Macmillan, gloomily concluded that the Soviet economy was likely sooner or later to outstrip its rivals.

Against this apparently favourable background, the Soviet leadership made its plans for achieving the material and technical basis of communism by 1980. By that date, three essential economic targets would be attained. The Soviet Union would have the highest per capita industrial and agricultural production in the world, the highest productivity of labour in the world, and the highest living standards in the world. In all three respects it would have far surpassed the USA. As regards living standards: 'In 1980 the real per capita incomes in the USSR will exceed the present level of incomes in the USA by about 75 per cent.' Real incomes in the USSR would increase by over 250 per cent in the coming two decades. People would have plenty of high-quality food and enjoy general material sufficiency; every family would have 'a separate, comfortable flat' for which it would pay no rent; and the working week would be the shortest, the most productive and the highest paid in the world.[10]

These were exhilarating prospects: to most Soviet citizens, the picture thus etched must have seemed like paradise. Yet the economic transformation, though astounding, was not in itself tantamount to the achievement of communism. What the new Programme predicted was that, by 1980, a communist society would be built 'in the main [*v osnovnom*]'. When Stalin had declared in the 1930s that socialism had 'in the main' been achieved, the qualification had been something of a formality. But in this case it mattered. What would have been achieved by 1980 was 'the material and technical *basis*' of communism. 'The construction of communist society', the Programme pointed out, 'will be fully accomplished in the subsequent period.'[11]

Those few words contained a great deal of content. They suggested a further refinement of Marx's original formula for the transition. Socialism would be followed not by communism but by the first of two post-socialist stages, whose theme would be the creation of the material requirements for communism. Only after that would a properly communist society begin to emerge. Stage one promised to transform living conditions for Soviet citizens, but stage two promised – and required – a still more dizzying transformation. Hardly surprisingly, no date was given for its accomplishment. For this final leap forward, there would have to be a transition to communist principles of distribution. People would work to their utmost without any financial inducement (there would be no money), and they would be rewarded in accordance with their needs. The new economic system in turn presupposed a fundamental moral change. People would no longer be driven by selfish desires; purged of the character-traits created by the old society, they would be wholly concerned with the general well-being, and their attitudes would be altruistic and collectivist. Communist society would, in addition, be remarkably homogeneous:

remaining class and cultural divisions would have disappeared. It would also have become completely self-regulating, a society without coercion, and those one-time coercive bodies, the Communist Party and the Soviet government, would have been dissolved back into the community and lost from sight. What had to be done by 1980, while daunting, was therefore equivalent simply to scaling the foothills and establishing a base camp for the subsequent assault. What rose beyond was a veritable alpine peak of change. Yet Khrushchev was confident that the peak could be conquered and full communism established in the reasonably near future.

His most urgent preoccupations were economic: the seven-year plan (1959–65), which aimed to increase gross output by 50 per cent, and overtaking America for industrial and agricultural production by 1970. But while economic growth would be the motor of the advance, other necessary changes – moral, social, cultural and political – could not be ignored until the material-technical basis was in place. There would have in fact to be a simultaneous attack on all aspects of the problem. The aim was nothing less than that people should learn 'to work and live in a communist way'[12] – to work and live, that is, as they had never worked and lived in Russia or anywhere else before.

5

If people were to work and live differently, they would have to *be* different. The 'old man' of capitalist society, prey to antisocial desires, would have to be replaced by someone who was public-spirited, egalitarian and living a life no longer marked by significant economic, social and cultural differences. Reshaping the human material had of course been the intention throughout. Yet Stalin had not attached a high priority to it. While the party held society in a vice-like grip and acted as the will and intelligence of the citizens, it was enough that they be responsive and efficient instruments. With communism on the near horizon, however, the party could no longer continue to act as surrogate for a passive and dependent population. Yet it could also not risk giving people the freedom necessary for communism unless and until they knew how to use it. The citizens could only be unleashed as fast as, and no faster than, they shed their old outlook in favour of a Marxist-Leninist one. That was why the moral reshaping of the population had became a matter of urgency.

The intensity of Khrushchev's campaign indicated how much of the 'old man' still remained. A 'vigorous struggle' was launched against

anti-socialist behaviour and attitudes: against 'indolence and parasitism, drunkenness and rowdyism, swindling and money-grubbing',
against national chauvinism, bureaucratism and maltreatment of
women, and against 'manifestations of individualism and selfishness',
including 'the remnants of private-owner psychology, superstitions
and prejudices'.[13] The final victory of scientific atheism over religion
now became a priority; as a result, the Orthodox Church was severely
repressed. As to what would replace bourgeois morality, that was
summed up in The Moral Code of the Builders of Communism.
Among the qualities emphasized were 'devotion to the communist
cause', 'conscientious labour for the good of society', 'a high sense of
public duty', 'an uncompromising attitude to injustice, parasitism,
dishonesty, careerism, and money-grubbing', and hostility to 'the
enemies of communism, peace, and the freedom of nations'.[14] At the
new creed's heart lay collectivism. Collectivist living and working
would bring the new person into being, and 'active collectivism'
would dissolve his 'selfish individualism' and instil the principles of
communism into him.[15]

The campaign for a communist outlook went hand in hand with the
drive to create a communist way of life. As people came to think differently, so everyday life would change, but developments in the second
respect could not outpace those in the first. Take work. For many,
Khrushchev declared, 'work is no longer simply a means of earning a
livelihood, but a social calling, a moral duty'.[16] The new attitude,
however, was not yet universal; for that reason, wage differentiation as
an incentive to effort had to remain. Preparing people for the life
without material stimuli which lay in the near future was nevertheless
vital. Material and moral stimuli would for the time being be held in
balance, but the tendency would be towards the moral. As a result, the
new Programme insisted that 'the disparity between high and compar-
atively low incomes must be steadily reduced'.[17] What this promise (or
threat) indicated was that peasants and workers would be brought
closer to the wage levels of white-collar employees, in preparation for
the time when income differences, and income itself, would disappear.

As economic differences were phased out, so too the more glaring
differences in manner of living and working would be erased and a
'classless society of communist working people' would come into existence. The gulf between mental and manual work would be narrowed
by making sure that all engaged in both sorts of activity. Manual
workers would be highly trained and educated – so much so that
leading farm workers would become 'veritable professors in their field'

(or so Khrushchev fantasized), while mental workers would be taken out of their ivory towers and made to do physical labour. In addition, the gulf between town and country would be steadily narrowed by the assimilation of rural life to urban. Collective farms would be amalgamated into much larger units, each with its own schools, shops, recreational and welfare facilities. The traditional village would in time be abandoned altogether and replaced by an 'agro-town', a new type of semi-urban community in the countryside. As machinery and electricity were used increasingly in agriculture, so farm work would more closely resemble industrial work. Material and mental change would, moreover, help create a peasant free of the 'private-ownership mentality'. Working on the super-productive and super-technological kolkhoz, and schooled in the new thinking, peasants of the future would find it 'unnecessary' to cultivate their own private plots and would voluntarily give them up. While rural life drew much closer to urban, there would be movement in the opposite direction as well: the new Soviet town would be green and spacious, a garden town, *rus in urbe*. And a general homogenization of town and country alike would be achieved by everyone living a communal existence in large apartment blocks, whose canteens would put an end to the 'wasteful' practice of home catering.[18]

Just as peasants would give up their private plots, so non-Russians would cease to cling to their national distinctivenesss. Khrushchev did, however, see the need for tact in dealing with the non-Russians. He had condemned Stalin for his deportation of nationalities, and was careful not to follow him in blatantly favouring the Russians. Yet in his attitude to the nationalities question Khrushchev remained a Marxist-Leninist zealot. He made it clear that communism would not 'conserve and perpetuate national distinctions'. He looked forward to 'the future single, international culture of communist society'. And he warned that 'even the slightest vestiges of nationalism' would be eradicated with 'uncompromising Bolshevik determination'.[19] National distinctions would, he admitted, linger on well beyond the completion of the first stage of communist construction. These distinctions were nevertheless doomed to eventual extinction as certainly as were all the other undesirable distinctions inherited from the old society.

6

The most sensitive aspect of Khrushchev's communist project, however, concerned the state and its relationship with society. The state had to be diminished and ultimately eliminated – that was unde-niable; it was also undeniable that the state would have a significant role for some time to come. Khrushchev nevertheless insisted on a very different state and a very different relationship with the citizens. The coercive methods and the sacrifices characteristic of the socialist phase had no place whatever in the building of communism. Only a democ-ratic state acting through people who willingly endorsed its aims was appropriate to the task. Creating such a state lay at the heart of his communist project.

Khrushchev knew of course that his more conservative Presidium colleagues, and many other members of the apparatus, would not welcome any encroachment on their prerogatives, and he made an effort to damp down their forebodings. He announced, for instance, that 'The state will remain long after the victory of the first phase of communism. The process of its withering away will be a very long one; it will cover an entire historical epoch and will not end until society is completely ripe for self-administration.'[20] And when would society be 'completely ripe'? Not until 'a developed communist society' had been built and not until socialism had been victorious worldwide. That, one might have thought, postponed the evil long enough. Yet Khrushchev left no doubt that the state's 'withering away' would be a continuous process. *Fundamentals of Marxism-Leninism* stated bluntly that the process was 'in effect already going on'; [21] the new Programme more cautiously implied the same. A developed communist society and the worldwide victory of socialism were, therefore, simply the conditions necessary for the *final and complete* elimination of the state. The building of communism would be guided by a state very different from the dictatorship of the proletariat. Socialism having been achieved, there was no further justification, Khrushchev insisted, for the dicta-torship of one class over the others. The exploiters had been removed, the problems created by continuing class-struggle no longer existed. The workers would, admittedly, continue to play a 'leading role'. The Soviet state would nevertheless from now on express the will of the whole people.

The 'state of the whole people' (*obshchenarodnoe gosudarstvo*) – as the Programme called the state at this juncture – was an idea unknown to Marx, Engels or Lenin. They had assumed a straight progression from the dictatorship to statelessness, while Stalin had insisted that the dictatorship would remain in full force up to the eve of communism and even beyond it. But here was Khrushchev suggesting, as an inter-mediary stage, a western-sounding state that was democratic rather than dictatorial. No wonder that many of his colleagues fought to prevent the new conception getting into the Programme.[22] If Khrushchev had his way, the redefined state would develop rapidly in a democratic direction. It would become increasingly responsive to citizens' wishes; state bodies would begin shedding their functions to voluntary ones; public control over executive organs would be made more effective; the 'elective and accountability principle' would be used more widely; and full-time officials and coercive methods would be steadily phased out.

All of this was the purest and most starry-eyed Leninism, heard again after decades of being silenced. Only a consciously committed citizenry could create communism. As *Fundamentals of Marxism-Leninism* put it:

> The edifice of the new society can be created only with the most active and energetic participation of the masses, of millions of people who must not be submissive performers of someone else's orders but conscious architects of the new forms of their social life.[23]

But how exactly would Stalinist petrifaction be got rid of? How would the Leninist ideal of government not only for but *by* the masses be realized? How would ordinary people be turned from 'submissive performers' into 'conscious architects'? In part by expanding the role of voluntary organizations, such as trade unions, kolkhozes and the Young Communists' League, which would take over many functions from the state. The great advantage of these organizations over state ones was that they did not dictate. Their decisions were made collectively; they reflected the interests of all involved; for that very reason, they were more likely to be implemented. Alongside this, a much larger role would be given to the soviets, which for the last four decades had been little more than a rubber stamp. The soviets in fact provided a crucial linkage between state and people since they were both organs of state power and popularly elected representative bodies. But their *representative* role was the one that from now on would be emphasized. They would assert control over the executive – ministers, for instance, would be made to account regularly to standing committees of the Supreme Soviet. The Programme even came up with the unLeninist idea of releasing Supreme Soviet deputies from their jobs and making them full-timers in order that they should perform more effectively.[24] But just as the soviets would be boosted vis-à-vis the executive, so the electors would gain in strength vis-à-vis the soviets. Deputies would be made more accountable to their constituents; and there would be a regular turnover in membership, with at least one-third of deputies being replaced at each election.

All of this suggested a democratizing tendency, yet despite it socialist democracy would remain very different from democracy in the west. The point, after all, of boosting soviets and voluntary organizations was to promote communism – and to promote it by the Leninist method of drawing the whole population into the task. The goal was centrally prescribed; the freedom Khrushchev offered was freedom to exercise maximum initiative in pursuit of it. Socialist democracy, *Fundamentals of Marxism-Leninism* pointed out, 'is not directionless democracy but *directed democracy,* i.e. democracy directed by the Party and the state in the interest of the further development of socialism and the building of communism'. Were the party's powers to be limited, then democracy would suffer: 'For the Party embodies in its activities the will of the masses ...'[25]

And far from wanting to curtail the party's role in the build-up to communism, Khrushchev had the opposite in mind. There would be 'a further enhancement of the role and importance of the Communist Party as the leading and guiding force of Soviet society'. As the state transferred its functions to public organizations, so 'the Party increasingly comes to the foreground as the leader of all of society and the guiding force among all public organizations'.[26] The party would as a result both supervise the state's withering away and direct the organizations which replaced it.

Was this not disingenuous? By boosting the power of the party as the state withered away, Khrushchev was surely undercutting the enhanced authority he appeared to be offering to soviets and voluntary bodies. Yet the party he envisaged carrying out this enhanced role would be fundamentally different from Stalin's – otherwise, it would be incapable of fulfilling its task. From now on, the party had to be open to new ideas and ready to tackle problems never foreseen by Marxism-Leninism's founders. It could not lead society towards communism 'unless it develops *democracy within its own ranks*'.[27] Election of officials mattered. Free speech on important and even controversial issues mattered. Greater turnover in membership of party bodies also mattered: one-quarter of the members of the Central Committee and the Presidium would be new each time, and there would normally be a limit on the number of successive terms served by Presidium members.

Not only should the party become more democratic; it should embrace far more of the population. Under Khrushchev's stewardship, membership expanded from under 7 million to over 11 million, and the increase represented, in absolute terms, the greatest growth in the party's history.[28] Khrushchev's ambition reached further, however. The party had begun as a drop in the ocean; it still remained a small minority; but as communist construction proceeded, its ideas and values would infuse all of society, until in the end every person had become 'a conscious communist'.[29] Party and society would thus become as one; and having carried out its mission of preparing Russia for communism, the party as a separate entity would be dissolved.

7

Such was Khrushchev's plan for rescuing the Soviet Union from the Stalinist cul-de-sac and bringing it, in two stages and relatively quickly, to communism. The plan was, needless to say, utopian; needless to say, it ran into trouble. This doctrinal highfalutinness, and the social and moral engineering that went with it, stirred widespread resentment. Creating a society fit for communism was an uncomfortable process for the many who had not yet reshaped themselves. Moreover, the political implications of the attempt caused indignation among those Khrushchev could least afford to antagonize – members of the party elite. There were signs, too, that the project would fail in its immediate aim, the creation by 1980 of communism's material-technical basis; signs, indeed, that the economic prognosis on which it rested was fundamentally mistaken.

That said, Khrushchev's achievements in the socio-economic sphere were remarkable. He raised living standards, launched a crash-attack on the housing problem, did a great deal for the peasantry. His promise of overtaking the Americans in material terms by 1970 for a time at least caught the popular imagination. In raising standards, however, he also raised expectations, and by the early 1960s his vision of economic transformation was looking at odds with the reality. Despite his vigorous efforts, there was very little increase in agricultural output. In 1962 a hike in meat and dairy prices touched people on a raw nerve; there were some serious disturbances, even cries of 'Down with Khrushchev!' A poor grain harvest in 1963 compounded the government's problems. This time it averted discontent by importing grain from the west, though it saved itself only by making what, in effect, was a humiliating admission of the weakness of collectivized agriculture. But it was not merely that Khrushchev had raised hopes he was unable in the short term to satisfy. From the beginning of the 1960s there was a marked downward turn in the underlying economic tendency. The rate of increase in investment began to decline. In 1963 and 1964, industrial growth rates fell below 8 per cent – an abysmal level by Soviet standards. Moreover, in 1963 growth in national income slipped below that in the USA. The signs suggested that the years of heroic economic achievement were over, that the dynamic was going out of the Soviet economy, that the growth rates on which the communist project had been based could not be sustained and would probably decline. These indications of economic slowdown made a mockery of Khrushchev's boasts about overtaking the Americans. They also turned the target date of 1980 for achieving the material-technical basis of communism into an embarrassment for the party. By 1964, those with access to the evidence could see that Khrushchev's dash for communism rested upon a false economic premise. There would be no short-term victory over the Americans, no short-term creation of abundance. The challenge the regime faced was not to meet the final requirements for communism but, rather, to maintain faith in the beliefs which justified it when the economic gulf between the advanced capitalist countries and the Soviet Union was likely to remain and even to widen. By the end of the Khrushchev period, the economic signs in fact indicated not imminent communism but the need for retrenchement and a goal set at a safely unspecified distance.

Problems were created, too, by Khrushchev's vigorous social and moral engineering. That was true even of his relations with the peasantry. This first-ever peasant ruler of Russia did much for the peasants – yet here, as elsewhere, his communist vision, his doctrinairism, got in the way of his humanitarianism. He wanted to do good to the peasants, but could not imagine doing it other than by fundamentally changing peasant life and work and transforming the peasants themselves. In the new Russia, traditional villages would be swept away by the bulldozer and replaced by the 'agro-towns' more appropriate to communism; but when peasants were resettled in the concrete wastelands of such a community, they had little reason to feel grateful. Among the amenities lost to them was, in many cases, the village church. The final years of the Khrushchev period saw a fierce anti-religious drive, which disbanded more than half the remaining Orthodox parishes and closed some ten thousand churches. But the greatest threat to the peasant way of life lay in Khrushchev's attitude towards the private plot, that crucial concession which had made life bearable for peasants after the collectivization. The private sector still provided about one-third of the country's agricultural produce. Khrushchev made it crystal-clear, however, that private plots had no place in communist society; and while he stopped short of banning them, intense pressure was exerted to reduce the land area and the livestock in private ownership.

Or take the very different case of those who wanted to think and create for themselves – the intellectuals and artists. They, too, had much to thank Khrushchev for. They naturally welcomed his loosening of controls, his readiness to trust, his belief that discussion and persuasion were preferable to commands and punishments, his desire to raise people out of the inert state to which Stalin had reduced them, his conviction that only a free and self-motivating society could create communism. The Khrushchev period was exhilarating for such people, but it was also something of a roller-coaster for them, and it created as many problems as opportunities for them. Intellectuals might not be threatened by the Gulag, yet they were far from free. They were still required to be 'party-minded'; Khrushchev was as remorseless as Stalin in harnessing art and thought to the party's purposes. His desire to mould minds was at odds with his desire to liberate personalities, his communist doctrinairism clashed with his commitment to a freer, more relaxed society, and the contradiction could not be resolved except by universal acceptance of his own beliefs. The result meanwhile was confusion, made more acute by his volatility, his tendency to swing from backslapping jokiness to angry outbursts and then back to emollience.

Yet if the limits of the permissible often seemed blurred, they were in principle clear enough; and they could be seen in the different treatment meted out to the writers Alexander Solzhenitsyn and Boris Pasternak. The hitherto unknown Solzhenitsyn was allowed to publish *One Day in the Life of Ivan Denisovich*, and its appearance in 1962 caused a sensation. Solzhenitsyn's qualities as an artist were not what mattered to Khrushchev. What did, was that his fictional account of life in the Gulag provided useful material against the Stalinists; moreover, the author's values and general outlook seemed quintessentially Soviet. (Little did Khrushchev guess that he had unleashed someone who would butt his head against the Soviet oak and one day help to topple it.) Boris Pasternak, by contrast, was a relic of the old intelligentsia, an 'internal emigré' whose writing breathed the spirit of bourgeois idealism, and thus well beyond the reach of Khrushchev's indulgence. There was no question of allowing *Dr. Zhivago* to be published or Pasternak to accept his Nobel prize; and while not formally punished, he was in effect harried to his grave. By his own lights, Khrushchev did much for freedom, but the freedom he believed in was freedom to work for the only principles he considered worthy of respect – those of communism. Yet the effect of the 'thaw' was to whet appetites for something he would never have contemplated granting: an unconditional and guaranteed freedom.

Intellectuals were part of that larger body known as 'the intelligentsia': the white-collar sector, labelled a 'stratum' rather than a class but in effect the Soviet middle class. By the late 1950s, some 20 per cent of the employed had non-manual jobs. This middle class of largely worker or peasant origin, created by Stalin's cultural revolution, grew rapidly from the late 1950s with the expansion of higher education. Its members were the managers, administrators, engineers, surgeons, scholars and general skilled professionals of Soviet society, and under Stalin they had achieved a comfortable lifestyle which Khrushchev's doctrinaire egalitarianism now put at risk. For Khrushchev was determined to prevent the 'middle-classing' of Soviet society – his hostility to anything bourgeois burned with unabated intensity. Peasants and workers would be raised up, but the 'white-handed' and the well-to-do could expect only to be levelled down. The new society would have little room for privacy, bettering yourself at others' expense, or self-regarding activity of any kind; all its emphasis would be on the public sphere, on collective living and working, and 'anti-social' inclinations would be firmly repressed. Khrushchev vented his scorn, for instance, on 'bourgeois housing': communism required that people live in large communal blocks and eat in public. In a similar spirit, he rejected private car ownership in favour of the large-scale provision of taxis and rented cars. Middle-class aspirations were threatened, too, by his drive to narrow the gulf between mental and physical work. His educational reforms were particularly offensive in this respect since they made secondary-school pupils do work in factories or on farms and allocated most university places to applicants with at least two years of employment behind them. The greatest threat to the middle class, however, lay in Khrushchev's attitude towards wages. Incentives for skill and effort might continue for the time being: but what the future held was a steady narrowing in material standards between themselves and the 80 per cent of manual workers. The privileged wellbeing this large and influential sector enjoyed would shortly be sacrificed, or so it seemed, upon the altar of communism.

Thus in a variety of ways Khrushchev's communist project rode roughshod over the interests and inclinations of significant groups. The non-Russians should perhaps be added: for any non-Russian with a sense of national identity, there was little to rejoice at in the future as Khrushchev depicted it. Yet none of these groups could directly challenge his position or his programme. The first secretary was at risk from the party elite alone.

8

Many in top positions had welcomed the initial de-Stalinization because of the enhanced security it promised them. The arbitrariness of personal dictatorship had now, it seemed, been replaced by the relative stability of collective leadership operating within clear, if largely unwritten, rules. Life and liberty were one thing, however; job security was another, and once Khrushchev had got into his stride that came under threat. 1957 saw a radical administrative reform which abolished most of the central economic ministries and devolved economic decision-making to some hundred regional councils. This decentralization won Khrushchev support in the regions, but it infuriated a huge army of Moscow bureaucrats, who either lost their jobs or had to transfer elsewhere, and it confirmed the feeling among many in the elite that Khrushchev was fundamentally unsound. Further offence was caused at the Twenty-Second Party Congress when he launched 'the systematic renewal of cadres', stressing the need for the introduction of 'new forces' in leading party positions. The rules laid down to boost turnover and limit the number of terms in office inevitably alienated those who had hoped to hold on to their jobs. And still more indignation was provoked the same year when Khrushchev reorganized the middle and lower levels of the party apparatus, splitting them into parallel structures for industry and agriculture and thereby causing enormous disruption.

Khrushchev did more, however, than play havoc with the machine of state. His administrative reforms were a major irritation; but his anti-Stalinism in its more radical form and the populist, anti-bureaucratic rhetoric which went with it posed a clear threat to the party's monopoly. True, many of the measures intended to speed the withering away of the state had little practical effect. The transfer of functions from state to voluntary bodies was no more than token, while the soviets did not significantly expand their powers vis-à-vis the executive. As for democratization of the party, that hardly went beyond publishing transcripts of Central Committee plenums and inviting non-party specialists to certain meetings. Khrushchev's increasingly radical talk was nevertheless threatening to the party, since its clear intention was to shake the masses out of their passive, uncritical obedience. Praise of socialist democracy was not in itself unfamiliar or worrying; what made it harmless was an interpretation of democracy that stressed defence of the people's *interests* – and what they were was decided of course by the party. Khrushchev, however, seemed to be adding what to many of his colleagues was an unwelcome second feature: socialist democracy was now concerned not only with the people's interests but with their *wishes*. This new emphasis went together with his insistence that reason and persuasion were better than coercion. Before long, he seemed to believe, the wishes of party and people would converge more or less spontaneously. Lenin had admittedly had similar far-fetched ideas. But grass-roots activism, thinking for oneself, standing up to officialdom – these had long since been rooted out from Soviet life. Such practices had been treated by Stalin as irrelevant or obstructive to the task of modernizing and strengthening the country, and their revival was deeply unwelcome to many in the hierarchy.

By the 1960s, Khrushchev had in fact antagonized many of his colleagues for two very different reasons. He had broken away from the constraints of collective leadership and carved out a clear-cut position for himself as Leader. Maintaining collective leadership would not in any event have been easy, given that there was no tradition of it in Russia; but what made it impossible was the lack, as things turned out, of basic policy agreement among the leaders. Under challenge, Khrushchev had defended himself in the only way open to him – by inflating his own position at his fellow oligarchs' expense. Yet this bullying and irascible First Secretary could not overcome resistance by outright Stalinism; instead, he resorted to the very different method of trying to mobilize the masses against his opponents, of exploiting Marxism-Leninism's more-or-less forgotten democratic potential. The would-be autocrat was thus at the same time a would-be democratizer – a disturbing combination for any apparatchik who wanted untroubled tenure of his office and enjoyment of its fruits. It is tempting to see this democratism of Khrushchev's as a cynical and self-serving stratagem, but it should not be forgotten that the communist project which lay at the heart of the dispute between him and his opponents required as an absolute condition for its fulfilment that the masses become genuine partners of the party and sooner or later supersede it.

For a mixture of reasons, then, Khrushchev had by the 1960s

adopted a position that could be seen as both neo-Stalinist and neo-Leninist, authoritarian-conservative and democratizing. He had broken with collective leadership and built up something of a cult of himself; he was also preaching a version of Leninism that resuscitated ideas which the practice of life had shown (or so many of his colleagues believed) to be both unrealistic and dangerous. The democratizing aspect was of course the novel one for a Russian leader, and it challenged a basic unspoken assumption of Russian political culture: that the country could not be internally stable and externally secure without a political system in which the masses gave unquestioning obedience to orders from above. What this democratizing trajectory might have led to is an intriguing speculation. A commission Khrushchev had set up to work on a new constitution was even considering proposals for free and multi-candidate elections, a proper, full-time parliament, separation of powers, and an independent legal system.[30] By the end of his life, he would go so far as to take back his previous blanket approval of all Stalin's doings up to 1934. In enforced retirement, an 'unperson', he condemned the coerced collectivization – 'an utter perversion of the policies Lenin bequeathed to us' – and the crushing of the right.[31] Such views were a natural follow-on from those he had first aired in 1956. They raised a question-mark against the whole Stalin revolution, of which coercion had been the essence, and thus against the achievement of socialism itself. They could only have convinced his former colleagues that he was indeed a wrecker and that the course on which he had set the party would, if continued, have led to disaster.

Yet whether Khrushchev would have brought about a real devolution of power is extremely doubtful. Frightening apparatchiks with the threat of popular retribution was one thing; establishing even a quasi-democratic system would have been quite another. He wanted to trust people and give them their heads, yet imposing effective constraints on the party would have gone counter to everything he stood for. He envisaged a freer and more spontaneous relationship between party and people with a two-way flow of energy and ideas; he would not, however, have wanted genuine pluralism or anything that jeopardized the party's ultimate control. His ideal was not a party reduced in power and authority but rather one capable of infecting the masses with its vision and its dynamism, of carrying them forward to the creation of communism. This neo-Leninist ideal was shared by a number of young party radicals, who in later years would do yeoman service on behalf of perestroika. But the party bosses wanted neither Khrushchev's neo-

Leninism nor his power hunger; and in October 1964 the maverick First Secretary was ousted.

9

Toppling a party leader was unprecedented, but by 1964 Khrushchev had made multiple mistakes and raised up an army of opponents against himself. He had mismanaged the economy, especially the agricultural sector. He had bungled badly in foreign affairs (the Cuban missile fiasco and the breach with China in particular). He was, however, more than an incompetent; many members of the ruling class now perceived him as a menace, someone who had too much power and used it dangerously. Furthermore, he had alienated the elite without winning a following among the masses. Too Bolshevik to appeal to the peasants, too peasant to appeal to intellectuals or the middle class, this moody, impulsive and rather boorish man was almost nobody's idea of what a Soviet leader ought to be. Even had he won an enthusiastic popular following, he would of course have been unable to translate it into effective support against his highly-placed opponents. The mechanisms simply did not exist; not until the late 1980s would a reform-minded leader be able to beat off his enemies by drawing the masses into the political process.

Khrushchev was left with nothing more, his son would reflect, than the support of 'a very thin layer' of radicals.[32] By the end, even many of them had tired of his erratic and authoritarian ways. As a result, he was helpless when, in October 1964, the plot against him was sprung. He was indicted before the Central Committee on various counts, but the essence of the case against him was that he had concentrated all power in his own hands, slighted and ignored his Presidium colleagues, and promoted a cult of himself which even outdid that of Stalin.[33] While his colleagues accused him of flouting collective leadership and acting arbitrarily and capriciously, they passed over in silence what they may well have regarded as his other major crime: that he had endangered the party by his headstrong pursuit of communism and his naive, all-too-literal Leninism. Maybe on that issue, unlike the others, they were not of one mind. The session in any event ended with the Central Committee formally approving Khrushchev's 'request' to be relieved of his duties 'in connection with his advanced age and the deterioration in the condition of his health'.[34] Of the real reasons why he had been removed, nothing whatever was said in public.

This time, unlike in 1957, Khrushchev had let events take their course. 'Could anyone', he asked his accusers, 'have dreamt of telling Stalin that he didn't suit us anymore, and suggesting that he retire? Not even a wet spot would have remained where we had been standing. Now everything is different. The fear's gone and we can talk as equals. That's my contribution.'[35]

It was a fair self-assessment. Khrushchev had done much to make the country freer, happier and more prosperous. Many radicals who supported him no more than half-heartedly at the end would come to lament his loss and to idealize the Khrushchev era as a lost age of opportunity. Two decades later, such people would begin a new reforming drive under a 'Back to Lenin' banner. Communism, however, would no longer be on the agenda. The failure of Khrushchev's bold experiment had raised a serious question-mark against the economic premise on which communism rested. It had suggested that reshaping the human material as communism required might well be impossible. And, if that were not enough, it had indicated that the Communist Party itself – irony of ironies – might be lukewarm about communism, might even present an insuperable obstacle to it. What as a result lay in the not-too-distant future was not a Marxist-Leninist fulfilment but a meltdown.

7
A Problem of Credibility, 1964–85

1

What line the new leadership would take was by no means clear. The things for which Khrushchev had been ousted were, however, obviously excluded. There would be no return to personal rule; there would also be no rash policies which might damage or discredit the party. Government would be genuinely collective, and the top jobs were accordingly divided – Alexei Kosygin became premier and Leonid Brezhnev took the more important position of party First Secretary. Power lay from now on with an oligarchy whose outer circle embraced no more than a few hundred persons, while policy-making reflected the interests of the perhaps two million people who made up the ruling class as a whole. The decades between Khrushchev and Gorbachev would in fact be the golden age of the Soviet ruling class. 'Stability of cadres' was the motto. Life was secure, predictable and governed by tacitly understood rules. High officials grew old in their posts, untroubled either by the supreme leadership above them or by the masses from below. Leonid Brezhnev was the ideal leader for such a regime. He was no Lenin, Stalin or Khrushchev, and the very fact that he was not brilliant, dominating or a 'character' was what recommended him to his peers. This dignified, amiable but essentially mediocre man had no very strong ideas of his own and let himself be guided by the consensus among his colleagues, who in return heaped honours upon him.

The Brezhnev era would go down as one of conservatism and stagnation. It was by no means obvious in 1964, however, that the new leadership had taken power with an essentially conservative programme. Khrushchev had been accused, after all, of would-be

Stalinism rather than reckless radicalism. The plan for communism by 1980 was, admittedly, quietly shelved and the idea of 'the state of the whole people' fell into abeyance. Yet while the fast track to communism was set aside, the new regime followed Khrushchev in making a firm commitment to improved living standards. Economic reform therefore remained very much on the agenda. Like Khrushchev, the regime maintained unrealistically low prices on the staples of life, guaranteed full employment, and boosted welfare benefits, the full range of which was now extended to the peasantry. All of this required a buoyant economy, and the statistics for GNP, industrial production and real per capita income showed appreciable increases for most of the Brezhnev era. Yet while the economy continued to grow, it grew more slowly than expected. Figures for the growth of GNP, industrial production, agricultural production, labour productivity and real income all pointed downward rather than upward. The leadership in fact had to face the same problem that had troubled Khrushchev in his later years, though in a more acute form: the dynamism had gone out of the economy. Why had this happened? And how could it be remedied?

Reform-minded economists diagnosed over-centralization as the basic fault in the system. There was too little scope for initiative by managers and too little incentive for efficient effort by workers. In 1965 Kosygin, who had charge of the economy, came up with a reform package which reflected this diagnosis and appeared to tackle the problem of declining growth head-on. From now on, enterprises would have more autonomy, including a limited freedom to deal with one another rather than simply with the centre. Managers would be allowed to draw on profits to make incentive payments to workers. Profitability would, moreover, be given greater importance as a planning criterion. The decision to abolish Khrushchev's regional economic councils and restore the central ministries tended, admittedly, in the opposite direction. Taken as a whole, the package nevertheless represented a clear, if modest, step away from hyper-centralization and towards a more realistic and efficient economic system. Some economists indeed welcomed it as a turning-point scarcely less important than NEP. Hopes that the Kosygin reform might lead to fundamental economic change were, however, to be dashed. The package ran into strong opposition within the party, and by the end of the decade the reforming impetus, with its emphasis on enterprise autonomy, profits, incentives and quality of production, had largely petered out.

Kosygin's reform fell victim to a conservative tendency which began very early in the new era and was in part a reaction to the dissidents. Outright defiance of the authorities had been unknown since the 1920s – under Stalin it would have been unthinkable ; its reappearance therefore came as a shock to many in the party. What was so disturbing about these dissidents who circulated forbidden literature, demanded their constitutional rights and even staged public demonstrations was that they challenged the regime's basic legitimation: its claim to represent the will and interests of the entire population. They were, admittedly, few in number and drawn almost wholly from intellectuals; in conservative eyes they were nevertheless the beginning of something potentially very dangerous. These rebels were Khrushchev's children: a proof of how destabilizing his reforms had been and a warning of what might happen if the party did not assert its authority by traditional methods.

There was no obvious link between dissidents and Kosygin's modest reform, yet for conservatives the reform was pregnant with alarming possibilities. Economic liberalization, were it to get going, would threaten not only the central planners but the power and privileges of the elite and, in the end, perhaps even the party's monopoly itself. That was why it had to be fought. And in the struggle with the reformers, it was the conservatives who held the commanding heights. The whole framework of the debate favoured them. The Soviet economy continued to be thought of as a single unit, like a factory, which needed to be run from the centre and subjected to strict hierarchical control. Anything that went counter to this image was suspect. Proposals for market mechanisms and increased material incentives could be criticized as a retreat from communism, while plans for enterprise autonomy were easily represented as an assault upon central planning.

Such attacks on the reform might have been warded off as scaremongering had it not been for the Czech events of 1968. The crisis of that year in Czechoslovakia played into the conservatives' hands because it seemed to bear out their main (if not openly stated) contention: that economic liberalization had extra-economic implications which posed a direct threat to the socialist system. Under the leadership of a new First Secretary, Alexander Dubcek, the Czech regime had begun a programme of full-blooded economic reform, aiming to increase incentives, broaden enterprise autonomy and introduce a range of market mechanisms. Similar reforms had been or would be carried through in other satellite countries without incurring

Soviet wrath. What, however, outraged Soviet conservatives about the Czech experiment was that economic change shaded quickly into political. In decentralizing their economy, the Czechs also democratized it, to the extent of allowing elected workers' councils with considerable powers over the management of enterprises. Democratization was not limited, moreover, to the economic system. Under pressure from its grass roots, the Communist Party began to reform itself: there would be elections by secret ballot and the right to express minority views. The party would keep its 'leading role', but other groups would be allowed to organize and even to stand against it. Such inroads into the party's monopoly were an intolerable provocation to Soviet conservatives. A majority of the Politburo (as the Presidium had been renamed) insisted that the Czech experiment should be liquidated. On 25 August 1968 Soviet troops invaded, under the pretext of resisting counter-revolution and defending socialism. Thus began the 'normalization' of Czech life.

2

The Czech crisis crystallized opinion within the oligarchy. Brezhnev, who had been wavering in the middle, swung to the side of the conservatives, and Kosygin fell increasingly into his shadow. A consensus had evolved within the ruling circle which would last until Brezhnev's death in 1982. Whatever the problems of the economy, they were by no means so grave as to justify risky experimentation. Technology, especially computerization, might in due course overcome the difficulty of running the increasingly complex Soviet economy from a single centre. In any event, reform of all kinds was ruled out. The party would from now on vigorously defend its monopoly and its control of all aspects of social activity.

Khrushchev's timetable for communism had, as we have seen, already been tacitly discarded. So had those aspects of his programme that had been intended to make society more independent and self-motivating in order to prepare it for communism. The foundations of socialism might have been laid, but this 'still did not make it possible to start immediately upon the transition to communism'. 'Victorious socialism', the regime's ideologists argued, 'must, as the founders of Marxism-Leninism foretold, pass through various stages of development, and only a developed socialist society provides the opportunity of advancing to the construction of communism.'[1]

'Developed socialism' was a new idea and an important one: it gave the slow-track approach to communism a theoretical justification.[2] Thanks to it, the regime had an escape from the pressure for reform created by Khrushchev's insistence that the socialist phase had been completed and that communism therefore lay immediately ahead. That, Soviet citizens were given to understand, was a misreading of the situation. Soviet society had, to be exact, reached the advanced stage of socialism – 'that stage of maturity in the new society which sees the completion of all social relations on the collectivist principles intrinsic to socialism'. Nor should people expect communism in the near future. On the contrary: developed socialism 'constitutes a relatively long period of development along the road from capitalism to communism'.[3]

'Developed socialism' thus had the effect of postponing communism to a safely distant and unspecified date. By doing so, it saved the regime from a commitment that would have seriously embarrassed and might even have undermined it. The emergence of 'developed socialism' did not, however, mean that the communist commitment had ceased to matter, that the party still paid lip-service to it simply because, as a *communist* party, it had to. Communism might be unattainable; it nevertheless continued to bear directly on everyday reality. Marxism-Leninism made it clear that the Communist Party alone could lead society to communism. That task it could not accomplish unless society was fully united behind it. Communism, in other words, could be achieved only if people accepted the party's leadership unquestioningly and did their utmost to fulfil its commands. Thus the communist goal lay immediately behind the mechanisms of direction and repression by which the party exercised its rule.

The post-Prague propaganda offensive laid heavy emphasis on the party's leadership role and fulsomely justified its monopoly. The party's role was even enshrined in the new constitution, which came along belatedly in 1977. The Stalin constitution had made no more than passing reference to the party. Coyness was now set aside, however, and the true situation was written into the constitutional record. 'The Communist Party of the Soviet Union', ran article six, 'shall be the guiding and directing force of Soviet society, and the core of its political system and of all state and social organizations.'[4]

Strenuous efforts continued to create the 'new Soviet person', though the intention was to make him or her a willing agent of the party rather than a builder of communism. People had it drummed into them that they should develop 'a high level of ideological commitment and dedication to their socialist motherland and the cause of communism'.[5] The order was in itself noteworthy: socialist motherland first, cause of communism second. Propaganda claims that this was a society united around the party and striving single-mindedly towards its goal needed of course to be taken with a pinch of salt. Yet the propaganda which portrayed a union of minds between party and people was not wholly misleading. Most people took the party's rule for granted; few would have questioned the statement that 'no other society has done or would ever do for the popular masses, for the working people, what socialism has done for them'.[6] Popular acceptance of party rule or at least acquiescence in it can be explained in part by the lack of alternative opinions and of any experience of life elsewhere. People knew only the party's opinions and only life in the Soviet Union. The apparent contentment of the Soviet masses cannot, however, be put down solely to ignorance. The fact was that ordinary people had never lived so well as they lived under Brezhnev.

3

For those in the know, the overall economic picture was still a gloomy one. Growth rates were falling; quality of production was declining; the technological gap with the west was become ever-wider. Ordinary citizens, however, were sheltered from any knowledge of the underlying tendency, and not until the end of the 1970s did the failings of the economy begin to repercuss directly upon them. People had every reason in fact to feel grateful to a regime that seemed dedicated to their wellbeing. Living standards improved steadily on the wretched levels experienced under Stalin. Basic foodstuffs such as milk, meat and butter became more plentiful; by the end of the Brezhnev era, most homes had a television set, a washing machine and a refrigerator. While these modest but very real gains were being achieved, the traditional advantages of the Soviet system – full employment, low food and rent prices, free education and healthcare – were retained. With some justification, Brezhnev could have said to the masses: 'You've never had it so good.'

The benefits had not, however, been spread proportionately across the community. Khrushchev's egalitarian wages policy had been continued, with the result that the income gap between manual and white-collar workers had steadily narrowed. During the decade 1965–76, the average wage of industrial workers had risen by 65 per cent and that of collective-farm workers by 86 percent. The wages of white-collar employees, on the other hand, had grown by no more than 25 per cent. Far from playing down the equalizing tendency, the authorities trumpeted it:

> The equalizing of the socio-economic and living conditions of industrial workers, white-collar workers and collective farmers, of town and village dwellers, is of enormous social and political signif- icance. In the Soviet Union today, differences in income, and in particular differences in pay, between these groups of the popula- tion is insignificant.[7]

The nominal purpose of equalizing was of course to prepare the way for communism. That, however, was now little more than a figleaf; by levelling incomes, the regime was taking care of its own and making sure of their continued loyalty.

The tacit deal between bosses and the labouring masses has been seen by some historians as an unwritten 'social contract'.[8] The regime gave people security, extensive welfare benefits and steadily improving living conditions, and it tolerated a laxity at work that would have been unthinkable in a private-enterprise economy. In return, however, workers agreed to be poorly paid and to give unconditional obedience as employees and as citizens. 'You pretend to pay us and we pretend to work' summed up the trade-off well enough. It was a deal, moreover, between two sides with a good deal of mutual understanding. The bosses themselves had only recently climbed out of the working class or the peasantry, spoke the same language as ordinary people and shared with them a culture very little affected by western attitudes and tastes.

All of this suggested that the regime would continue for the foresee- able future without any serious challenge. An obvious problem was presented by the middle class, whose members were effectively excluded from the social contract; but their discontents, which will be discussed in the next chapter, did not for the time being break the surface. Only the dissidents put up any overt opposition, and their numbers were tiny. A mere seven, for instance, demonstrated in Moscow in August 1968 against the invasion of Czechoslovakia. The dissidents could, admittedly, count upon a great deal of passive support. Their weakness, however, was that there was almost no support, active or passive, for their aims and attitudes outside the middle class. While anti-regime movements in eastern Europe were attracting a cross-class coalition in which workers rubbed shoulders with intellectuals, nothing of that kind seemed remotely likely in the

Soviet Union. Blue-collar workers were at best indifferent to the dissidents, at worst positively hostile to them. A yawning and unbridgeable chasm of culture in fact separated the regime's courageous and often highly distinguished opponents from the masses. And the regime, playing the old tsarist game of 'divide and rule', did its utmost to exploit these cultural differences. When dissidents went on trial, they were portrayed as traitors who had been working for the west, and the case against them was often embroidered by the suggestion that they were Jews or embezzlers. The dissidents were helpless against this exploitation of popular prejudices, this stirring up of age-old resentment against the west and westernized Russians. There was simply no common ground, many felt, between themselves and the masses. 'To the majority of the people', wrote Andrei Amalrik, 'the very word "freedom" is synonymous with "disorder". As for respecting the rights of an individual as such, the idea simply arouses bewilderment.'[9] Another dissident commented on the masses despairingly: 'I'm not yet demented enough to risk my head trying to "help" them. Do you understand that they feel *I'm* the enemy – not the brutes who enslave them?'[10] Isolated, outnumbered, widely seen as fifth-columnists colluding with the enemies of Russia and Russianness, the dissidents were engaged in a hopeless crusade, and by the end of the 1970s their movement had in effect been crushed.

While the dissidents were dealt with fairly easily, the non-Russians proved more troublesome. Part of the problem was demographic: the Russians were a declining proportion of the population – by 1979, no more than 52 per cent of the total. This decline in numbers presented no immediate threat, given that Russians still overwhelmingly dominated the higher levels of the party. The Russian hold was, moreover, strengthened by the migration of Russians to non-Russian republics (especially Estonia, Latvia, Kazakhstan and Ukraine) and by vigorous promotion of Russian as the common language of the Union. Such measures to bolster the imperial centre would hardly have been necessary of course had the basic assumptions underlying the nationalities project been borne out. Socialist consciousness and the material benefits of Soviet rule should by now have undercut national self-awareness and brought about a voluntary bonding. If the regime's ideologists were to be believed, this was precisely what had happened. Developed socialism, they claimed, had seen the formation of a historically new social and intellectual community – the Soviet people.[11] Many intellectuals from the national minorities, however, saw this idea of a Soviet people as simply another russifying device, and in areas such as

Ukraine, where a strong national awareness had existed before the Stalin terror, the new idea provoked a considerable resistance.

The revived national movements were helped here and there by tact or even sympathy on the part of local party first secretaries, most notably Pyotr Shelest in Ukraine, who did his utmost to soothe wounded national feelings. Sensitive treatment was not always enough, however, to curb passions; and a glimpse of what lay repressed just beneath the surface came in Lithuania in 1972, when the suicide by burning of a student provoked violent anti-Russian demonstrations and demands of 'Freedom for Lithuania!' The authorities were perplexed and disturbed by this revival of attitudes which the 'national in form but socialist in content' approach should by now have disposed of. In the case of Jewish protesters, they could at least deal with the problem by allowing them to emigrate. But those who wanted not to leave but to stay put and to change or break up the Soviet Union were more difficult to manage; and the authorities were particularly galled by a new breed of nationalist who claimed that the party had deviated from Lenin, that its current nationalities policy was simply Great Russian chauvinism in socialist trappings.

As the general line hardened after 1968, so too did the attitude towards nationalists and those local leaders who were treating them with some indulgence. As in the 1930s, Ukraine turned out to be the eye of the storm. The lightning struck in 1972, when Shelest was sacked as party boss there in favour of a hard-liner, and about a thousand officials were purged with him. Throughout the other minority areas, nationalist and dissenting voices were similarly silenced. Repression was, for the authorities, the obvious solution. It was what they were good at, and on the surface it dealt with nationalism as effectively as it had crushed the dissident movement in Russia itself. Yet what this showdown between Moscow and the periphery made plain was that the union of minds which Lenin had seen as essential to the building of socialism among the Soviet peoples was no more than a chimera. The regime had no idea of how to make it a reality, had long since given up even trying to make it a reality. What had been achieved instead was compliance based on repression; and repression, though still effective, was no longer the force that it had been.

4

In its final years, Brezhnev's Soviet Union presented an awesome facade to the outside world and to its own subjects. It had five million men under arms and had equalled if not overtaken the military capacity of the United States. Its control over its own subjects and over its outer empire of the satellite states seemed complete. It had even taken on a new defence commitment, in 1979, by sending in 100 000 troops to prop up a puppet Marxist regime in Afghanistan. So impressive and so menacing was the façade that few people, be they Soviet citizens or outside observers, guessed that the regime and the entire Soviet experiment were within a decade of collapsing. Yet beneath the surface things were going badly wrong. The most obvious problem was economic.

During the second half of the 1970s, the decline in growth rates had suddenly accelerated. In 1966–70, GNP, for instance, had been growing at over 5 per cent per year; by the second half of the 1970s, the rate had slowed to 2.5 per cent. There was a similar slump in the growth of labour productivity. In the opinion of a leading Soviet economist, Abel Aganbegyan, the final years of the Brezhnev era saw 'practically no economic growth' at all, while living standards actually began to fall. Summoned before Kosygin to explain why the economy was performing so badly, Aganbegyan could only describe its current state as 'catastrophic'.[12]

The declining improvement in labour productivity was especially worrying, all the more so since everyone knew Lenin's admonition that 'In the last analysis, productivity of labour is the most important, the principal thing for the victory of the new social system.'[13] There were various reasons for the shortcoming. Failure to update equipment and to introduce modern technology was one. Lack of entrepreneurial drive and spirit of innovation was another. Part of the problem, however, lay with workers rather than with planners or managers. Labour discipline was getting worse. The old evils – absenteeism, shoddy workmanship, drunkenness on the job, pilfering and embezzlement – were becoming rampant. Worker motivation was, needless to say, crucial. It had always been accepted that cultural change would lag behind socio-economic, that communist attitudes towards work could not be achieved until the objective prerequisites for communism were in place. By the end of the 1970s, however, the argument that worker attitudes were simply changing rather more slowly than the socio-economic environment was wearing very thin. All the signs were that morale and motivation were actually deteriorating. And the link between low morale and economic failure was becoming obvious.

The regime's economic successes had been achieved above all by dint of its ability to galvanize. It had transformed backward Russia into an industrial power by inspiring people, striking fear into them, and stimulating them by material incentives. By the end of the 1970s, however, all three levers – belief, fear, and material inducement – were ceasing to be effective. The loss of belief was especially important. The dominant attitudes of the workforce as it entered what, by Khrushchev's reckoning, should have been the decade of communism were apathy and cynicism. Admittedly, most people still saw capitalism as unjust and exploitative. Many still believed that the Soviet system provided at least the framework for a better life for the masses than capitalism could achieve. The utopian beliefs by which the party justified itself had nevertheless lost their credibility. Communism implied freedom, equality and abundance; it conjured up a vision of a new society peopled by new human beings. But there would be no such transformation, no leap forward into a different order of existence. Things would bump along much as before, maybe getting a bit better, maybe getting a bit worse. The elderly men who lined the Mausoleum on the great holidays were in any event incapable of kindling faith or generating enthusiasm. They talked of communism, but a communist future was not believable. They talked of the increasing unity and homogeneity of Soviet society, but it was all too apparent that society was becoming increasingly divided and differentiated. They talked of the high morality, selflessness and social conscience of the new Soviet man; but they themselves were widely seen as greedy, selfish and lacklustre old men, in all senses, who were doing what the rulers of Russia had always done – looking after their own interests behind a façade of fine-spun phrases. Thus it had been, thus it would always be: words and reality were impossibly far apart.

Belief was dying, then. Moreover, in the Soviet Union of the late 1970s there was little to fear, provided you did not openly challenge the authorities. There was no requirement to work hard: your job was safe and nothing short of outrageous conduct would jeopardize it. Nor was there much incentive to exert yourself. There were of course monetary rewards for skilled and hard work, but these were decreasingly effective since it was becoming ever more difficult to spend your money. Unrealistically low prices and rising incomes had created a huge consumer demand which the supply of food and goods simply could not satisfy. By the end of the Brezhnev era, meat had virtually disappeared from shops and some areas of the country had food rationing. As a result, people spent longer and longer queuing for basics. The obvious solution was to raise prices to more realistic levels; but bitter memories of riots provoked by earlier price-rises made the regime balk at that. Soviet citizens had come to regard low and stable prices as a right, a fundamental aspect of socialism, a part of the unwritten contract between rulers and ruled. Shortages could be put up with provided they did not get any worse (but they *were* getting worse). And for those willing to pay more, the burgeoning black market offered an alternative to shopping around and queuing. The growth of this 'second economy' was tolerated by the authorities because it eased hardship, yet it pushed a further wedge between the idealized world of their pronouncements – in which society was progressing steadily towards communism – and the realities of life as the ordinary citizen experienced them. Meanwhile, unspendable money piled up in bank accounts.

None of this suggested an upheaval in the offing. The Sovietologist Seweryn Bialer, writing just after the Brezhnev era, diagnosed a 'crisis of effectiveness' but, understandably enough, saw no evidence of a 'crisis of survival'.[14] It was only drunks, not rioters, who created disorder in the streets; the regime's outward control was as complete as ever. People grumbled, they cracked jokes about the authorities, yet few could imagine a future for the country that was not Soviet and socialist – even if communism now seemed a fairy tale. Western observers generally agreed that the demise of the Soviet system was not yet in sight. Edward L. Keenan, an influential American observer, explained the stability of society by arguing that the current oligarchy embodied a tendency which, in a less obvious form, went far back into the pre-revolutionary past. Oligarchy was in fact the natural form of government for Russia.[15] The emigré Alexander Zinoviev found different reasons for the regime's likely longevity. 'It is a mistake', he argued, 'to regard Communism as something foisted on people by force and fraud. It constantly wells up from below, from the cells.' The Russian people were naturally collectivist and uninterested in individual freedom. Soviet society was as a result 'not only stable: it is in the highest degree stable'.[16]

The apparent rock-like stability of Soviet society suggested that prudent reforms were unlikely to endanger the regime. And if there were risks in policy changes intended to stir people from their apathy, it was also becoming clear that there were long- if not short-term risks in doing nothing. The country's international situation was being made more difficult by the determination of President Reagan to re-establish America's military supremacy. But in the absence of a dynamic economy, military parity could be maintained only by putting increased pressure on the consumer. Even without such pressure, the current stagnation promised lengthening queues and declining living standards. Rank-and-file Russians were unlikely to revolt on behalf of civil rights or the dissidents; but they might in the end create trouble if meat, milk and bread became still harder to obtain. Communism was not a make-or-break issue; living conditions might well be.

The glaring economic problems of the country as it entered the 1980s touched on deeper issues. The economic system reflected the regime's commitment to the creation of a new human being whose actions were unselfish and motivated only by the general good. By now, however, anyone who was not blinded by ideology could see that such a human being had not been and would not be created. Human character and motivation remained in essence what they had been before October 1917. To admit or even imply this was, however, unthinkable. The practical experience of constructing socialism, the ideological handbook of the era stoutly maintained, 'refutes the claims of bourgeois ideology that men are inherently flawed ...'[17] The political and economic systems and the basic values of Soviet society all rested upon the assumption – stridently asserted – that flaws in the human character could be and were being eliminated. To challenge that would be to challenge the communist project and the Communist Party itself. Yet the result of maintaining this fiction and the institutions and attitudes that went with it was that the regime in a sense fell between the stools. It could not, despite its protestations, transform the human material at its disposal; but neither could it get the best out of the stubbornly unreformable people who worked in its factories and on its farms. There were no new people, nor would there be, and the human beings the regime was left with worked extremely badly under a system based upon a fundamental fallacy.

The economic problems and the ones that underlay them were hardly likely to be tackled by Brezhnev – though even he in a moment of unusual candour in 1978 admitted that the economic problems were becoming bad enough to threaten the country's stability. But he died in November 1982 after a long illness, and he was replaced as general secretary by someone of very different mettle.

5

Yury Andropov's credentials as a reformer were not, on the face of it, very promising. He had been Soviet ambassador in Hungary during the 1956 revolution, and perhaps because of that he had taken a tough line towards the Czechs in 1968. He had also spent fifteen years in charge of the regime's security as head of the KGB. Yet he had not fitted easily within the post-1968 consensus, and Brezhnev seems to have viewed him with disquiet. The two men were very different. Andropov lacked Brezhnev's easy-going charm and his hedonism; he was austere, reserved and wholly untouched by the corruption and extravagance of the later Brezhnev era. He was also intelligent, well-read, sophisticated in his tastes, and not without sympathy for the reformist tendency in eastern Europe, especially in Hungary. Moreover, in his pre-KGB days he had gathered around him in the Central Committee a kitchen cabinet of young progressives, some of whom would play a major role in the Gorbachev period. Any pretensions he might have had as a reformer were stifled during the long years in which Brezhnev made him serve at the KGB. His election as general secretary in November 1982 nevertheless aroused fervent expectations among the reform-minded. The age of stagnation and complacency had, it seemed, been buried with Brezhnev. Now the country's problems would be addressed.

The hopes aroused were not wholly disappointing. From the outset, Andropov recognized the gravity of the economic problem. He complained forcefully about low productivity, lack of innovation, the wasteful use of resources. He called for greater freedom for enterprises and for lessons to be learned from the other socialist countries. He even attacked the wage-levelling policy adopted since Stalin – Marx, he declared, had been 'a decisive opponent of levelling' and had categorically rejected 'naive ideas of socialism as "universal equality" in distribution and consumption'.[18]

Yet as a reformer Andropov was more puritan than liberal, and his years at the KGB had left their mark. The root of the problem, as he saw it, lay in the lax attitude towards work tolerated by his predecessor. His remedy, therefore, was to reassert discipline through increased use of coercion and punishment. So he came down hard on absenteeism, drunkenness and poor production standards, and he sent police to seek out absconding workers. The attack on indiscipline was accompanied by a fierce anti-corruption drive, aimed not only at dishonest workers but also at corrupt practices among the elite. Thousands of arrests were made; some of the more flagrant offenders were even executed.

There was, however, a touch of desperation about these measures. In an article written to mark the centenary of Marx's death, Andropov was remarkably open about the difficulties of the task ahead. Individual psychology, he conceded, had proved far harder to change than had been expected. Experience had shown that 'the turning of what is "my own" and privately owned into what is "ours" and common to all is no simple matter'. People were still unable to understand that society's wealth now all belonged to them; they had failed to grasp this truth 'economically, politically and, if you want, psychologically, and failed to become collectivist in outlook and behaviour'. The reality was that 'Even when socialist production relations are finally established, some people preserve ... individualist habits, a striving to profit at others' expense, at the expense of society.' Yet without a change in human nature and human relationships, 'any "model" of socialism, however attractively presented, will prove unviable and will continue to live only in the imagination of its creators'.[19]

These were sobering reflections. So far, Andropov warned, the country was only at the beginning of developed socialism, 'a long historical stage which, in turn, will naturally have its periods and stages of growth'.[20] How much tone and attitude had changed in twenty years! Brezhnev had escaped from Khrushchev's optimistic timetable for communism by introducing the notion of developed socialism. Andropov was now stretching out the timetable still further by suggesting sub-divisions of the sub-division. He had exposed the failings of the economy; he had also come close to admitting a fundamental flaw in the whole communist project – that it made unrealizable demands of human nature, which was not the malleable clay the project required it to be.

For some of his progressive proteges, there was an evident link between economic failure and the recalcitrance of human nature. If humans could not be modified to suit the project, then the project would have to be modified to suit humans. It would have to be rethought in such a way as to release people's hitherto repressed mental and physical energies. But while Andropov had glimpsed what was wrong, he was not prepared to accept any such radical cure. The project would not be rethought, even if the timetable for its accomplishment had to be spun out. As for the economy, the only ways of gingering it that he would permit were those traditionally sanctioned – exhortation and indoctrination accompanied by coercion and punishment and eked out by limited material incentives. This was the closed circle within which Soviet economic planners had chafed for decades. Andropov would not contemplate them breaking out of it.

Above all, he rejected any suggestion of democratization as a therapy. This was so sensitive a subject that he did not limit himself to praising Soviet democracy – he launched an attack upon those who might doubt its merits. They should not, he warned, misunderstand what the Marxist goal of 'self-government' implied. 'It goes without saying that an interpretation of self-government as inclining towards anarcho-syndicalism, to splitting society into independent corporations competing with each other, to democracy without discipline, to the notion of rights without duties, is deeply alien to us.' In the Soviet Union, the interests of the state and those of the citizen were identical. 'But regrettably there are people who are trying to counterpose their selfish interests to those of society and its other members. In this regard', he added, 'there is a clear need to educate and sometimes to re-educate certain persons ...' (Here one catches an echo of the KGB chief, who had despatched many a dissident to a psychiatric hospital for 're-education'.) Under the Soviet constitution, the citizen had broad rights and freedoms; the constitution nevertheless emphasized 'the priority of public interests, service to which is indeed the supreme manifestation of civic duty'.[21]

The message was clear – 'don't presume to know better than the party!' What had begun as a perceptive analysis of Soviet problems finished as a clichéd defence of the party's monopoly. Andropov had sensed the depth of the economic problem, even something of the utopianism of the whole project, but he had drawn back from these alarming insights to the safe terrain of traditional thinking. Some of his admirers would wonder whether, given longer in power, he might not have responded to the challenge more adequately.[22] It seems unlikely. He had anyway become seriously ill after a few months in office, and within fourteen months of being elected general secretary he was dead.

Andropov's successor, Konstantin Chernenko, a crony of Brezhnev's, was older still and was already ill when he assumed office. Soviet affairs were now in the hands of a sick mediocrity whose entourage consisted largely of elderly men who had been in high position since the war or even the 1930s. Chernenko and this cohort all too strikingly symbolized the decadence of this once virile and idealistic party. The end of the traditional Soviet order now seemed in sight. Did this mean, however, that the Soviet experiment in socialism was doomed? Among the regime's critics, there were some who fervently rejected such a suggestion. The death of the old order, they believed, was precisely what was needed to revive the experiment and bring it to completion. Escape from this petrified *ancien régime* was the one thing that might yet save socialism in Russia. Those who thought along such lines belonged to the Alternative Tradition. Their moment, it seemed, had come.

8
The Alternative Tradition

1

The Alternative Tradition was a cluster of beliefs which had sustained the defeated and the repressed. At its heart lay the conviction that the Soviet experiment had been right at the beginning, had gone tragically wrong under Stalin, but could yet create a socialist society – provided the leadership democratized, made real economic reforms and returned to a proper conception of socialism. The origins of the Tradition went back to the 1920s and early 1930s, to the struggle against Stalin's hijacking of the revolution and perversion of its purposes, though not until Khrushchev's thaw had 'alternative' views begun to be heard. They were then voiced strongly through the 1960s, most of all by economists, who came up with ideas for change that had implications which went well beyond the economic. Alternative viewpoints also emerged in literature, literary criticism, history and most branches of the social sciences. The Tradition's home was *Novy Mir* (*New World*), journal of the Union of Soviet Writers, which under the inspired editorship of Alexander Tvardovsky stood for a democratic socialism wholly purged of the Stalinist perversion. 'We believed', one of Tvardovsky's colleagues wrote, 'in socialism as a noble ideal of justice, we believed in a socialism that was human through and through and not just with a human face. We regarded the democratic rights of the individual as incontestable.'[1] The post-Prague crackdown and Tvardovsky's enforced resignation in 1970 brought *Novy Mir's* campaigning to a halt. For the remainder of the Brezhnev era, alternative voices were severely muffled, if not silenced altogether. The coming to power of Yury Andropov in 1982, however, gave the reform movement a new lease of life, and in important respects its critique now became more radical.

Alternative thinkers went further than Khrushchev in distinguishing between Leninism and Stalinism, between the 1920s and the 1930s. They were fervent Leninists, but their Leninism differed markedly from the official cult. The Lenin they admired was not that embodiment of iron will and revolutionary resolve, that icon with the raised fist and thrusting chin who stood in the main square of every town and sanctioned even the most repressive acts of government. Rather, it was a thoughtful and human Lenin, a political genius and natural leader, yet someone capable of questioning himself and even of making mistakes; a man burdened by the enormous responsibility of having installed the world's first socialist regime and grappling with the problems of creating socialism in a country not remotely ready for it. This Lenin – the real Lenin, they believed – had not found a way out of the wilderness until the early 1920s, when he discovered that the way forward lay through NEP and cultural revolution. His final thinking about the road to socialism had, however, been ignored; and, with the partial exception of Khrushchev, Soviet leaders had since proved wholly unreceptive to any suggestion that the cultural revolution had done its work, that culture had by now 'caught up' with politics and that the time was therefore ripe for implementing Bolshevism's democratic principles.

Alternative thinkers had different opinions as to whether Stalinism could have been wholly avoided; some reluctantly justified Stalin's creation of the command economy as necessary in the circumstances of the 1930s. They nevertheless unanimously rejected any suggestion that Stalinism provided an appropriate model for socialism, that universally valid guidelines for the construction of a socialist society could be deduced from it. Stalinism was an unmitigated and avoidable disaster for some, while for others it was a tragically necessary diversion from proper socialist practice and one that had long since outgrown its usefulness. Either way, it had inflicted enormous suffering and in some respects at least retarded the socialist cause; and the continuation under Brezhnev of a modified form of it was entirely unjustified.

The party had, then, made terrible mistakes. There were grave deficiencies in what it had achieved. Despite all, however, its record was more good than bad and its claim to be an agent of socialism remained valid. It could still bring about a socialist society, but on one condition – that it returned to the spirit of its origins. The early Soviet experience was a resource still available for guidance and inspiration, if only the leadership would heed it. What, above all, had to be rediscovered was that early, if necessarily imperfect, Bolshevik democratism. Democracy was indispensable to socialism; only by adopting it could the party reinvigorate itself and lead the country from the current counterfeit to genuine socialism.

All of this made alternative thinkers critics of a special kind. They deplored much about Soviet life – the corruption and complacency of the ruling class, the apathy and cynicism of the workforce, the pervasive official hypocrisy. Yet they were socialists, Marxists and Leninists, they accepted the framework of the Soviet system, and what they asked for was more socialism rather than less. They were quite different, therefore, from the regime's dissident opponents in that they did not in principle reject the Soviet state and its purposes, nor did they believe in making any public challenge to it. Heroic defiance was not the Alternative Tradition's style. Alternative thinkers saw themselves rather as a 'loyal opposition': tactful, essentially positive critics whose task was to bring about change from within by exerting pressure and opening the leadership's eyes. Their reading of Marx and Lenin was so evidently correct, and so evidently what the current situation required, that the leadership was bound sooner or later to accept it – or so they assumed. And from 1985 the leadership began doing just what its alternative critics had hoped for.

2

The Alternative Tradition was part of a wider reaction within the Soviet bloc countries against the Stalinist economic system and the Stalinist model of socialism. Alternative thinkers in the Soviet Union were stimulated by the economic reforms in Czechoslovakia, Hungary and elsewhere; they in turn influenced and were influenced by such theorists of reform as Janos Kornai in Hungary, Wlodzimierz Brus in Poland and Ota Sik in Czechoslovakia – who, in emigration, would emerge as the leading exponent of the 'Third Way'.[2] There was also a lively awareness of America. That country was not, and could not be, a model for the reformers, but their disparagement of America was often, to the discerning eye, criticism of Soviet evils in thin disguise.[3] Horizontal links with other countries were supplemented by vertical links with the deeper Soviet past: some leading activists, notably V.S. Nemchinov and V.V. Novozhilov, had made their mark as reform-minded economists in the very period now being idealized – the 1920s.

The reformers began in the Soviet Union, as in eastern Europe, with a critique of the economic system. The economy was performing badly; it had lost its earlier dynamism; and the principal reason for the failing, the reformers suggested, was excessive centralization, the reliance upon commands and directives as the basic operational method. Such a system ignored economic realities; it let planners impose essentially subjective views in defiance of the objective needs and tendencies of the economy. It was both inefficient and arbitrary – inefficient because arbitrary. What was needed was to replace 'administrative' by 'economic' levers – that is, to let market forces, operating through prices and profits, do the work of directives. The market, the reformers tirelessly insisted, was not alien to socialism, was in fact intrinsic to socialist production; and the 'socialist market' – not to be confused with its capitalist counterpart – was essential if planning was to function effectively. Enterprises should be given a wide area of autonomy; they should be put on a 'cost-accounting' (*khozraschet*) basis, under which they would be responsible for covering their own costs and would be guided in their decisions above all by the criterion of profitability.

The existing system was unrealistic; and its most glaring failure of realism lay in its attitude towards the workers, whom it treated as if they were robots or at best a 'labour resource'. Reformers were strongly critical of this tendency to dehumanize the workers and regard them as work-performing objects. Machines did what they were told, but only human beings were capable of showing initiative, of being creative. 'A machine will never replace human beings in the process of economic creativity,' Alexander Birman insisted.[4] A system concerned only with what could be got out of the workers lost sight of the whole purpose of a socialist economy, which was not production for production's sake but the satisfaction of people's material and spiritual needs, including those of the workers. The focus of attention at the workplace should therefore, Birman argued, be not so much the work done as the workers who did it: 'To what extent can they fulfil their dreams, wishes and plans, which of course are not limited to smelting more iron or making more shoes?'[5]

Socialism, the reformers emphasized, aimed to develop *all* the faculties of man; in a fully realized socialist society, work would no longer be a burden and would be done voluntarily and eagerly because it fulfilled a basic need in human beings – the need to be creative. What had begun as a critique of the economic system thus broadened into something else: a critique of Soviet society that cast some doubt on its claim to have achieved socialism.

But what was it that made Soviet society socialist? The official view ran something like this. The Soviet state had eliminated exploiting classes and placed the means of production in common ownership. It had as a result created a society without social antagonisms, indeed without serious internal divisions or conflicts of any kind, a society that was united in its aspirations and was becoming ever more homogeneous. These conditions allowed the Soviet state to do what no capitalist state could – to define a general social interest, one that embraced the entire population. This interest the party represented and fully satisfied through the policies it promoted.

Much of this analysis the reformers readily accepted. The socialization of the means of production was an immense advance – without that socialism would be unthinkable.[6] Socialism's great advantage over capitalism was that by abolishing private ownership of production means it had created the potential for a single, non-conflictual social interest. The restructuring of property relationships was, however, not enough by itself to remove all significant social division and conflict. The reality was less neat and more complicated than the official view suggested. Conflicting classes indeed no longer existed in the Soviet Union, but the country still had distinct social *groups,* each with its own interests, and these in turn consisted of separate individuals, each with their own needs and motivations.

Serious thinking about the importance of groups and interests within socialist society had been stimulated by Ota Sik, whose *The Economy, Interests, Politics* had been published in the Soviet Union in 1964.[7] Sik argued that workers think and act not only as a class but also, and above all, as individuals living in a particular social milieu. Only an economic system that took account of these individual interests could be effective. And it was only through their individual interests that workers would, in time, come to an awareness of their common interests. These views were fiercely combated by traditionalists, for whom any suggestion that Soviet society was less than a monolith, that groups within it had interests of their own, was heresy.[8] The reformers nevertheless persisted. Their view, they were convinced, reflected the reality. It was the key to revitalizing the economy. It was intrinsically socialist. Moreover, it presented no threat to the party. The revival of sociology, after years of being banned, indicated that they were making progress. And it was a sociologist, V. Shubkin, who, in 1965, put their case most explicitly: 'within classes there exist definite social groups, the differences between which are created not by the forms of ownership of the means of production but by such factors as profession, level of qualification, education and income.'[9] Unless these groups were taken into account, Shubkin suggested, unless their needs, tastes, attitudes and motives for acting as they did were given some attention, the concrete economic problems of the country could not be solved.

The cry was taken up. Interests were vital. Pay the worker decently. Pay him above all in accordance with how well he worked – 'to each according to his work' was, after all, a fundamental principle of socialism. Then economic performance would improve. 'Human beings', Nikolai Petrakov pointed out, 'need to feel a direct relationship between the work they do and the satisfaction of their needs.'[10] But if workers were to be converted from passive and lacklustre performers of tasks into active and imaginative builders of socialism, more needed to be done than rejig pay scales. 'The need to work', Petrakov went on, 'is linked inseparably with creativity, with a sense of participating in the decisions taken.'[11] However, for decades workers had been bludgeoned into an inert obedience; every flicker of initiative had been crushed in them. If the economy was to revive, there would have to be a very different culture at the workplace. Nothing less, it seemed, than the democratization of the entire economic system would do.

'Democratization of management is necessary', the veteran V.V. Novozhilov urged, '... for the development of the creative activity of the popular masses. The larger the creative participation of the masses in developing the economy and culture, the quicker the rate of economic growth.'[12] The workers, then, had to be involved in day-to-day administration. The very fact of involving them would raise their level of creativity, Alexander Birman said; it would also make their physical work 'incalculably more stimulating'.[13] Only then would they begin to show initiative. And that was indispensable. As Otto Latsis put it:

'Workers' initiative is an Aladdin's lamp which will solve all of the previously unsolvable economic problems.'[14]

All that remained to be discovered was the genie of the lamp.

3

That the economic system needed to be democratized was the reformers' main argument. But their interest in democracy did not stop at the workplace. Democratization of the economic system was, in the end, inseparable from democratization of life in general. That democratization at work would boost economic performance could be said openly enough. That it would have the further beneficial effect of helping to democratize the public sphere in general could not be said openly but was nevertheless a recurring theme in the reformers' writings.

The advantage of the cost-accounting (*khozraschet*) system, V.S. Nemchinov argued, was that it would create 'a reliable filter against relics of voluntarism' (that is, against arbitrary action by the authorities).[15] V. Shubkin pointed out that concern for interests and interest groups would assist 'the development and strengthening of democratic instincts and of democratic methods of administering socialist society'.[16] Alexander Birman openly linked democratism at work and in the wider sphere by saying that socialism's essence lay in 'the direct participation of the labouring masses in the administration of production and of the entire country. And not just participation in administration – the word "participation" is inadequate – but administration by the masses themselves.'[17] Nikolai Petrakov turned a discussion of the pros and cons of planning into a thinly veiled criticism of the authority enjoyed by 'experts'. Experts were by no means infallible, he suggested, and needed to recognize that their knowledge was but relative and limited. They had the right to recommend, but no right to impose their views. People had to make their own free choices; only through market preferences could mistakes by the planners be exposed and corrected.[18] Petrakov was commenting on the economic system, but the significance of his remarks for the Soviet system as a whole was obvious. What, after all, were the party leaders but 'experts' who made absolute claims for the validity of their knowledge and imposed their views upon everyone else?

Soviet reformers could not of course say outright that without general democratization there could be no economic recovery, still less any real socialism. What many may well have wanted to say was, however, said in 1965 by a Czech who has especial interest for us. At Moscow University in the early 1950s, Zdenek Mlynar had become an intimate of Mikhail Gorbachev, and the two remained closely bonded until the 1968 disaster drove them apart.[19] Mlynar's ideas anticipate the political reforms implemented in the Soviet Union from 1987. Indeed, they may be seen as a model for the within-system reformism which, after much initial success, was to be discarded in 1990 for an approach that broke with Soviet tradition entirely. Yet in the context of the 1960s, what Zdenek Mlynar had to say was nothing less than mould-breaking.

Diversity and even conflict of interests within socialist society should, Mlynar argued, be welcomed. For these group interests represented dynamic forces which should not be ignored, still less stifled, but should instead be made use of through representative institutions. In such institutions, 'the interests of society as a whole are defined in the process of a confrontation of different, and sometimes contradictory, interests and approaches'. Collisions would inevitably occur, and in the course of them 'the contradictions are resolved and proper expression is found for the real interests of society'.[20]

In suggesting that the general interest should be defined not simply by the party from above but in a process of interaction between top and bottom through representative institutions, Mlynar was saying something extremely radical. For all its radicalism, his thinking nevertheless reflected an underlying optimism about the socialist project. The group conflicts were, he was at pains to point out, *non-antagonistic*. Had he said otherwise he would of course have got into serious trouble. Yet Mlynar was doing more than pay lip-service to an unavoidable orthodoxy. For in the democratized society he envisaged, the task of 'resolving contradictions between various group interests' would fall to the party. If it was to discharge the task properly and to resist pressure from sectional interests, its leadership role, far from being diminished, would have to be strengthened.[21] The party, then, would act as an above-group arbitrating and integrating force; it would – and it alone could – subsume a mass of conflicting particular interests into a comprehensive general interest. This view of the party's function in a democratized, but still one-party, state could hardly, however, have survived any serious suggestion that the leadership had sectional interests of its own for the sake of which it would block changes necessary for the general good.

That the leadership did indeed promote its own interests in ways that put it in an antagonistic relationship with the rest of society had been hinted at by the Polish economist, Wlodzimierz Brus.[22] It was implicit, too, in Petrakov's remark that 'the planner is himself a consumer' – the planner, in other words, was likely to be influenced by subjective criteria of his own, and was not a disembodied intelligence guided by an objective science. Hence the need for a market mechanism to curb him.[23] Such remarks were subversive of any suggestion that a genuine community of interests might be achieved within a democratized, one-party state. They pointed instead towards western-style politics, towards parties representative of different interests vying within a system whose aim was government based not on a 'general will' but rather on a *majority* interest.

Yet most alternative thinkers of the 1960s seem to have believed that, given the necessary changes, a full coincidence of interests could indeed be achieved. Alexander Birman is a case in point. Birman argued powerfully in favour of increasing the rights of individuals and of local institutions. He emphasized in particular how important it was for soviets to be able to express local interests and even resist the central economic authorities. The 'territorial principle' was vital 'because it creates the necessary organizational forms to involve the initiative of millions of workers ...' The relationship between central and local authorities would, however, be collaborative. No serious conflicts could occur between them. Quite the contrary: 'Joint work will quickly give rise to a common language, since the disagreements will not, after all, be antagonistic and the debates will be between Soviet people, who are equally interested in the success of the common cause.'[24]

There spoke the authentic voice of the Alternative Tradition!

4

The Tradition appeared at its most radical, but also its most optimistic, with Roy Medvedev. In March 1970 Medvedev, a historian recently expelled from the party, was a co-signatory, together with the physicists Andrei Sakharov and Valentin Turchin, of a letter to the leadership which said things that could not have been said in the official press. The economy was showing signs of 'breakdown and stagnation', which nothing less than fundamental change would correct. The country, moreover, was missing out on the technological revolution and falling further and further behind America. This did not mean that socialism was inherently incapable of beating capitalism in economic competition. The difficulty, the authors insisted, lay not with the socialist system as such but rather with 'those qualities and conditions of our life that run counter to socialism and are hostile to it. Their cause – anti-democratic traditions and norms of public life – arose during the Stalin period and has not been completely liquidated to this day.' The solution they suggested was a cautious democratization, which should be carried out 'at the instigation of, and under the control of, the highest authorities'. Such a democratization – allowing, for instance, a choice of candidates in elections – was essential. Without it, 'We will fall behind the capitalist countries in the course of the second industrial revolution and be gradually transformed into a second-rate provincial power ...'[25]

Predictably enough, the leadership ignored the request. This rebuff did much to destroy what remained of Andrei Sakharov's attachment to the Soviet state and socialism and to turn him into an out-and-out dissident; he would spend the rest of his life as a tireless campaigner on behalf of a liberal-democratic Russia. Roy Medvedev, however, remained within the Alternative Tradition, if only just. Unlike other alternative thinkers, he had come out in open opposition to the party. Yet, unlike Sakharov, he continued to believe in socialism and the basic Soviet framework and in the possibility of achieving a genuine socialism within it. However, partial democratization was not enough: nothing less than full and uninhibited democracy would do. Democracy was not, as many party members seemed to think, a Trojan horse which once admitted would destroy the citadel. It was a *sine qua non* for the success of the socialist project.

Medvedev was in effect taking Bukharin's central thesis and applying it to politics rather than economics. Bukharin had justified the mixed economy by arguing that in conditions of economic pluralism the virtues of the socialist economic system would shine out.[26] Almost mimicking him, Medvedev insisted that it was precisely through exposure to the ideas and policies of non-Marxist parties that people would come to appreciate Marxism and the party that embodied it. Just as Bukharin had seen a fully socialist economy being achieved by way of the market, so Medvedev argued that the practices of western democracy were necessary to bring about the triumph of a true socialism. The party should give up its monopoly. It should establish civil liberties and allow other parties to compete with it. There should be a clear-cut division between executive and legislature. The Supreme Soviet should become a proper parliament whose deputies were full-time and competitively elected. These proposals were grounded in Medvedev's conviction that 'Any political organization grows weak and decays without the stimulus of real political conflict ...' The reforms would not, therefore, undermine the party, quite the contrary: 'The point about open dialogue with dissidents is that it will strengthen communism and the Communist Party ...' Socialism would always be 'the ideology of the overwhelming majority'; it enjoyed a natural majority position which only continuing monopolism could jeopardize. Were real socialist democracy to be established, then all non-Marxist parties would be 'deprived of a mass base and therefore would present no threat to the future of socialist society'.[27]

It followed that the party needed democracy and had every reason to embrace it. Given free competition, policies based on Marxism-Leninism would inevitably prevail. In such conditions the party would revitalize itself and win the vigorous and widespread support that would enable it to accomplish its task. Much as the economic reformers argued that plan and market were complementary rather than contradictory, so Roy Medvedev had convinced himself that party domination was fully compatible with the practices of democracy.

This was alternative thinking taken to a radical extreme. Yet if Medvedev was a radical, he was also an optimist, a true believer who knew that the Soviet experiment would come right in the end. The economy was in his view basically sound, even if there was a çase for some private enterprise in the service sector and in small-scale industry. The country needed pluralism of ideas, but its social structure was and would remain fundamentally homogeneous. As for the nationalities problem, that had in essence been solved. Thus in all respects but one the conditions for a proper socialism existed already. Democracy alone was missing; its absence was the sole serious impediment. The Prague Spring, however, was proof that a communist party could liberalize and regenerate itself without renouncing the basic values of socialism, and Medvedev was optimistic that by the end of the century the Soviet Union would have become 'a truly socialist nation'.[28]

But how would the change be brought about? How was a jealously monopolistic party to be transformed into one that accepted democracy? Certainly not by outright opposition. A dissident himself, Medvedev stood aloof from the dissident movement and urged those who shared his outlook to remain in the party and work for change within it, rather than engage in futile skirmishings. These 'party democrats' were not numerous so far, but their numbers and their influence would grow. Before long, more far-sighted people would enter the leadership, and an alliance might then emerge between these reformist leaders and 'the best of the intelligentsia'.[29] However, in order to persuade the elite to accept changes that transformed the party's very nature, it would surely take more than the rationality and good sense of the democrats' arguments. And what was needed was seen most clearly by an observer on the other side of the Atlantic who might be regarded as an honorary member of the Alternative Tradition – the historian, Moshe Lewin.

Lewin's career showed striking parallels with Roy Medvedev's. Like Medvedev, he had written extensively on Soviet history of the 1920s. Like him, and unlike most American observers, he viewed the early revolutionary period positively and believed that the Soviet socialist project might yet be redeemed. Like Medvedev, he foresaw a situation in which enlightened politicians would join with intellectuals in a 'new coalition of forces' which would transform not only the economy but the whole political system, bringing it 'into accord with the growing complexity and modernity of society'.[30] But while Medvedev had been writing *On Socialist Democracy*, Lewin had spent the early 1970s in a study of the economic reform movement that emphasized the similarity between current reformist thinking and the thinking of the 1920s. And this genealogy gave him the key to the reform coalition's likely success. The reformers would win not simply because their arguments were more rational and sensible than their opponents'. They would win because they could relate themselves 'to important and acceptable trends in the Soviet past', because the solutions they proposed would be 'well in line with certain traditions inside the party'.[31] A case based on rationality and effectiveness would thus be strengthened and given a deep emotional resonance by an appeal to the collective memory. The party would be invited to go forward by going back, to shape its future by recovering its past, to complete its mission by returning to the springs of its original inspiration. And the focus of attention would be Lenin, especially the late Lenin, the Lenin of NEP and the 'political testament'.

5

In October 1968 readers of *Novy Mir* were treated to a highly charged piece of Leniniana by an Old Bolshevik, Yelizaveta Drabkina.[32] The piece began in a mood of devotionalism as Drabkina described Lenin's final days and death and 'the endless, aching anguish' she felt whenever she revisited the place of his dying. Reverence for Lenin was standard enough, but the intensity of feeling, the sense of real dependence upon the leader, set this well apart from conventional hagiography. Drabkina had fought for the Bolsheviks, had had a fervent commitment to socialism, but then had fallen victim to the purges and spent long years in Siberia. The importance of Lenin, for such a person, was that he offered a way of coming to terms with personal and national tragedy without sacrificing those original beliefs, without admitting that one's life and a whole era of Russian existence had been built upon a destructive illusion. By being a genius whose 'behests' had been ignored or flouted, he was able to redeem the tragedy.

When she thought of 'the tragedy of 1937', Drabkina thought not only of 'the great inquisitor and his contemptible executioners but above all of those who were their victims – communists and Soviet people whose faith in the party and in communism could not be destroyed either by torture or by the scaffold'. Communism was not Stalin, she insisted; it was 'Lenin, Sverdlov and Frunze – people with the purest conscience and the highest ideals to be found on earth'.[33] For Drabkina, Lenin and Stalin had thus become antipodes; the blacker Stalin appeared, the more Lenin shone out. But if Lenin was to be an anti-Stalin and a solvent of Stalinism, attention had to focus on the years when he was at his most mellow and unStalinlike, when he had come closest to reconciling practical politics and the ideals of socialism. That was why Drabkina and alternative thinkers in general gave special attention to 1921–4, the period of NEP and the 'political testament'; that was why they saw the late Lenin as the true one and the 'testament' as an indispensable distillation of his wisdom.

All of Lenin, for Drabkina, was in those last writings: 'his mind, his heart, his unusual clarity of thought, his concreteness, and the link between great theory and living reality'. With the 'testament' Lenin had 'spread out his warm and powerful wing over party and country and all of labouring mankind ...'[34]

That the revolution had gone astray at the end of the 1920s and not yet returned to its proper path could not be said openly. Alternative thinkers nevertheless circled endlessly around the theme of the 1920s, creating a mood of nostalgia for what they seemed to regard as a golden age before the Fall. None among them stirred nostalgia for the lost ideals of the 1920s more effectively than Mikhail Shatrov, a playwright from an Old Bolshevik family many of whose members, including his father, had been swept away by the purges. And in 1966–7 Shatrov's play *The Bolsheviks* electrified Moscow audiences by dealing directly with the fate of the revolution and seeming to ask – 'did things have to turn out as they did?'

Set in August 1918, *The Bolsheviks* begins with party leaders discussing their plight as a tiny minority of the enlightened amidst a sea of ignorant and hostile peasants. 'Don't you realize', says Lunacharsky, 'that in an overwhelmingly peasant country like Russia the danger of our being overwhelmed by the petty bourgeoisie is real and threatening?'[35] He fears that the party may be taken over by 'vermin' with 'red rosettes' – careerists who merely mouth socialist slogans. But such fears are then thrust into the background by the dreadful news that Lenin has been struck down by a would-be assassin. Despair seizes his colleagues. Never before have they felt their dependence upon him so acutely. 'Vladimir Ilich can't be replaced by anyone', says Sverdlov, speaking for them all.

In this crisis they rush through decrees establishing terror and concentration camps, though some endorse the decrees with profound misgiving, knowing well how terror had got out of control under their Jacobin predecessors. The prophetic warnings about the dangers of dispensing with legality are underlined by voices from the street – 'Let's follow the example of the French Revolution! In revenge for the blood of Comrade Lenin ... let the blood of the bourgeoisie and its lackeys flow in torrents!' But then comes the news that Lenin is recovering, and it leads to an explosion of joy: 'We're on our way again!' [36] With Lenin at the helm, nothing, it seems, can go wrong – the party is safe from both external enemies and those within its own ranks. His near-death nevertheless raises the question: what if Lenin should die – what then? And the audience is left with the feeling that, had it not been for his premature death a few years later, the outcome would have been not Stalinism but genuine socialism.

Like Mikhail Shatrov, Roy Medvedev had lost his father to the purges; like him, he would fight against the Stalinist perversion; like him, he would be driven by an idealized view of early Soviet socialism whose psychological root may well have been devotion to the father taken from him by Stalin. But whereas Shatrov insinuated the idea that the Stalinist perversion had been a cruel accident, Medvedev spent much of the 1960s writing a book that would put the idea of Stalinism's fortuitousness on a firm historical basis.[37] There was always of course a danger that the masses would swamp the enlightened, that peasant culture would in the end degrade the culture of socialism rather than be remade by it. Nevertheless, had Lenin not died in 1924, then 'the victory of genuinely socialist and democratic tendencies would have been more probable than the victory of Stalinism'. Stalinism's triumph, Medvedev suggested, was the outcome of two fateful historical accidents: the early death of Lenin, the genius of the revolution, and the criminal character of Stalin, 'the embodiment of all the worst elements in the Russian revolutionary movement ...'.[38] It followed that the Stalinist episode, however bloodstained, did not discredit the party or devalue the achievements of the early Soviet state. Stalinism – 'the negation and bloody annihilation of Bolshevism'[39] – simply made it all the more necessary that the party should return to the principles that had animated it in the 1920s, that it should resume the work so tragically broken off then, that it should lead the country from pseudo-socialism to the genuine socialism of Marx and Lenin.

Not all alternative thinkers agreed that the 'great turn' of 1929 could have been avoided. They were, however, at one in thinking that Lenin would have abhorred Stalinism and that he had been guided by an utterly unStalinist concept of socialism. Medvedev spoke for all in suggesting that Lenin had been a genuine democrat, even if at times he had been forced to act against his own convictions:

> Early on, Lenin envisioned Soviet power functioning as a pluralistic system, allowing for free competition within the soviets among all parties representing the workers ... Lenin, you see, was convinced that the Bolsheviks would come out ahead of all other parties in any free competition.[40]

Adverse circumstances, but also their own mistakes, had then forced the Bolsheviks to flout democracy. The elections to the Constituent Assembly had been bungled; held a few weeks later, they would have given the Bolsheviks a popular mandate. War Communism was a mistake, but Lenin had learned from it; and with NEP, his greatest theoretical innovation, he had laid the foundations of a truly democratic socialism.

Across the Atlantic, Moshe Lewin was suggesting something not dissimilar. In *Lenin's Last Struggle* he showed the dying leader being haunted by the evils, actual and potential, of Soviet power and battling to purge or pre-empt them, to imbue the party with properly socialist values and a sense of what still had to be done to achieve socialism. Lenin had not, Lewin argued, begun by envisaging a monolithic state, nor had he wanted a strictly monolithic party. The dictatorship of the party over the proletariat was never part of Lenin's plan; it was, rather, 'the completely unforeseen culmination of a series of unforeseen circumstances'.[41]

Those who wrote in the official press had to be more cautious, but heavily emphasized the Leninist inspiration of the changes they wanted. Lenin had been pro-market and pro-peasant, had seen NEP as a long-term policy and War Communism as no more than a regrettable short-term necessity, and had tried to prevent Stalin's brutal treatment of the nationalities. Lenin as the reformers presented him in fact questioned not only the command economy and Stalinism but fundamentals of the Soviet system as it still existed. Socialism for Lenin, Birman insisted, had been 'not only a certain fairly high level of material production and not only the socialization of the means of production'; it had also meant direct participation by the masses in administering the state.[42]

And so, subtly and not so subtly, alternative thinkers diffused a mood of regret for the dashed hopes and unrealized ideas of the 1920s, and suggested that these ideas might yet help bring the country to socialism. But if the reformers needed to convince a ruling class that was deeply suspicious of change, they also needed to convince themselves. Lenin was both a flag of convenience and an inspiration for them. As they portrayed him, he was not only a marketeer, a democrat and an embodiment of humanity; he was also someone who had grappled successfully with the contradictions thrown up by the attempt to create socialism in a society utterly unprepared for it. This facet of Lenin's appeal was underlined by a leading reformer somewhat later: 'His ability to reconcile seemingly irreconcilable things continues to astonish one with every re-reading of his works.'[43]

That, perhaps above all, was what drew the reformers to Lenin. For this 'outstanding dialectician' had reconciled the irreconcilable – on paper at least. Market and plan. Self-determination of nations and the integrity of the Soviet state. Self-determination of individuals and the leading role of the Communist Party. With NEP he had maintained centralized direction of the economy while providing wide scope for individual initiative. Battling against Stalin, he had etched a plan by which non-Russians could be persuaded to give the Soviet state their voluntary support. And while insisting that the party dictatorship was for the time being indispensable, he had envisaged a steady convergence between party aims and popular wishes which before long would have made any coercion by the party – any 'bossing' – unnecessary.

Lenin had thus confronted the very dilemmas that lay at the root of the current Soviet malaise – dilemmas that the regime had sidestepped by going off into a pseudo-socialism deeply influenced by the autocratic inheritance. Could you not have a planned economy and yet encourage the initiative essential to economic growth and efficiency? Could you not create conditions in which the non-Russians joined willingly in the common enterprise? Could you not give people wide freedom of expression and action in a way that did not jeopardize the party's objectives but, rather, bonded party and people more tightly than before? Lenin as the reformers read him suggested that you could. To the various dilemmas he indicated one and the same solution – a carefully implemented democratization. Without that, the party would never fulfil its mission; without that, socialism would remain beyond reach. This belief in the saving power of democracy was what, more than anything else, united those party intellectuals who chafed under the Brezhnev regime and rejected the ideology of 'developed socialism'.

6

The early 1980s saw a wave of new thinking from economists, sociologists and others who, unlike Roy Medvedev, stopped short of outright defiance of the regime. The election of Yury Andropov as general secretary had given reformism a very considerable boost; and the deepening problems of the Soviet economy had made its arguments all the harder to ignore. Admittedly, all was still quiet in the streets. There had, however, been disturbances in neighbouring Poland, where the government's repressiveness and its mishandling of the economy had brought workers and intellectuals into concerted opposition to it. Nothing similar to the nationwide and cross-class Solidarity movement was likely in the Soviet Union, where dissidents were, as we have seen, tiny in numbers and isolated from the workforce. Yet if the Polish troubles did not touch a nerve, they were not entirely irrelevant either. The policies that had led to crisis in Poland were remarkably similar to Brezhnev's. If Prague had shown the dangers of liberalizing too much, the revolt which erupted in Gdansk flashed a warning of the hazards of continuing with policies of economic conservatism and political repression.

Even before Brezhnev was dead, an article in the official press had come out with 1960s-type arguments for democratizing the economic system but gone beyond them by arguing in addition for *political* democratization – for 'a gradual decentralization of authority functions'.[44] Anatoly Butenko added urgency to his plea by directly linking the current situation in the Soviet Union with the crisis in Poland. That, he suggested, had been the result of a lack of democracy within the party and in society in general, and in the Soviet Union too, he predicted, there would be social tension and even 'open political conflict' if the ordinary worker remained excluded from decision-making and if he continued to see the political and economic systems not as 'his' but as 'external and alien forces'.[45]

But was this not an increasingly homogeneous society? Had Soviet society not been purged of social conflict and 'antagonistic contradictions'? Not so, said Butenko. There was in fact a 'basic contradiction' between society's production forces and the existing system of production relationships, as a result of which the development of production forces was being held back. What he was saying in this Marxist language was that the existing political and economic systems were benefiting the ruling elite, or elements within it, at the expense of society as a whole. This was a dangerous idea even to hint at, and before long the editors of *Questions of Philosophy* would be forced to eat humble pie for having published it. That Butenko should have publicly floated such a heresy was nevertheless a remarkable sign of how the party's hold on society was weakening.

Butenko's case was developed the following year by a leading, Siberian-based economist and sociologist, Tatyana Zaslavskaya.[46] Zaslavskaya's paper was less obviously provocative since it did not argue directly for political democratization or raise the spectre of possible Polish-type eruptions. Her paper was not in fact intended for publication at all – simply for discussion within a small circle of academics and leading functionaries. The implications of the paper were nevertheless deeply radical, and its leaking to the west caused a sensation. The failures of the Soviet economy sprang, Zaslavskaya suggested, from inherent deficiencies in the economic system and therefore could not be eliminated without fundamental restructuring. The system treated workers as 'cogs' and expected them to behave 'just as obediently (and passively) as machines and materials'. The result was 'low labour- and production-discipline, an indifferent attitude to the work performed and its low quality, social passivity ... and a rather low level of moral discipline'. In short, the country had not yet achieved 'a genuinely socialist type of worker' or a 'genuinely socialist attitude to labour'.[47]

That was a swingeing enough comment on a society that claimed to have reached the high plateau of developed socialism. But Zaslavskaya became more radical still when she took up Butenko's point about the conflict of interests within society. The orthodox view, she reminded her audience, held that 'under socialism there is no group interested in the preservation of outmoded production relations and therefore their perfection takes place without social conflict'. But this was wrong: there *were* divergent interests, and therefore no improvement could be achieved without conflict. The existing system suited lazy and apathetic workers because it demanded so little of them; it also, she implied, suited many in the economic hierarchy since it gave them unlimited control over a passively obedient workforce. Both elements – bosses and workers – had an interest in obstructing reform. How then might it be achieved?

Two things, Zaslavskaya suggested, were necessary. First, realism. Theory had to recognize the existence of groups dedicated to keeping outmoded production relations. What was needed in fact was a new model of production relations which took into account 'the "multi-dimensionality", and frequently even the conflict of interests, of the groups operating in the economic structure ...' Changes to ideology were not, however, enough. In addition, it was necessary to develop 'a well-thought-out socialist strategy', whose purpose should be 'to stimulate the activity of groups interested in changing production relations and block the actions of groups capable of obstructing this change'.[48]

Quasi-reform, as a fellow reformer put it, was inadequate. Nothing less than real reform would do, and that would have to be 'carried through despite the resistance of conservative and inert elements in the state apparatus'.[49] This insistence on the need for a concerted and planned struggle against conservative elements showed how much had been learned from the failure of reform in the 1960s. A partial reform of the economic system in isolation from the broader power structure would be futile. Nothing less than an overall restructuring would do. That, however, would provoke fierce resistance from those whose personal power and privileges would be threatened. Economic reform could not be separated from political. What was at issue in the end was power, which remained in the grasp of a small group of conservatives who guarded it jealously. That was why strategic thinking was necessary, that was why it was vital to build a coalition in which intellectuals joined together with reform-minded members of the governing elite.

It was not only social scientists who were rebelling. A glimpse of how grave a situation the authorities now faced was provided in late 1983 by *Novy Mir* (now a neutered version of its former self), in an article which deplored the current tendency to abandon 'the revolutionary-democratic tradition in Russian literary criticism' in favour of views that challenged 'our whole tradition of cultural history'. The fashion now was for 'asocial views of history, morality and culture', which were making an appearance 'both in belles lettres and in ordinary people's attitudes'.[50] The most revealing words in this lament were 'ordinary people' and 'asocial'. It was not intellectuals alone, or so it seemed, who were going astray. People at large were becoming less party-minded, were beginning to think for themselves, to define and work towards goals of their own. No wonder that alarm bells were ringing! The guardians of orthodoxy were still at their posts of course, and in the final years of the old order they would tighten their vigilance, but their position was becoming desperate. In its heyday the party had persuaded or coerced the population into accepting its right to be the arbiter of all opinions. Now, however, persuasion hardly worked any more, and the agents of coercion were having an uphill struggle.

7

The socialist critics of Soviet society who have been grouped together in this chapter as 'the Alternative Tradition' were not of course wholly of one mind, and the differences between the radical democrat Roy Medvedev and the moderates of the alternative mainstream were obvious. Both sides, however, were essentially optimistic about the outcome of the Soviet socialist experiment. In Medvedev's case, the optimism was an act of faith, and it rested upon largely unexamined assumptions about the health of the economy and the wellbeing of Soviet society in general. The moderates, by contrast, were empirical scholars who were well aware of the economic problems and social tensions (though they tended to share Medvedev's blindspot about the nationalities). Yet most of them, too, were optimists, and their optimism derived from the belief that under socialism there were not and could not be any antagonistic contradictions, that the party, once democratized, could construct a general interest out of a myriad partial interests and guide the country towards a fully realized socialism.

Among the moderates some, however, even in the 1960s, feared that no easy resolution of conflicts could be achieved simply because the party itself, or elements within it, now pursued an interest of its own. The sobering experience of the 1970s could only confirm and deepen this suspicion. The 1965 reform – which Alexander Birman had once hailed as equivalent in importance to NEP[51] – had been killed off by a conservative leadership which saw its vital interests being threatened by it. The disjunction between the general interest as the party chose to define it (in effect *the party's* interest) and the interest of society as a whole had become glaring. The economic downturn of the late 1970s only underlined how much the wider interest was now being sacrificed. What had happened raised a clear question-mark against Mlynar-type ideas of consensual, general-interest government by a democratized but still monopolistic party that was capable of acting as an above-group integrating force. It seemed to point instead towards the uninhibited democracy advocated by Roy Medvedev. But was this perversion of the party into an interest group inevitable and unalterable? Might not genuine socialists win back control and so restore the party to its proper function? Most alternative thinkers agreed with

Medvedev that this could well happen, and developments of the early 1980s only encouraged the belief.

There was more, in the end, that united the reformers than divided them. What united them above all was socialism itself. That socialism was in principle a juster system than its capitalist rival they took for granted. That Russia would remain Soviet and socialist for the foreseeable future they likewise scarcely questioned. The party's recent performance had disillusioned many of them, yet few doubted that the party, once recaptured from the conservatives, could achieve its original objectives. All saw democratization if not full democracy as vital and were convinced that there could be no real socialism without it. All, moreover, had ceased to take communism seriously and had come to regard socialism as an end rather than a preliminary to something transcendently different from itself. They no longer believed in the new person or the classless, stateless society or in 'from each according to his ability, to each according to his need'. All this had gone into the museum of antiquities.

That set them fundamentally apart from Lenin, whose belief in achieving a relationship of genuine mutuality between party and people had been inseparable from his communist perspective. They were holding on to the husk of his vision of mutuality and failing to notice that the kernel was missing. Yet the vision, however misunderstood, mattered – they could see no way forward except through a return to Lenin. For he had solved, or at least etched solutions to, problems that without his magic seemed unsolvable. His colleagues, his mortality and, above all, cultural backwardness had prevented the implementation of his ideas. Now, however, the time was ripe – more than ripe – to do what Lenin had been unable to do: to enact his vision, to unleash the people as a creative force, to make Soviet society democratic and fully socialist.

One other thing bonded these critics of the regime: the very fact that they were reformers, rather than revolutionaries or armchair dreamers. They wanted change that was achievable and could be achieved by peaceful, within-system methods, even if it would finish by transforming the system. Their task, therefore, was to persuade and cajole, to make influential friends, to push at doors that were already half-open. But did they have any real chance of success? Moshe Lewin apart, western observers almost unanimously thought not. Unless crisis struck, the party would remain true to its autocratic and intolerant character. To democratize, to accept accountability to its own grass roots and to society as a whole, was so obviously contrary to the leaders' self-interest as to be, in any circumstances other than a crisis, unthinkable.

Yet one factor spoke in favour of such a change: the ongoing and rapid modernization of society. Soviet society of the 1980s was, needless to say, vastly different from the society that had nurtured the Bolsheviks. This was a highly educated and a preponderantly urban society – by 1970, 70 per cent of Russians lived in towns. It was, in addition, a society with a sizeable and influential middle class. By the end of the Brezhnev period, there were some 35 million members of the intelligentsia – in the Soviet sense of white-collar, non-manual workers. Many of these were engineers or technical specialists, but a significant number were intelligentsia in the traditional sense of having the educational and cultural background likely to breed independent thinking and the capacity and inclination for reasoned criticism of authority. Moreover, middle-class people had done relatively badly out of the economic transformation since Stalin's time; they in effect had been the losers from the regime's 'social contract' with the blue-collar classes. Wage differentials had narrowed considerably since the 1950s, and by the later Brezhnev era doctors, teachers, engineers, office administrators and the like tended to be less well-paid than skilled manual workers. The middle class had grievances of a different kind as well. It, above all, had suffered from the withdrawal of the partial and precarious freedoms granted by Khrushchev, and its more talented members had been badly hit by the return to intolerance and oppressiveness. They provided a natural constituency for alternative thinking, could it only establish itself within the party; and they would almost certainly respond to any leader who promised to curb state arbitrariness and to widen the scope for individual initiative.

A changed society was reflected in a changed party. The party's formal commitment to the working class remained, but it was now far from being the working-class stronghold that it had been in the early 1930s. As society became more highly-educated and more white-collar, so had the party. By the early 1980s, at least half the members, and a higher proportion of the elite, had an intelligentsia (in the official sense) background. The typical party member was now an ambitious and well-qualified member of the middle class who had joined for reasons of career advancement rather than because of a primary ideological commitment; and if he or she had broader aims, it was to mould the party to the needs of society rather than to use it as an instrument for reshaping society. For the time being, power remained with men of Stalinist vintage and of worker or peasant origin who did not in the least sympathize with middle-class values and aspirations. Yet the party was coming under increasing pressure from within its own ranks to do what middle-class society wanted: to grant those freedoms that were necessary for the talented to fulfil themselves and at the same time – or so alternative thinkers argued – were a precondition for the creation of a genuine socialism.

During the early 1980s reformers such as Zaslavskaya were building bridges with figures in the leadership who might one day work towards a democratized and genuinely socialist Soviet Union. Each party to the relationship needed the other. The reformers were of course dependent upon open-minded and pragmatic people in the leadership; but they in turn could only welcome 'new thinking' that promised to restore dynamism to the economy and to society in general without jeopardizing the party's monopoly. The denouement of the Soviet tragedy thus began with a rapprochement between the leadership and 'the best of the intelligentsia', for which two decades of alternative thinking had prepared the way. With Mikhail Gorbachev's election as general secretary in March 1985, the Alternative Tradition's moment had come. And the general secretary who was to lead party and country into what seemed an auspicious new era was of course none other than the former Moscow University friend of Zdenek Mlynar.

9
A New Socialism, 1985–91

1

Till the very eve of the Gorbachev era it remained an article of faith among western experts that the Soviet Union would in the short term remain impervious to change, that its rulers would ward off any attempt at serious reform.[1] When perestroika began, therefore, most experts reacted with extreme scepticism – 'Don't be deceived!' was the characteristic response.[2] The changes would be no more than cosmetic; real change under the Soviet regime was out of the question. Once the seriousness of the reform had become undeniable, this stance was of necessity modified. Yet it was an easy shift from denying that reform would even be attempted to asserting that it would not and could not achieve its aims. And when the system eventually collapsed, those who had cast doubt on the very possibility of reform declared themselves vindicated, even if the collapse had been brought about by something they had never contemplated – a drive for fundamental change.

This approach was seen at its most striking in the writings of Martin Malia.[3] Perestroika, in Malia's view, was the last throw of 'soft communism', and largely the work of a master tactician, a supreme apparatchik, a wheeler-dealer who lacked any strategic vision or principled commitment to reform and was in the end destroyed by the progressively more radical measures he had against his will been driven to adopt. The reforms, in short, had not been intended but had been blundered into by a manipulator who remained incorrigibly wedded to Sovietism and suffered in the end the fate of the sorcerer's apprentice: that he and his work were swept away by the very forces he had himself unwittingly unleashed.

However, Andrzej Walicki, who in earlier sections of this book has appeared almost as Malia's twin, interpreted the perestroika experiment very differently. Repudiating Malia's view that perestroika had been six wasted years and that real reform began only after the collapse of the Soviet Union, Walicki portrayed Gorbachev as a heroic, though too little appreciated, liberator, as someone who had brought about 'truly epochal change' through reforms that were not merely within-system but transformed the very nature of the system, 'removing its totalitarian features, destroying its legacy of fear and mental bondage'. Gorbachev could not therefore be dismissed as a failure: he might have been defeated as Soviet president, 'but not as a reformer whose priority was freedom for the Soviet people'.[4]

The great strength of Walicki's interpretation was that it highlighted what mainstream Sovietologists had tended to gloss over, if not to deny outright – perestroika's remarkable *success*, the fact that it had ousted a dictatorship which had appeared impregnable, achieved 'an incredibly quick and peaceful dismantling of the entire edifice of the communist tyranny', and put in its place the institutional framework for democracy. Walicki's account was less satisfactory, however, as an explanation of why and how perestroika had succeeded to the extent that it did. The focus was almost wholly on Gorbachev, giving the impression that he had carried out the liberation single-handed. The liberator appeared, moreover, as a deeply divided self, committed to freedom yet unable to shuffle off his loyalty to Soviet socialism. Hence his 'strained, inconsistent and lamentably unconvincing' attempts to defend Lenin.[5] What Walicki could not allow was that these two potentially conflicting commitments – to democracy and to Marxism-Leninism – might be harmonized for Gorbachev, as for many others, by the Alternative Tradition. Gorbachev's achievement and his personal drama, which did indeed become acute once the Tradition's failure stared him in the face, have to be seen in their wider intellectual and social contexts. The success of the reforms owed much to a movement which pushed and exhorted a sometimes reluctant general secretary and refined and deepened his thinking; and behind the movement's more technocratic concerns lay a commitment to achieving democracy, without sacrificing traditional Soviet objectives, which gave it something of the character of a crusade.

That said, the personal contribution of Mikhail Gorbachev was indispensable. And what he was mattered almost as much as who he was, for with his election as general secretary, in March 1985, a new generation and a new type of person came to the leadership. Those who had run the country until then had been shaped by Stalinism, had kept a living link with the early Soviet period and even with tsarism. Gorbachev, born in 1931, had been reared in very different circumstances. Tsarism and the revolutionary struggles he knew only by hearsay; he had been too young to take part in the war, and Stalin had died while he was still a student. True, like many of his predecessors in the Soviet elite he was of peasant stock. This boy from the farm had, however, made his way to Moscow University, shed his peasant self, and become a sophisticated professional well able to understand the frustrations and the aspirations of his middle-class contemporaries. His predecessors in the leadership had risen in a turbulent world; their rigidity and intolerance were hardly surprising. But there had been little to cast Mikhail Gorbachev in the same mould. Even as a student, his Czech friend Zdenek Mlynar noted, he had been inclined to question fossilized truths and outdated practices.[6] As leader, he would respond to problems imaginatively and be willing to rethink fundamentals.

Well before 1985, reform-minded intellectuals had been looking to this bright and energetic man, evidently a rising star, as someone who might one day implement their ideas.[7] What now lay ahead was a coalition held together by alternative ideas and assumptions, a coalition in which, much as Moshe Lewin and Roy Medvedev had envisaged it, party leaders and intellectuals would make common cause against an entrenched conservatism. The ideas were far from clear-cut – there was no programme, no blueprint. The reformers were, however, bonded by a feeling that 'Everything is rotten',[8] that things could not go on as they were, that real and radical change was urgently needed, that the inspiration and genuine socialist commitment of the early revolutionary years had somehow to be recovered. The very vagueness was an advantage: people with different aims and degrees of radicalism could cluster more easily around a mood and some general propositions than around a blueprint. What was attractive about the Tradition, moreover, was its underlying *optimism*. That things would yet come out all right seemed to be the message. Alternative ideas had the attraction, too, of offering change without apparent risk. Here was a new approach to the economy, a way out of the impending crisis, which did not endanger fundamental party principles. There would be no challenge to central planning as such, still less to the party's vanguard role. Quite the contrary: alternative thinking – 'new thinking', as it would become known – was presented as the only way of strengthening the party and safeguarding its position.

Yet if alternative ideas were reassuringly within-system, they had implications that reached well beyond the system. One way of thinking about the Tradition might be to imagine a long row of inter-connecting chambers leading off a main hallway. The hallway was orthodox Marxism-Leninism – but the further you penetrated from it, the more exotic and unSoviet the surroundings became. For many whose radicalism had been no more than latent, the Tradition would prove a school of self-discovery, leading them by gentle stages to a drastically different notion of socialism and even to views that lay outside socialism altogether.

The way things would go had already been suggested by Zdenek Mlynar in his reflections on the Prague Spring. The initial aim of the Czech reformers, Mlynar explained, had been to renew the existing system by liberalizing the Communist Party, making it subject to social control and bringing about a limited pluralization:

> These were, for us, far-reaching measures, and we decided that we would first have to see how these reforms worked out in practice before asking ourselves the next question – namely whether the system thus reformed was ripe for extension, and whether unlim-ited freedom of the press and political pluralism, including possibly a multi-party system, could be accommodated.[9]

In the Soviet Union, this 'next question' would force itself on to the agenda early in the reform process.

A glittering array of the talented – academics, writers, professionals of all sorts – rallied to the cause of 'perestroika' (reconstruction), as the reform movement became known. There were echoes here of the excitement of 1905–6, when the *beau monde* of Petersburg and Moscow had flocked to the Kadet Party and its campaign to create a liberal-constitutional Russia. As liberalism had conquered public opinion then, so alternative socialism seemed to sweep all before it now. These fervent alternative socialists were, above all, the 'children of the Twentieth Congress'. After long years of repression their moment had come, and they would prove to be the shock troops of the reform movement. By 1987 they had won a commanding position in the media. Old orthodoxies, unable to withstand the onslaught, seemed to crumble on all fronts. Roy Medvedev came in from the cold and would before long join the Central Committee. Mikhail Shatrov caused scandal and delight by putting the new philosophy on the stage. A former Khrushchev aide spelled the issue out in the clearest of terms. There were two rival models of socialism: War Communism and NEP.

The first was the socialism of Stalin and Trotsky, the second the socialism of Marx, Lenin and Bukharin. A choice had to be made; that could only be 'to return to Lenin, return to Marx and the sources of socialism'.[10] As a volume of essays written by the leading alternative lights put it – *There Is No Alternative*.[11]

What had come into being, one contributor to the volume argued, was 'an alliance, unique in our history, of the intelligentsia and the political leadership of the country'.[12] And in this respect the difference between the late 1980s and that earlier period of reformist excitement was striking. Then the reformers had battled in vain against an obdurate regime which fobbed them off with mere concessions. Now they held the commanding heights. The way seemed open for them to create the new socialism – that is, to create real socialism.

2

Brezhnev's idea of 'developed socialism', with its complacent assumption of solid achievement, was soon discarded. Socialism, it turned out, was not 'developed' at all; it was simply 'developing', and so far only 'its most minimal possibilities' had been revealed.[13] Given that socialism in any real sense still lay well ahead, communism now receded into the remote future and in effect dropped from sight altogether. The 500 pages of *The CPSU on Perestroika*, published in 1988, contained no more than a single reference to communism. Gorbachev himself almost never referred to it after the Nineteenth Party Conference of that year.[14] Freed at last from the shadow of communism, socialism had become an end in itself. But this new independence raised a question – if socialism was not after all the stepping-stone to communism, what was it? The further they moved from the certainties of Marxism-Leninism, the more that question would haunt the reformers.

As communism disappeared, so did the grandiose ambitions associated with it. There would be no more talk of enormous feats of moral, political and socio-economic engineering. The 'new person', the intended achiever of these feats, had vanished; socialist society would instead get the best it could out of unreformed human beings. There would be no 'withering away of the state', no stateless self-administration; the aim, rather, would be to humanize and democratize the state, making it a genuine servant of the community. And there would be no moneyless economy, no abolition of 'bourgeois right', no distribution of goods and services in accordance with need. People would be rewarded according to how hard and how creatively they worked, on the assumption that by bettering themselves they would better everyone else. All of this suggested a narrowing of the gap between rhetoric and reality – in place of grandiose schemes, there would be real, if modest, improvement. Avoiding communism and the 'new person', the reformers talked of 'a new society', a 'new life' and 'a new condition of socialism'.

Perestroika began of course as a response to a looming economic crisis, and two decades of alternative thinking about the economy lay behind its economic reforms. The 1987 Law on State Enterprise liberalized the economic system considerably, increasing the powers of enterprise-managers vis-à-vis central ministries and of workers vis-à-vis managers. The 'cost-accounting' (*khozraschet*) principle was brought back and emphasized as a key to enterprise efficiency. The market was legitimized; entrepreneurial and self-bettering attitudes were encouraged – within limits. The rethinking of economic fundamentals reached as far as ownership. Diversity in the forms of ownership was now seen as necessary; state ownership would continue to dominate, but alongside it there would be municipal, cooperative, and even joint-stock and private ownership. The proprietorial instinct itself, long frowned upon, was, moreover, rehabilitated – Gorbachev noted with approval how 'our people have yearned for the proprietorial role'.[15] Cooperatives were, however, especially favoured, in part perhaps because of their Leninist credentials, and they developed rapidly from 1988 in the retail and service sectors.

These were significant changes, yet they were soon overshadowed by unexpectedly radical political changes. That liberalization of the economic system should be accompanied by some political relaxation was not surprising – how futile it was to attempt the first without the second had been made plain in the 1960s. The need for all-round reform had, after all, been implicit in alternative thinking about the economy. Without a climate that encouraged individual initiative and ambition and discouraged passivity and unthinking conformism, the reforms would get nowhere. Economic change required political and cultural change; the socialist market required socialist democracy. And in January 1987 the reform was given a dramatic change of emphasis. 'Democratization', Gorbachev told his no doubt astounded Central Committee colleagues, 'is not simply a slogan but the essence of perestroika.'[16]

'Democracy' and 'democratization' were, admittedly, familiar terms to any reader of the Soviet press. What they meant in the Soviet lexicon was activating the masses, getting them to work harder and to endorse the party's policies more wholeheartedly. From 1987, however, Gorbachev discarded the traditional meaning and came up with a different and distinctly unSoviet one. Democracy as he now presented it was about *empowering* the masses; it implied making the government accountable, having officials elected rather than simply appointed, and giving ordinary people a right of criticism. And in 1988 he dispelled any lingering hopes or fears that his democratization might be no more than cosmetic by making a blistering attack on the sham of Soviet democracy:

> the proclamation of democratic principles in words and authoritarianism in reality, incantations about democracy from the tribune but voluntarism and subjectivism in practice, talk about democratic institutions and an effective flouting of the norms of a socialist way of life.[17]

This denunciation of Soviet so-called democracy heralded a 'cardinal reform' of the political system, which began at the Nineteenth Party Conference in the summer of 1988. The aim of the reform was to draw a sharp line between the roles of party and state – in effect to restrict the party to a strategic and guiding role – and to resuscitate the soviets, rescuing them from the comatose condition in which they had been since the 1920s. The outcome was a new legislature, the Congress of People's Deputies, chosen in 1989 by competitive elections, and a smaller body derived from it, the Supreme Soviet, which would do the day-to-day work of legislating. The reform was not so radical that rival organizations were allowed to challenge the party. But although the elections took place under the one-party system, they stirred immense interest and were fiercely fought. A number of former dissidents, including Andrei Sakharov, managed to overcome the obstacles put in their way; so too did the disgraced former Moscow party boss, Boris Yeltsin. The new legislature, almost at once christened a 'parliament', provided what no forum in living memory had: real debate on issues of public importance. Together with it, there appeared a new chief executive – the chairman of the Supreme Soviet. Since Gorbachev combined the new post with being general secretary of the party, and since the party kept its monopoly, no real alteration in power relationships occurred. That the chief executive of state was no longer a party appointment but was appointed by and accountable to a legislature elected relatively freely by the whole population nevertheless put down a marker for the future.

These were changes 'from above'. But there were also changes 'from below', encouraged by the dying away of fear and the new doctrine of 'socialist pluralism'. As fear diminished, grass-roots activity increased. Unofficial organizations began to be set up in 1987, and during 1988 their number mushroomed. Forbidden topics, such as crime, disasters, pollution, social deprivation, were openly and even obsessively discussed. Public opinion polls appeared. Even the church came back into the limelight, and in 1988 it celebrated a thousand years of Christianity in Russia with much panache.

These various changes were significant, yet within-system: the scope and pace of the change were dictated by the party, which was careful to protect itself. In the economic sphere, the state would continue to play the dominant role; as under NEP, cooperative and private enterprise would be restricted to the small-scale sector. Capitalism was praised for its adaptability and for having drawn 'enormous lessons from our revolution';[18] it was nevertheless seen as a mixed blessing whose evils had to be excluded and whose market practices needed to be tightly regulated. The liberalization under the 1987 State Enterprise Law had been somewhat formal, and the ministries in practice clawed back much of the power they had lost on paper. As for agriculture, a law of 1989 allowed land to be leased to private farmers, but *sale* of land on any large scale was forbidden. By the end of the decade, a few thousand private farms had been set up, but it looked very much as if Soviet agriculture would continue to be overwhelmingly collective.

The changes in the political sphere, while bold, were likewise within-system. The one-party state and the vanguard role of the party remained sacrosanct. The system of elections to the new legislature had been strongly biased in favour of party-approved candidates, and almost 90 per cent of deputies turned out to be party members. What qualified Gorbachev to be chairman of the Supreme Soviet was that he was party general secretary; and while in his new capacity he was nominally responsible to the legislature, his real accountability was still to the party's policy-making organ, the Politburo. The same policy of reviving the soviets but binding them to the party was applied at lower levels: regional soviets too were, at Gorbachev's insistence, to be chaired by the first secretary of the local party committee. 'If the soviets are to begin to work,' he argued, 'we must reinforce their authority with the authority of the party.'[19] The soviets would thus at one and the same time be encouraged to play a more active part and be held very firmly in check.

The aim of the reforms was in fact to achieve a modernized and democratized socialism which would incorporate the best of western practice while keeping the essence of the Soviet system. The new society would 'activate the human factor'; in plain language, it would encourage people to work harder and more effectively. Key beliefs were revised accordingly. Like Andropov, Gorbachev rejected any suggestion that equality meant levelling; but he went further and redefined it in terms of rights rather than material conditions. What was important, he insisted, was to achieve 'social justice', a new notion which implied that talent and effort should be rewarded commensurately and that the same laws and demands should be applied to everyone.[20] A safety net of welfare provisions would be kept; but social protection would be somewhat reduced, and the basis of the new society would be 'labour and only labour'.

As equality fell victim to the new thinking, so too did other basic values of Soviet socialism – collectivism, unthinking conformity, passive obedience to authority. What the new society required was a questioning, driving, risk-taking spirit. The fully realized socialist society would be 'a society of people with initiative', and pride of place in it would go to 'the innovator'.[21] The 'bourgeois vestiges' only a few years before condemned by Andropov as incompatible with socialism were thus in effect rehabilitated. There would be no more attempts to convert 'mine' into 'ours' or to replace the pursuit of private interest by selfless dedication to the public good. People would pursue their own creative ends and better others by doing so. All of this implied a more favourable view of the individual than any Russian government had taken before. There was no question, of course, of swinging to the ultra-individualism of the west. The deep-rooted belief that the individual who actively pursued his own ends was a threat to the general wellbeing and needed to be curbed nevertheless dropped away. What had to be done, Gorbachev argued, was to find a balance between the needs of the unfettered individual and those of the social whole, to achieve 'an organic blending of collectivist and individualist principles'.[22] Just as public and private interests had been reconciled under NEP, so they would be reconciled again, and still more effectively, in the new socialist order.

The individual could now, within wide limits, say what he wanted. Individualism implied diversity of opinions rather than a core of received wisdom which had to be accepted by all. But that was a disturbing and dangerous idea in a country where the state had always acted as if it possessed a monopoly of truth and as if any conflict between its interests and the citizens' was unthinkable. Andropov had hammered home the latter point as recently as 1983. Pluralism never-theless became a key concept of the reform programme. Socialism, Gorbachev declared, had to be 'a society of growing diversity in people's opinions, mutual relationships and activities'; it had to be marked by 'a huge diapason of opinions, convictions and judge-ments'.[23] There was a John Stuart Mill-ish flavour to this which, in a general secretary of the Communist Party, was astounding. Gorbachev's argument appeared to be the classic liberal one that all truths are partial and relative; that no opinions which are not mani-festly harmful should be repressed; that competition between ideas is vital. In January 1989 he poured cold water on the belief 'that some hold the truth in their hands while others are people who raise the banner of false values'. Six months later, he went as far as to deny that the party 'is infallible and possesses the absolute truth'.[24] Such an admission appeared to destroy the very bedrock of the party's monopoly. Yet Gorbachev seemed to see no incompatibility between that and his new-found liberality. The pluralism that would be permitted would be 'socialist' and clearly tagged as such. Moreover, the only pluralism in question was of *opinions;* there was no sugges-tion, as yet, of extending pluralism to political organizations.

The political system appropriate to the new socialism was, of course, democracy. Only democracy could 'end the deeply rooted apathy and give a powerful impetus to the socio-political activity of working people'. Only democracy could 'combine the interests of the indi-vidual with those of the collective and society as a whole'. Like pluralism, democracy would be 'socialist', and socialist democracy, Gorbachev insisted, had nothing in common with 'all-permissiveness'. There would in fact be 'an organic union of democracy and discipline, of independent action and responsibility, of rights and obligations ...'[25] 'Organic', incidentally, was a favourite word of the perestroika thinkers. But how could people be persuaded to use their rights 'responsibly' (another favourite word)? Only by increased mentoring. In the development of democracy, Gorbachev pointed out, 'a huge role belongs to party propaganda and agitation'.[26] That of course was the purest Leninism. You gave people freedom, but you first made sure that they would use it correctly.

This, then, was the new socialism. The interests of the individual and of society would be reconciled through democratization and a mixed economy. The outcome would be a Leninist mutuality in which people gave willing and active support to policies that were seen to reflect their own wishes and interests. A party that had returned to the correct path and an innately socialist population would thus be bonded, and any attempts by anti-socialist elements to come between them would be doomed to failure.

There were nevertheless areas of ambiguity and points of potential conflict within this Leninist framework. Perestroika activists called for the rebirth of civil society. They demanded that the state should be subordinated to this reborn civil society. They launched attacks on 'monopoly' and 'monocentrism'. Georgy Arbatov, for instance, put the case for non-party mass organizations which could act as a forum for critical ideas.[27] None of these suggestions necessarily violated perestroika's neo-Leninist framework. Subordinating state to society was not, after all, the same as making the party subordinate: the point of the 1988 political reconstruction had been to detach party from state and restore it to a genuinely Leninist vanguard role. The need for competition and diversity beneath the one-party umbrella had been recognized by Gorbachev himself. As for non-party organizations, they, Arbatov insisted, would be 'loyal' as well as 'critical'. 'Loyal but critical' was a characteristic notion for this stage of the reform process. Clash of ideas was healthy and necessary; what would emerge from the debate were correct policies, a fortified party, and further progress towards socialism. These were nevertheless dangerous ambiguities for the leadership, since they could easily be exploited by those who were ceasing to believe, or had never believed, in a Leninist framework for the new socialism.

As the reform process advanced, so the criticism became sharper and less loyal. The critics came, moreover, from both ends of the political spectrum. From the 'right' (as Soviet usage had it), that is, from party traditionalists who feared that the reforms were jeopardizing the party and its socialist mission; but also from the 'left', that is, from those who wanted the reform to go further and faster and even to leave socialism behind altogether. Gorbachev's reaction was to treat both sets of opponents as extremists who were challenging a golden mean of moderation and common sense. Those on the right mistakenly distrusted the masses and underestimated their commitment to socialism; those on the left were 'ultra-radicals' and 'adventurers' who wanted to 'jump stages' and were advocating 'borrowed', that is, unSoviet, values. Both were, in their different ways, anti-socialists and spoilers. The party, Gorbachev insisted, was the sole integrating and consolidating force; it alone was capable of 'assuring social stability on the basis of revolutionary changes'. The party would synthesize opinions, unite the various layers of society, and accomplish 'the complex work of harmonizing different interests'.[28] It would in fact perform that unifying and guiding function, that vanguard role, which Lenin had envisaged. And, with public opinion behind them, its leaders would rapidly, though democratically, extinguish their opponents' challenge.

3

But there was no surge of public opinion to the leadership's side, no sweeping of its opponents into oblivion. On the contrary, left and right encroached steadily on the centre's following. Something was going badly wrong with the reform project. The most obvious problem was economic.

It had been clear from the outset that economic and political reform had to be mutually dependent. Without democratization, there could be no economic reform. That in turn, however, would repercuss upon politics; and if the party was to continue to dominate a democratized state, the success of its economic policies was vital.

That economic reform would have beneficial effects had been little questioned in the reform camp. Economic liberalization and a limited tolerance of the market had boosted support for the party during the 1920s; in the admittedly different conditions of the 1980s, they were likely to do the same. Belief in the 1920s precedent was strengthened by a flurry of articles which suggested that NEP had improved living standards significantly and that the NEP approach to socialism had remained viable up until Stalin's arbitrary destruction of it.[29]

But not only were conditions in the 1980s vastly different from those of the NEP decade. The assumptions underlying the two reforms were far from similar. Market relations had been accepted in the 1920s as a temporary deviation from socialist practice. That the socialist economic system was inherently superior and that its advantages would sooner or later be generally recognized had not been doubted by NEP's supporters. 'Overcoming the market through the market' had been Bukharin's maxim. The market would bring the peasants to socialism; in doing so, it would liquidate itself.

By the 1980s, the market was seen very differently. Socialism had long since been formally achieved; the inadequacies of the socialist economic system had become glaring; and few, other than party diehards, now denied the effectiveness of the capitalist alternative. Market principles could not therefore be passed off as a temporary expedient, as something that would help the transition to a fully realized socialist economic system. The market would have to be permanent – a continuing and vital corrective to socialist centralization, a gingering element without which the system would ossify. The superiority of socialist economic principles would nevertheless still be asserted; the market would be tightly restricted; and two mutually antagonistic economic systems would be locked together in an uncomfortable permanent embrace. Not surprisingly, critics soon began to point out that the systems were incompatible and likely to harm one another, that a choice between them had to be made. But the most damning comment on the attempt to splice plan and market came from the performance of the economy itself.

Andropov's disciplinarian measures had had good effects which continued into the early perestroika period. In 1988, however, a downturn in economic performance set in as the impact of liberalization began to be felt. Industrial output declined. Wage increases ran ahead of increases in productivity. The state budget plunged deeply into deficit. Essential goods became hard to find. Food-rationing was introduced over an increasing area on goods such as meat, butter and sugar. By the end of the 1980s, a number of staple foodstuffs had become virtually unobtainable in state shops. What could not be bought in the shops could still be got via the black market or the new cooperatives, though only of course by those who could afford high prices. Scarcity was at least a familiar enough problem. But price inflation, which made itself felt from 1988, was, by contrast, an unfamiliar evil – stable prices had been one of the benefits of the Soviet economic system and they had done much to make people feel secure. Full employment had been another such source of security. That too, however, now seemed in jeopardy. Some reformers were even recommending unemployment as a necessary stimulant for the economy. To the ordinary citizen, economic reform began to look like a licence for the few to better themselves at the expense of the many. The reformers had promised a synthesis of two contrasting economic systems which would preserve the best and discard the worst of each. By the end of the decade, however, their policies seemed to be having entirely the opposite effect.

While the economic reform was failing badly, the political reform was proving a runaway success – mid-1989 saw the meeting, amidst scenes of euphoria, of the first-ever Soviet parliament. The two reform processes had thus become wildly asymmetrical. Political reform, seen originally as a necessary auxiliary to the more important economic task, had outgrown that modest role, become an end in itself and succeeded beyond all expectations. It began to look, however, as if the asymmetry in the two processes would lead each to damage the other. Worker discontent was being expressed in strikes, go-slows and other forms of disruptive activity unknown to the command economy, and this was making the economic downturn sharper still. No wonder that some perestroika supporters had second thoughts about carrying out economic and political reform simultaneously. Economic reform, they decided, should have come first and should have been introduced with an 'iron hand'.[30] Admiring glances were even cast in the direction of General Pinochet. But just as political reform was blighting the chances of economic renovation, so the performance of the economy was damaging the party's popularity and its chances of continuing to dominate Soviet politics. What was happening in fact was an NEP effect in reverse. Improving living standards would no doubt have consolidated the party's hold upon society; but nothing was more likely to weaken and destroy that hold than a collapse in living standards.

And not only in the economic sphere were things going wrong. It began to look as if the renowned stability of Soviet society, which had been one of the party's proudest boasts, had been based less on socialist consciousness than on fear. As fear diminished, so discipline gave way. Violence, corruption and dishonesty of all kinds escalated. The fabric of everyday life was in danger. So too was the Union itself.

The economic reforms might have made things worse, but they had at least been an attempt to tackle a widely recognized problem. The nationalities problem, however, had not appeared on the original reform agenda at all, and right-wing opponents of the leadership claimed that it was largely of perestroika's own making. That was hardly fair: perestroika had not created the problem, but it had allowed long-suppressed grievances to come into the open. By 1989, Soviet rule was under serious challenge in various parts of the periphery, especially the Baltic states, Georgia and Moldavia. In the Baltic states, for instance, popular front organizations with widespread support were rejecting the legitimacy of Soviet power in their territories and the very idea of Soviet nationhood. This unexpected rebellion bewildered and shocked many Russians. They were having to accept loss of the 'outer empire', that buffer zone of satellite East European states created by Stalin after the war. That was disturbing enough. But now the 'inner empire', which had belonged to Russia far longer, and was home to many millions of Russians, was under threat as well. It began to look as if perestroika had opened a Pandora's box of evils.

Reacting belatedly to the non-Russians'revolt, the government fell back on Lenin – it condemned previous violations of Leninist principles and assured the non-Russians that nationalities policy would from now on be completely Leninist. A policy statement in September 1989 confirmed the right of self-determination, but distinguished between that and secession and firmly rejected what it called 'separatist nationalism'. A few months later a new law confirmed the right of secession, but hedged it about with such conditions as to make it in practice a dead letter. Lenin's nationalities policy had rested of course on the assumption that socialism would dissipate national consciousness, that Soviet identity would get the better of separate national identities. The revolt of the late 1980s was proof that nothing of the kind had happened; even in Russia itself, national awareness was on the rise. Decades of repression in the name of socialism had in fact had the effect of strengthening national feeling where it already existed and even of creating it in some areas where it had previously been non-existent. The new nationalities policy was as a result wholly inadequate. In the rebels' eyes, this was mere chicanery in Leninist trappings, and the government's attempt to fob them off simply made them pursue their cause more determinedly.

Faced with a spreading revolt, what could the government do? It could fall back on the traditional methods of force and fraud. Alternatively, it could turn the right of self-determination into a reality. The first course, however, would flout the most basic principles of the new socialism; as for the second, it seemed madness to let the Union disintegrate at the very time when a Leninist policy was at last being implemented and when, in addition, the nations of western Europe were moving in precisely the opposite direction – away from national self-sufficiency and towards economic and even political integration. Yet these were clear-cut and potentially viable policies; the government, it began to appear, had no clear-cut or viable policy. Finding a Leninist middle way in the nationalities question would be as difficult as in the economic. Converting the Union to that voluntary basis envisaged by Lenin appeared no more than a pipedream. Either the minority peoples continued to be coerced, or else those who so desired were allowed to depart. These were the obvious options, but both were repugnant to the reformers. They could only procrastinate; as they did, the rebellion spread.

4

Perestroika and the new socialism were in crisis: of that by the later part of 1989 there could be no doubt. There were few if any signs of Leninist mutuality, of dialogue and cooperation between a party and people agreed on essentials. The party was increasingly divided by raucous conflict; ordinary people were becoming weary, disillusioned and scared of the prospect of losing the traditional securities of Soviet life. The reformers' hope had been that an imposed conformity would be replaced by real consensus. Instead, society was becoming deeply polarized. Much of the middle class was swinging to the left, while party hard-liners were trawling for support among a troubled and aggrieved working class.

In September, one of the reform's original supporters came out with the claim that Marxism-Leninism had exhausted its potential, that nothing less than a completely fresh start would do. Still more devastatingly, this renegade declared that the party had 'led the country nowhere' for seventy years.[31] A chorus of voices would soon be saying the same: the country had been taken down a blind alley, what was necessary was to go back not simply to 1929 but to 1917 itself.

Suggestions that the October Revolution had been a mistake predictably enough provoked the right into an impassioned defence of Soviet pieties. These polar opposites were, however, agreed on one thing: that the Leninist *via media* was a make-believe. There was not and there never had been any such middle way. The choice was simply between a traditional Soviet way and a liberal way. Either plan or market. Either authoritarian state or democracy. Either firm restraint of the non-Russians or a real right of self-determination. The leadership had in fact to give up its present position, which was unviable and crumbling by the day, and move to right or left – either go back to collectivism and authoritarianism or go forward and reconstruct society on a fully individualistic basis.

The case for individualism had been put most cogently by Igor Klyamkin. Russian society, Klyamkin argued, had been transformed during the Soviet years, but the transformation had not yet been reflected in the political structure. Peasant Russia had given way to urban Russia; the 'obedient peasant', who was patriarchal in his thinking and accepted a collectivist 'we' created for him by the elite, had been replaced by the 'unfettered and obstinate townsman', who demanded a new 'we' that resulted from 'the interaction of millions of free "I"s'. The idea that freely interacting 'I's might create a new kind of societal coherence, and not simply lead to mayhem, was, Klyamkin admitted, relatively recent in Russia. But this new idea reflected a new reality. It was, he might have added, what a burgeoning middle class which had at last found its voice was clamouring for.[32]

If the individual was to be freed and society reconstructed to enable him or her to achieve fulfilment, then every aspect of the reform programme would have to be rethought: its economics, its politics, its attitude to the nationalities, its basic self-justification. The economics of the reform had been openly savaged as early as May 1987. The very term 'market socialism', L. Popkova declared, was an absurdity. 'Where there is socialism, there is no place for the market and the liberal spirit.' Socialism and the market were fundamentally incompatible. 'Being a little pregnant is impossible. Either plan or market – either directives or competition.' Social-democratic ideas of a 'Third Way' had failed; the west, Popkova pointed out, had outgrown this illusion and had rediscovered the advantages of a pure market economy.[33] In early 1987 such ideas were startling; but as the economy plunged into crisis they grew rapidly in appeal, and by the end of the decade economic thinking in left-intelligentsia circles was more Friedmanite than Leninist.

The swing towards the free market was reflected in attitudes towards NEP. Till 1988 the comment was overwhelmingly favourable. 1988 saw in particular much euphoric comment on 'the Bukharin alternative', unleashed by Bukharin's rehabilitation early in the year. From 1989, however, the comment became more critical: the successes of NEP had, it appeared, been exaggerated, while its intrinsic deficiencies had been overlooked. As Bukharin's appeal faded, so a new star rose in the firmament: Peter Stolypin, chief minister of Russia from 1906 to 1911, whose attempts to replace the communal system by independent peasant proprietorship would have led, it was suggested, to a prosperous agriculture – had the October Revolution not cut them off.[34]

The political counterpart to the economics of individualism was of course uninhibited representative democracy. The democratized one-party state was no more acceptable to the left than the strictly regulated market; from mid-1989, there were increasing calls for abolition of the party's monopoly and a complete separation of party and state. Among the 300–odd left-oppositionists in Congress, there emerged a 'Democratic Platform' within the party and in due course an organization called 'Democratic Russia'. The democrats were, however, heavily outnumbered in a parliament of 2250 deputies. Moreover, unlike in Poland or even the Baltic states, in Russia democracy had little appeal outside the educated middle class. There was no nation-wide movement for democratic reform, no pressure for it from the factory and the farm. That was why the democrats needed Boris Yeltsin, the disgraced former Moscow party boss who against the odds had barnstormed to a sweeping electoral victory in Moscow. Yeltsin on the face of it had little in common with the democrats, many of whom viewed him at first with deep suspicion. A rough-hewn provincial of peasant origin, he had no roots in the Alternative Tradition and had come only belatedly and somewhat opportunistically to a democratic position. But he had what the intellectuals of the left lacked: political flair, an unerring populist touch, an ability to reach out to the masses. Thanks to him, 'democracy', presented as an outright challenge to Gorbachev's democratization and as an implicit alternative to socialism, became a highly effective political slogan.

The democrats inevitably clashed with the leadership on the nation-alities issue. As consistent democrats, they could hardly not defend the minorities. The collective rights of peoples were inseparable from the rights of the single individual; the two clearly stood or fell together. But if there was principle in the democrats' stand, there was also self-interest. Their defence of the minorities may have been less than whole-hearted, but the national principle enabled many of them to become enthusiastic nationalists – *Russian* nationalists – for reasons that were largely self-serving. In the Soviet parliament they were no more than a small minority; but in the Russian parliament, due to be elected in fairer conditions in March 1990, the democrats, under Yeltsin's charismatic leadership, had a good chance of emerging as the dominant force. Were that to happen, they would inevitably tilt for the rights of the Russian parliament as against those of the parliament in which they were powerless. Russian nationalism in fact gave the democrats a cause which they could use against the leadership far more effectively than the middle-class one of democracy. By turning themselves into Russian nationalists, the democrats uncorked emotions which the Soviet state had long since bottled up – and, once uncorked, those emotions could hardly be put back.

The left, then, assailed the leadership for its inadequate economic policies, for its half-hearted democratization, for its mishandling of the nationalities issue. The attack reached deeper still, however – to the distinction between Stalinism and pre-Stalinist Bolshevism, whose work the leadership claimed to be carrying on. This distinction, indis-pensable to the reformers' case, was demolished in the winter of

1988–9 in a remarkable series of articles by the philosopher Alexander Tsipko.[35]

Far from representing a counter-revolutionary break with Bolshevism, Stalinism, Tsipko argued, had been a natural outgrowth from it, a product of the Russian revolutionary milieu with its utopianism and its lack of compassion and of realism. The political mechanisms of Stalinism had all been created under Lenin by the Bolshevik Old Guard. True, near to the end of his life 'Vladimir Ilich renounced the naive belief in pure socialism'; but the majority of party activists did not join him in this volte-face. Stalin faithfully reflected what most activists continued to believe in, and the affinity between him and them was the fundamental reason for his victory over Bukharin.[36] The implication of Tsipko's remarks was that the drama of Lenin's final months was a beguiling irrelevance – even had he lived, Lenin would have been unable to prevent the Stalinist outcome.

In Tsipko's wake, many other commentators took up the same theme: that Stalinism's roots lay in the work of Lenin and the Bolshevik Old Guard, that the 'administrative-command system' was not created by Stalin but merely brought to completion by him. The same message was thundered from abroad by Alexander Solzhenitsyn, whose *The Gulag Archipelago* was published in the Soviet Union in 1989. Solzhenitsyn provided the Soviet reader with a massively documented account of how the regime had maltreated its opponents in prisons and labour camps, and by tracing the Gulag system back to the very origins of the Soviet state he wiped out any suggestion of a sharp qualitative distinction between Leninism and Stalinism. A steady flow of other publications exposing cruelty and repression during the early Soviet years further eroded the impression that the regime had got off to a relatively humane start. By the end of 1989, the idea of Stalinism as a counter-revolutionary coup, an aberration unrelated to the early years of Soviet power, had more or less been swept away. The Soviet experience, it began to look, was all of a piece. It had to be accepted, or rejected, as a whole. With that at least, the right agreed.

Many right oppositionists, like many on the left, had begun as perestroika supporters: among them Yegor Ligachev, the right's eventual leader, who remained as Gorbachev's deputy in the Politburo until 1989. The future rightists had accepted the need for significant economic reform, had put a traditional gloss on Gorbachev's utterances about democracy, had taken seriously his claim that reform would only strengthen the party. Well before the end of 1987, however, these conservative reformers had been undeceived. Their outrage at what was happening, their sense of having been duped, was hardly surprising. Gorbachev, it seemed, was trying to turn the party into what it had never been – a democratic and publicly accountable body, a political party proper. He was justifying his actions by an interpretation of early Soviet history that was unrecognizable to them. And his policies had taken so radical a turn that they were threatening more than the power and privileges of the elite; the dominant position of the party itself was being jeopardized by the unleashed hordes of anti-socialists and nationalists.

The right's fight-back began in March 1988 when a certain Nina Andreeva published, most probably with Ligachev's connivance, a broadside against the reforms. The target of her attack was 'left-liberal intelligentsia socialism', which contrasted 'the inherent worth of individuality' with 'proletarian collectivism' and preached 'the democratic charms of contemporary capitalism'.[37] Andreeva attacked conservative nationalists as well, but for her they were clearly a sideshow. What was looming, she indicated, was a battle between left and right: between liberals masquerading as socialists and genuine Soviet socialists, who continued to emphasize the leading role of party and working class. This was in its way a prescient enough analysis. And, traditionalist that she was, Andreeva could not resist calling her opponents 'cosmopolitans', that is, lackeys of the west and of international Jewry.

In 1989 the issue was fought out in published proceedings of the Central Committee, with Ligachev insisting that party and nation faced a crisis that could be staved off only by firm action against anti-socialist and nationalist forces. The party had been infiltrated by pseudo-socialists bent upon breaking up the Union and creating a multi-party political system:

> And in the economic system they aim at a transition to a full market economy and to private property – which means, though for the moment they are quiet about this, hired labour, unemployment, a profound social stratification, the worsening of the living conditions of millions of people, and the enrichment of a handful.[38]

Party bosses were by now an endangered species. Their revolt was natural; what made it serious was that they could look to important sources of support. First, traditional Russian nationalists. There had been a strong undercurrent of Russian nationalism in the later 'stagnation era', and this had now broken the surface. Traditional nationalists were very different from those former perestroika supporters now turning to liberal nationalism in that they staunchly opposed both liberalism and socialism. A 'red–brown' alliance was nevertheless emerging between the traditional nationalists and party diehards. The two sides were brought together by a common attachment to Russia's great-power role and by their hostility to the west. The ending of the cold war and the likely loss of the 'outer empire' inflamed these feelings. Moreover, they had a common commitment to defence of the Soviet welfare state. And their pro-welfare and anti-western views came together in a fierce rejection of 'marketeers' as people who wanted to stratify society, destroy traditional Russian morality, and turn Russia into an economic appendage of the west.

While party diehards reached out to nationalists, they also looked confidently to the armies of the working class, whose members had suffered a double blow from perestroika. The tacit contract under which, in return for loyalty, the regime favoured the working class and satisfied its basic material requirements had been set aside. In addition, the working class had been dethroned from the privileged position formally accorded it. Class values had been replaced by 'all-human' ones , and these supposedly class-neutral values were in effect skewed towards the middle class, which emerged as the new favoured class. It was middle-class people who had enthusiastically welcomed perestroika and identified Gorbachev as one of their own. As for the workers, they, with good reason, had been no more than lukewarm towards a socialism that was culturally alien to them and tilted towards the enterprising professional. One of perestroika's strategists had warned, rightly enough, that the reforms could not serve the immediate interests of every section of society and that most workers, faced with higher prices, unemployment and other 'minuses', were likely to make common cause with party conservatives.[39]

The 'minuses' in the end proved worse than could have been predicted. No wonder that by 1990 party traditionalists were going on the offensive. And while they attacked the reformers for having betrayed socialism, the working class and the Soviet heritage, the left was assailing them for not being full-blooded democrats and for not having made a complete break with the past.

The basic assumption of the reform had been that elements of capitalist economics and western democracy could be grafted onto Soviet practice in such a way as to rejuvenate the socialist movement. By the end of the decade, that assumption was looking threadbare. There could, it seemed, be no viable and lasting compromise solutions in either economics or politics. The 'safe' course of major but within-system reform had in the event turned a potential crisis into a real one.

Behind the new thinking there had been a one-sided reading of Lenin and the early Soviet experience, a reading in which truth had mingled with a great deal of make-believe. Lenin had indeed wanted a relationship of genuine mutuality between a party and people agreed on essentials. Such a relationship had, however, by no means been achieved in his own lifetime, and the economic and cultural transformation he had seen as necessary to achieve it had still lain well beyond the horizon. Six decades after his death, conditions were markedly different. People lived much better, yet the socialist economic system had clearly failed to produce abundance or to outperform its capitalist rival. People were well-educated, yet cultural revolution had not reshaped human nature or replaced self-seeking by a socialist dedication to the public good. In such circumstances, 'going back to Lenin' and relaxing central controls were bound to have effects very different from those intended. Far from strengthening the party and the socialist cause, the new Leninism had proved destructive of both. The leadership would continue to put a Leninist gloss upon its policies. However, the great belief in the transformative power of a Leninist, within-system reform – that belief which had inspired the perestroika revolution – had by the end of the 1980s been more or less killed off.

5

Where did the leadership go from here? Gorbachev's commitment to socialism remained unshakeable. He continued, moreover, to count on the innate socialism of ordinary Soviet people, their willingness to make a 'socialist choice' and to uphold socialist values. But Marxism-Leninism had become an anachronism, while alternative socialism, after the briefest of heydays, had exhausted its usefulness – in this situation it was by no means clear what socialist values now were and in what direction a socialist choice pointed.

Movement in some direction was, however, essential. The one-party state was no longer tenable; the mixture of socialist and free market principles was creating chaos in the economy; the revolt of the nationalities was spreading; and in the autumn of 1989 Gorbachev began moving away from the assumptions on which the new socialism had been based. A watershed was being crossed, that he recognized clearly enough. The analogy, he suggested, was with NEP. That had been 'a revolution within the revolution', one 'no less profound, perhaps,

than the October Revolution'. What was happening now was, similarly, 'a revolution within the revolution', 'a realistic path forward to
the new society'. Now, as then, 'new economics, a reorganization of
the political system, a genuinely federal state' were needed.[40]

That NEP represented a change for the better was basic alternative
thinking. Gorbachev was, however, going beyond that. Just as NEP
had been a 'revolution within the revolution', so the reconceived new
socialism was a clear departure from the policies and principles
adhered to since 1985. Lenin, Gorbachev was at pains to point out,
had made major changes at critical moments. In particular, he had
profoundly changed his attitude towards socialism in 1921, though his
colleagues had failed to recognize the profundity of the change.
Gorbachev too, the implication ran, had fundamentally rethought his
view of socialism; and he too was being plagued by colleagues who
failed to understand the need for a new conception.

Gorbachev was moving in effect from the mainstream alternative
position to one that more clearly resembled Roy Medvedev's. Yet the
circumstances in which he was adopting a more radical strategy were
very far from the ones envisaged by Medvedev. The leadership was
under assault, the economy was in free fall, the Union was being challenged by insurgent nationalists – that was not the background against
which Medvedev had seen the party sweeping to victory in a fully
democratized polity. Gorbachev had little choice, however, since he
had set in motion forces which now threatened to engulf him. Public
opinion was demanding more rapid and more radical reform; by going
with it, by riding the tide of opinion, he might yet manage to direct
what he had unleashed.

In February–March 1990 Gorbachev acted decisively to end the
anomaly of the democratized one-party state and extricate himself
from the absurdity of preaching democratic socialism while insisting
on the party's monopoly and rejecting multi-partyism. At a dramatic
Central Committee meeting the party agreed to renounce its
monopoly and allow an amendment to the clause of the constitution
(clause six) which enshrined it. This was a bitter pill for traditionalists,
one of whom rightly enough pointed out that what passed as democracy now was not what Gorbachev had offered the party in April
1985.[41] As a sweetener to them, the party's vanguard role and democratic centralism were in principle retained. The vanguard role was,
however, defined in such a way as to be little more than a totem, while
democratic centralism was largely nullified as an instrument of
oligarchic control by Gorbachev's strong emphasis on the democratic

component. There was no way of disguising the historic defeat suffered by party traditionalists, who had given up, at least on paper, the monopoly position which the party had in practice occupied since 1918. They had surrendered to the leadership but even more to public opinion; and what had stung them most was not liberal attacks but abuse from rank-and-file party members demanding democracy within the party itself. *Pravda*'s editor justly enough commented that what had happened was 'in the literal sense a revolution (*perevorot*)'.[42] The party had been put on a more or less equal footing, constitutionally speaking, with other socio-political organizations, and the way had been opened for the creation of a multi-party system.

A follow-up to this demotion of the party came in March, when Gorbachev transferred to a new chief executive position – president of the USSR. As president, he would have greater powers than as chairman; but, more important, the new position was wholly detached from the party. In his new capacity he would look for advice to a non-party body, the Presidential Council, and he would be accountable solely to parliament. Crucially, he would have nothing to do with the Politburo, whose remit was henceforth limited strictly to party affairs as newly defined. Thus, almost casually, the body which had run the country since Stalin was pushed to the sidelines. True, Gorbachev remained as party general secretary. He made it plain, however, that the presidency came first. As president, he would act not on behalf of 'some separate layer and political tendency' but would strive to be 'the representative of the whole nation'.[43] With that, the divorce between party and nation was finalized. For seventy years, the party had insisted on the complete identity between its interests and those of the people, whose will it claimed to embody. Now it had accepted demotion to the humble status of a separate political tendency.

In his economic outlook, too, Gorbachev became more radical. In May 1989 he had called for a 'full-blooded socialist market' and added that 'no more effective and democratic method of economic management has been devised by mankind'. In November he endorsed capitalism with the comment that Marx had 'underestimated' its capacity to perfect itself and assure a high level of wellbeing for most people.[44] During 1990 he gave up describing the market as 'socialist', spoke out in favour of private enterprise as the motor of economic growth, called for price reform, and argued that only the market and private property could underpin democracy. But how sweeping should the conversion to market principles be? What in particular should the scope and speed of privatization be? Debate on these issues intensified in the summer of 1990 when the

Shatalin Plan, prepared by radical economists and backed by Yeltsin's Russian government, proposed a 500–day transition to a market economy, with large-scale privatization of enterprises, major cuts in government spending and considerable devolution of financial power to the republics. A more conservative alternative, put forward by Nikolai Ryzhkov, the Soviet premier, envisaged a'regulated market', a much slower pace of privatization and retention of financial control by the Union government in Moscow. Gorbachev's inclination, or so it seemed in the summer of 1990, was for the former.

Pressure from the republics was meanwhile radicalizing his attitude towards the Union. The Baltic republics, Georgia and Moldavia wanted to break away completely – Lithuania even made a formal declaration of independence in March 1990. The other republics seemed ready to stay within the Union; but, with a Yeltsin-led Russia to the fore, they were demanding that they, rather than the centre, should determine what rights they should possess. Most issued declarations of 'sovereignty' – a high-sounding bluff which implied the right to secede rather than any immediate intention of doing so. Gorbachev tried to span the gulf between himself and the rebels with the slogan 'a strong centre and strong republics'. In March 1990, however, he made a major concession: the treaty of 1922, by which the Union had been created, would be revised. From then on, the nature of the new treaty was the central issue between the leadership and those republics still prepared to stay within the Union. In April 1991, Gorbachev and nine republican leaders agreed on the broad outlines of a new treaty, under which wide powers would be devolved to the republics. Membership of the new Union would be voluntary. That being so, those republics which had *not* signed the agreement – the Baltic ones, Armenia, Georgia and Moldavia – would evidently be outside it.

Gorbachev's radicalism was, however, all too often half-hearted and begrudging, and a vein of contradiction ran through it. The political reforms were the most radical, yet even these fell short of what many on the left demanded. The party might have lost its monopoly, but it had kept its 'vanguard role'. As president, Gorbachev claimed to represent 'the whole people'; he had not, however, risked a popular election and had been voted into office only by Congress deputies, themselves elected under the now discredited 1989 electoral system. The democratizing president thus by no means had a democratic mandate; and his lack of a proper mandate would be highlighted in June 1991, when Boris Yeltsin swept to a convincing victory for the presidency of Russia in a genuinely popular election.

There was similar shilly-shallying on the economic front. Gorbachev had seemed to give his support to Shatalin's plan for rapid transition to a market economy; but in September 1990 he had second thoughts and asked for the two rival plans to be conflated. In reality, he had given way to conservative objections to a plan that would have entailed large-scale privatization, massive cuts in government expenditure, and a transfer of economic powers from the centre to the republics. And it was on the ultra-sensitive nationalities issue that he came under greatest pressure from a now militant right. In January 1991 army and KGB units made a cack-handed attempt at repressing the independence movements in Lithuania and Latvia. The right had acted without Gorbachev's authorization; but he felt unable to dissociate himself from what had happened, still less to punish those responsible, and his weak-kneed response destroyed what credibility he still retained with the democrats. After the bloodshed in Vilnius, 'a humane and democratic socialism' could hardly be taken very seriously.

6

Thus Gorbachev twisted and turned, torn between what a fast-deteriorating situation seemed to him to require (drastic economic change, major concessions to the nationalities) and what conservative elements in the leadership and the military would allow him. Beyond these immediate battles, however, lay the question of what kind of society was being created. That the new society would be socialist, more completely and genuinely so than Soviet society had ever been before, was basic. Yet the new socialism had had to come to terms with democracy, the market and federalism, and in adapting to these alien elements it had become very different from what had always passed as socialism in the Soviet Union.

Soviet socialism had throughout been strongly collectivist in its nature and its doctrines. It spoke above all to the working class. It stressed the need for central planning and public ownership. It took pride in providing a high level of welfare services. It aimed to create a society based on cooperation rather than competition, a society that was homogeneous both materially and in its members' fundamental assumptions. It appealed to the instinct for group solidarity. It cultivated nationalist and anti-western emotions. It had a strong statist emphasis, and it counted on the party playing an unchallenged 'leading and guiding role' for the foreseeable future.

Socialism understood in such terms had, however, been largely discarded by the time the Central Committee confronted the issue of the monopoly. One speaker in the debate pointed out that the party now accepted much that until recently would not have been seen as belonging to socialism at all – 'Individual freedom as the supreme value, political pluralism, the market, a multi-faceted economy, variety in the forms of property, parliamentarism.'[45]

The 'revolution' of February–March 1990 completed a sea-change in the official understanding of socialism. But were these new values not the 'borrowed values' which Gorbachev had once accused his opponents of adopting? Had the party not been led into the old heresy of social democracy? Friendly gestures were indeed made to western social democrats, and credit was claimed for ending the historical schism within the international socialist movement; but when asked whether he was not more of a social democrat than a communist, Gorbachev not surprisingly side-stepped the question.[46] The larger issue of where the leadership stood in relation to the socialist idea could not, however, be ducked. In essence there were two problems. How did the new socialism relate to the 'classical model' – to Marx, Engels and Lenin? And what was specifically socialist about it?

As for the classics, the approach taken was 'creative'. The main feature of Lenin's thought had been 'anti-dogmatic breadth and freedom', or so the party's leading ideologist insisted, while Marx's favourite motto, Gorbachev pointed out, had been 'Question everything.' Such 'creativity' cleared the way for a free-and-easy attitude to the classics. Their legacy would still be taken into account, but interpreted undogmatically, and in interpreting it due weight would be given to 'the historical experience of the twentieth century'.[47] In reality, Marxist socialism had been discarded. A tenuous link was kept with Lenin by the suggestion that in the early 1920s he had fundamentally changed his view of socialism, but it was kept only by in effect detaching him more or less completely from Marx.

The question of interpretation was brought to a head by the pressing need for a new party programme to replace the now glaringly out-of-date 1961 one (according to which the threshold of communism should of course have long since been passed). Major changes to the existing programme had been approved by the Twenty-Seventh Party Congress in 1986 – but by now nothing less than an entirely new document would do. Amidst fierce debate in the summer of 1991, Gorbachev insisted that the old model of socialism was bankrupt. There had to be 'a fundamental change in our entire viewpoint on socialism – we will not find answers to our problems in the framework of the old model'. And when the draft of the new programme came out, it made some bows to the classics but went on to argue that socialism's 'arsenal' needed to include 'all the wealth of our own and world socialist and democratic thought'.[48] Eclecticism indeed!

The wider the party cast its net, however, the harder it became to put a recognizably socialist gloss on what it caught. The question 'What *is* socialism?' became unavoidable. Until the reforms, such a question would simply have elicited the restatement of long-acknowledged truths. The old certainties had by now, however, been swept away; and the deeper the reform cut, the more urgent the need for a new definition became. Gorbachev admitted the need early in 1988 – 'We proclaimed the slogan "More socialism!" – and must decide what values and principles should today be considered truly socialist!' By November 1989, the need had become urgent enough to require a whole paper from him on 'the socialist idea'. 'The idea of socialism, as we currently understand it', he declared, 'is, above all, the idea of freedom.' 'Democracy and freedom', he continued, 'are the great values of human civilization, which we have inherited and are imbuing with a socialist content.' The content, however, remained elusive; and as late as July 1991 Gorbachev would still be talking of the need to 'fill our socialist choice' with 'a new content'.[49]

But this was to put the problem the wrong way around. The new content had been largely decided – qualified parliamentary democracy, a regulated market economy, its entrepreneurial ethos softened by welfare provision that was, however, less lavish than before, and a federation of republics loosely controlled from the centre. What remained was the presentational task of persuading people that the new policies were indeed socialist; and that was made no easier by the ill-effects of the new policies.

Socialism as an idea nevertheless retained its appeal – opinion polls at the beginning of 1991 showed that two-thirds of the population still approved of it.[50] Gorbachev's insistent emphasis on 'our socialist choice' and 'our socialist values' therefore made sense – he was trying to tap a deep vein of socialist loyalism. But it was the pre-reform socialism that people clung to. This new socialism without roots in Russian or Soviet tradition was in danger of finding itself without a constituency. The professional classes were rapidly abandoning it, while those who still had socialist loyalties were by now more likely to see perestroika as a betrayal of socialism rather than as a fulfilment of it. The new socialism, in short, had gone too far from socialism's traditional moorings for much of the population – and yet not far enough for many of its initial supporters, who would be satisfied with nothing less than a complete break with the past.

Since 1989 there had been a stream of defections from among the initial supporters; the once-so-effective perestroika coalition had in fact fallen apart. Some of the defections had come as no great surprise. Yury Afanas'ev and Alexander Tsipko, for instance, had always given the impression that they would turn liberal at the first opportunity. There was a similar inevitability about Boris Yeltsin's defection. Gorbachev, however, suffered a severe personal blow from the loss of his friend and confidant Alexander Yakovlev, who had emerged as the chief ideologist of the new socialism. In the summer of 1991 Yakovlev made a much-trailed renunciation of the entire Soviet epoch and of Marxism, and rounded it off by declaring that 'socialism has been defeated'.[51] Losses to the left were balanced by defections to the right – the most important being that of Yegor Ligachev, who in 1990 became an outright critic of the leadership. Yet many who defected to left or right had come lately to the reform movement and had remained on one or other of its wings. Defections from the heart of the movement were more serious. Of these, the most striking was the loss of Tatyana Zaslavskaya.

This distinguished economist and sociologist had seemed the living embodiment of the alternative outlook. More than a mere theorist, Zaslavskaya had thought more hard-headedly about the strategy needed for a successful reform movement than anyone else. During the early 1980s she had come to know and admire Gorbachev and had pinned her hopes to him as a future reformer. She had then welcomed perestroika as a continuation of the long-abandoned work of October, indeed as 'the second socialist revolution', and had worked hard on its behalf.[52] But in 1990 the downward spiral of events brought her to a personal crisis. Socialism, she decided, had failed. It could no longer serve the country's needs. People now saw that the path followed for the last seventy years 'was all a mistake and led us up a blind-alley'.[53] The great majority now rejected socialist ideas; Gorbachev should do the same. The only way forward for Russia, this once most committed of perestroika supporters now believed, lay through the free market and parliamentary democracy.

With Tatyana Zaslavskaya's defection the Alternative Tradition had run its course; her words can be taken as an inscription upon its tomb. Alternative thinkers had correctly diagnosed the underlying malaise. They had explained the economic failure, the tendency away from social homogeneity, the apathy of the workforce, the general demor-alization and sense of exclusion. They had rightly pointed out that a monolithic economic and political system no longer corresponded to the needs of an increasingly sophisticated, diversified and stratified society. Their analysis had had an inspirational effect, gathering around it that coalition of would-be reformers without which pere-stroika would never have got going. Yet the Tradition's belief that the cure lay in resuscitating Soviet socialism's lost democracy, that democ-racy would stimulate economic growth and create the framework of a civil society, within which generally acceptable solutions to problems could then be found – that belief had proved utterly mistaken. The hoped-for consensus around redefined socialist goals never arrived. Far from setting an example of democratic unity, the party itself had split into bitterly feuding factions. This degeneration into factionalism put paid to hopes that, once freed from the oligarchs' grasp, the party would resume its proper function as embodiment of an evident general interest. As events spun out of control, it became clear that the unity of party and society, on which Soviet spokesmen had so prided themselves, had been due to coercion rather than anything else. The alternative to dictatorship was not consensus and a steady advance to socialism – it was conflict, fragmentation, a downward spiral into chaos and criminality. That conclusion, if borne out, had the most depressing implications for the Tradition's belief that socialism was unattainable without democracy and that a democratized party was the natural instrument of it.

That Soviet citizens would have difficulty in adjusting to something as unfamiliar as democracy came as no great surprise, of course. What had not been predicted, however, was that democracy would run counter not only to the culture of the masses but also to their imme-diate interests. Economic democratization produced problems rather than opportunities for blue-collar workers, who were less able than professionals to take advantage of the new freedoms and more likely to suffer from their ill effects. As for political democratization, that opened the door to division and conflict and thereby offended people who had been brought up to believe in solidarity and consensus. It appeared to pit social group against social group and ethnic group against ethnic group and thus to introduce the apple of discord into a society that had previously enjoyed harmony. Democracy had a stronger appeal to members of the middle class; yet by 1990 few of them still regarded socialism as its natural and necessary partner. Liberals had passed through the Alternative Tradition's school and left socialism behind altogether; rightists had long since rejected the Tradition's perversion, as they saw it, of Soviet history; indeed, few people of any persuasion took its analysis seriously any more. The Tradition had achieved a great deal, but its achievement had been negative rather than positive. It had done much to destroy an ossified political-economic system, but the alternative it had etched had quickly proved unviable, and by now its negative success was having altogether unanticipated adverse effects.

Gorbachev's personal popularity had by 1991 fallen almost to zero. The new socialism itself did little better, or so the results of the Russian presidential election of 12 June 1991 suggested. The outcome was a run-away victory for Boris Yeltsin, who took 57 per cent of the vote. Nikolai Ryzhkov, standing for a conservative version of perestroika, got a mere 17 per cent. The greatest loser, however, was the reformist candidate, Vadim Bakatin. Had the reforms been going to plan, then he, as representative of the new socialism, should have swept to victory. In fact, Bakatin got 3.5 per cent of the vote and came last of the six candidates, trailing even a neo-Stalinist. This election – the freest in Russia since 1917 – had in effect been a referendum on socialism and the CPSU in their old and new guises, and in it the party's standard-bearers had been crushed by a renegade who was promising to build a liberal-capitalist Russia on the ruins of the Soviet experiment.

Gorbachev continued to talk as if a democratic socialist way forward still existed. It did not. A resolution of the crisis created by a collapsing economy and the rebellion of the republics could not be far off, and when that occurred it would swing the country to the right or the left.

Meanwhile, what of Lenin?

7

The image of the founder had had to be reshaped. No longer the embodiment of party power and omniscience, Lenin had been turned into a human being, benevolent, democratic, struggling in difficult circumstances and burdened by a heavy sense of responsibility for what was happening. That was how Mikhail Shatrov portrayed him in his new play, *Onward, Onward, Onward!* , which stirred furious controversy when it was published in early 1988. The new Lenin invited not only admiration but sympathy; clearly a genius, he was also a fallible human of whom, in the end, too much had been asked. 'I entirely accept', Shatrov had him say, 'the moral guilt and the responsibility for what happened' – that is, for Stalinism.[54]

The reformers were, however, walking a tightrope: by making Lenin human they were in danger of making him merely ordinary and thus of robbing him altogether of his charismatic power. If he had indeed undergone a fundamental change of view in 1921, then the door was open to suggestions that he had got things seriously wrong before 1921. That was said clearly enough in May 1988, when for the first time in living memory he was publicly criticized. Lenin had rendered a 'great service', Vasily Selyunin stated, in turning the country towards NEP, but that had been a corrective to what, Selyunin indicated, had been a previous disservice – the course on which he had set the country in October 1917.[55] The view that Lenin had agonized at the end of his life and sensed a possible drift to disaster also opened him to attack. And if Lenin alone would have been capable of stopping Stalin, as Shatrov seemed to say, if he alone stood between the country and disaster, then had the revolution not been an irresponsible gamble? Alexander Tsipko, for one, saw his conversion to a sensible socialism coming too late and being too unrepresentative to have made much difference. The most that could be said for him was that he would have tried and failed. Before long, however, Tsipko had given up even that half-hearted defence: Lenin had not, he decided, changed his views after all.[56]

Muted and respectful criticism had by 1989 given way to outright condemnation. Vasily Grossman's novel *Forever Flowing*, published posthumously in June 1989, portrayed Lenin as the product of a thousand years of Russian servitude and as the apostle of a new and still more terrible slavery. Lenin in fact had been marked by 'implacable cruelty and contempt for the holy of holies of the Russian revolution – freedom'.[57] The image of benevolence was further dented by well-documented accusations that Lenin had been responsible for mass repressions, for example, of the Kronstadt mutineers. The writer Vladimir Soloukhin, moreover, broadened the accusation: Lenin, he charged, was responsible for more than individual killings – he had committed an act of genocide against the Russian nation as a whole. Indeed, Soloukhin claimed, 'Lenin was ready to destroy 90 per cent of the population in order that the remaining 10 percent should live under communism.'[58]

Not only was Lenin fiercely attacked – he was in danger of being sidelined. After decades in which 'Thou shalt have no other God but Lenin' had been the implicit first article of the party's creed, rival and long-suppressed symbolic persons returned to the stage. A cult developed around Nicholas II, whose thin, dignified face became a subject for pavement artists, and the cult added Nicholas to the line of saintly rulers of Russia by emphasizing the martyring of himself and his family, for which some now held Lenin directly responsible.[59] Peter the Great was another symbolic person whom Lenin had displaced, if less brutally, and he too now threatened a comeback: in September 1990, 20 000 people gathered in Leningrad's Palace Square to demand that their city be renamed St Petersburg. Of the rival gods, the most formidable, however, was God himself. Religion could now be practised openly, church bells rang out, and the Orthodox Church had even begun holding services as close to the epicentre of the Lenin cult as St Basil's Cathedral. Lenin meanwhile still lay in the Mausoleum and some at least still went to revere him there. Evicting him would of course be the ultimate desacralization. That idea was first publicly mooted in April 1989. From then on, anti-Leninists regularly suggested, to the horror of true believers, that the founder would be better off buried beside his mother. Burying Lenin would be tantamount to burying Leninism, a guardian of the shrine protested;[60] but that of course was precisely what the burying lobby wanted.

Party traditionalists naturally enough reacted with fury to such blasphemy. Left and right might agree that Lenin's democratic credentials were a fraud, but beyond that they parted company completely. While the left wanted to banish Lenin, the right was determined to wrest him back from the reformers. Its central claim, made openly and insistently from 1990, was that Lenin had been all of a piece – he had not, Yegor Ligachev and others reiterated, changed his views on socialism.[61] Retrieving Lenin from the reformers was not, as it proved, very difficult. By 1990, Lenin had turned from an asset to perestroika into a liability – the democratic image of him had been riddled with holes and damaging charges were being levelled against him. Come the May Day holiday in 1990, his name was markedly absent from the parade slogans. Perestroika, it appeared, no longer needed or wanted his validation; there was no mention of him whatever. By the 7 November holiday, however, the traditionalists had claimed him back. Now it was not Lenin but perestroika that the slogans passed over in silence. 'Comrades', rang out the second official slogan,' let us be faithful to the ideals of October and stand up for the name and the cause of Lenin!'[62]

By this stage, Lenin did indeed need to be stood up for. Attacks on him had gone beyond the verbal, and frequent acts of vandalism against Lenin monuments were being reported. These desecrations were, however, limited to the non-Russian areas, and in the Russian heartland they provoked indignation. Opinion polls in 1990–1 suggested that Lenin still enjoyed far greater respect than any other figure in recent Russian history. Yet if Lenin was an asset for the traditionalists, he was a diminishing one. The polls showed that among Muscovites and the young his stock was in rapid decline.[63] What Moscow thought today, the rest of the nation would probably think tomorrow. Time was evidently not on the traditionalists' side.

How could they best exploit Lenin's still considerable charismatic powers? Restoring the icon of the regime's previous propaganda was out of the question. The image of Lenin as human, sensitive and suffering was there to stay ; but that, too, lent itself to the traditionalists' purposes. And on 21 January 1991, within days of the bloodshed in Vilnius, *Pravda* launched a new cult of Lenin under the banner-headline – 'Forgive us, Vladimir Ilich!'[64] At this time there were, one might have thought, more pressing matters for the readers' attention – war was raging in the Persian Gulf and troubles were continuing in the Baltic states. But 21 January was, as it happened, a special day in the Lenin calendar: the anniversary of his death.

Until recently, celebrations of Lenin had focused very much on his birth rather than the anniversary of his death, and *Pravda* had given the latter little more than a ritual nod. But no longer. Lenin's death – to be exact, his dying – lay at the heart of the new cult. What followed the banner headline was a lengthy, poignant and pietistic account of Lenin's final days, written as if the death had occurred only recently. Its tone was of overwhelming grief. Grief above all for the premature death of someone indispensable; but grief, too, that Lenin's colleagues should have so little understood and even maltreated him; and grief, in addition, for what he had suffered posthumously at the hands of 'stagnation' ideologists and recent radical critics. The former had turned him into an unlovable icon, a machine for generating optimism, while the latter had come up with a still greater falsification. He was a fallible human, certainly; yet he was also someone of 'limitless humanity' and 'limitless superiority' who had done what he had to in a spirit of selflessness, for he had 'loved not himself in politics but politics in himself'.[65]

Pravda thus returned to an image which official propaganda had long since discarded – of Lenin as *saint,* almost a Christ-figure in his combination of human weakness with superhuman selflessness and wisdom. Here was no all-conquering hero proof against doubt or error or pain but instead someone who had sacrificed his life for his people as the saintly rulers of old Russia had sacrificed their lives for their people. Here was the ruler's passion – his agony of body and spirit; his willing sacrifice of himself; his humility and closeness to ordinary Russians; and his suffering at the hands of disciples who misunderstood, maltreated and even betrayed him: 'Again we are drawn by the need to talk to Lenin and to confess to him.'

That, incidentally, recalled what had been said of Stalin: he too had known his people's innermost thoughts, he too had been a father-confessor to them.

And then, in the manner of a litany:

> Forgive us, Vladimir Ilich, for having failed to fulfil many of your wise counsels, for having allowed the Stalinist camarilla to convert Leninism into Stalinism, for having for many years not read your wise books but instead got by with quotations and extracts made for us by solicitous ideological minders, for having allowed rogues of all kinds to call themselves 'true Leninists'. Forgive us, Vladimir Ilich!'[66]

Thus traditionalists, with their backs to the wall, tried to save the party by exploiting what remained of Leninist sentiment. They would re-enact the trauma of Lenin's death, reopen that long-healed wound, and so revive the Lenin cult by restoring the lost link between it and popular religiosity. The old Soviet order could not be saved by guns and authoritarian methods alone; candles and piety too were needed. Dying, Lenin might once more rescue the party; people would rally to him and it in its peril, as they had rallied to the party out of devotion to him sixty-seven years before. The contexts were, however, very different. Then the cult had been spontaneous; now it was being fabricated by beleaguered and desperate reactionaries. Then the grief had poured from a largely peasant population; now the cult was being relaunched in order to create that devotionalism which in 1924 had created it. Lenin and Lenin's party had in a sense fallen victim to their own modernizing efforts. With its right hand the party had done what its left hand (the one that fostered the Lenin and Stalin cults) would have least wanted – it had cut down the number of the credulous and multiplied that of the sceptical and free-thinking.

And so as radicals vilified Lenin, party traditionalists tried hard to resanctify him. In the matter of Lenin, as of policy in general, it began to look as if there could be no middle way. The Lenin of the Alternative Tradition had vanished from sight, finally disposed of by a critic who pointed out that the 'political testament' represented a complete rejection of Lenin's previous view of socialism, an admission of a tragic and criminal mistake, an acceptance that his opponents had been correct. Perestroika had not gone back to Lenin; what it had turned to, rather, was 'that Lenin who killed the Lenin in himself'.[67] Lenin, then, had come to see the error of his ways too late; the miseries heaped upon the nation were a consequence of that fatal blindness. In the transformed and increasingly surreal landscape of 1991 Russia, only two views of Lenin as a result survived. He was either a devil or a saint – either the scourge of the Russian people or their once and future saviour. Either he towered above the landscape, or else he suffered the fate of all too many monuments to himself and was cast down. What he was not and could not be was the wishy-washy democ-ratizer, the agonizing Chekhovian intellectual, whom reformers, with the best of intentions, had tried to turn him into.

Conclusion

1

The right's solution was tried first. On 19 August 1991 eight of Gorbachev's close colleagues, including the vice-president, the minister of defence and the head of the KGB, seized power on the pretext that the country had become ungovernable and needed to be saved from anarchy. In a manifesto which, avoiding anything Marxist, appealed to the traditional right as well as to party conservatives, the plotters laid heavy emphasis upon 'Russian' values – patriotism, community, material security. Within forty-eight hours, however, the coup had collapsed; and the democrats, who, under Yeltsin's leadership, had bravely defied it from within the besieged Russian parliament, then emerged as masters of the country.

The democrats' triumph reflected the determination of a relatively small minority, drawn mainly from the middle class, that the freedoms gained within the last six years should not be snatched from them. Outside the middle class, and outside the capitals, there was little active support for the democrats' cause. If ordinary people preferred Yeltsin to his opponents, it was because they saw this bear-like muzhik of a man as a symbol not so much of democracy as of Russia. *'Rossiya! Rossiya!'* – 'Russia! Russia!' – chanted the crowds outside the parliament. The conspirators had affronted not only the democratic values of the minority but the patriotic instincts of many who were indifferent or even hostile to democracy. That, plus lack of firm leadership, indeed downright incompetence, sealed the conspirators' fate.

Counter-revolution turned rapidly into revolution. A newspaper headline caught the mood of the moment: 'Perestroika is over – thank God!' 'I arrived back', Gorbachev himself commented of his return from captivity, 'to a different country.'[1] Not that he sensed straightaway how radically different the situation had become – on his first day back he restated his belief in Leninist socialism and argued that, despite its role in the coup, the party was still a potential force for progress. But two days later, after some rough handling by Yeltsin, he accepted the new realities. Power now lay with those who had saved him. His power had been the power of the party, and the party was broken. On 24 August he resigned as CPSU general secretary. On 29

August he suspended the CPSU itself, froze its assets and had all its buildings sealed. Not until 6 November was the Communist Party actually banned on Russian territory; however, by the end of August the organization which for seven decades had been the mainspring of all activity in the country had been excluded from the political arena.

The Soviet Union had a few more months to live, but the Soviet era was rapidly fizzling out. Functions performed by the Soviet government were transferred to its Russian counterpart. *Pravda* disappeared from news-stands; and when it reappeared it was no more than a whingeing voice of opposition. The country went back in some respects to the agenda discarded in October 1917 – one sign of that was the red, white and blue flag of the Provisional Government fluttering everywhere. People stopped calling one another 'comrade' and reverted to the pre-revolutionary 'Mr' and 'Mrs' (*gospodin* and *gospozha*). A seventy-four-year detour seemed to have ended. The reformers had talked a lot about perestroika as a 'revolution'; this was the real thing, and it was accomplished quickly and relatively bloodlessly.

Gorbachev devoted his final months in office not to socialism, which was evidently a lost cause, but to defence of the Union. A new Union treaty had been about to be signed when the plotters struck. Could something not be retrieved even now? However, the collapse of the Communist Party, and the powerful position acquired as a result by Yeltsin's Russian government, made that difficult. The other republics were unlikely to welcome a Union dominated by a nationalist-inclined Russian government. Yeltsin on his side might well regard loss of the Union as a price worth paying for getting rid of Gorbachev, whom he now detested. Moreover, the acknowledged failure of socialism had removed what had always been seen as the necessary cement of the Union. The issue was finally decided in the largest of the non-Russian republics, Ukraine. The Union could survive without the Balts or the Caucasians; it could not survive the loss of Ukraine. On 1 December 1991 the Ukrainian electors voted in a referendum by an overwhelming majority to end the centuries-old union with Russia.

On 25 December Gorbachev made a farewell broadcast as the president of a state that was about to pass into history. Once he had finished, the Soviet flag was lowered from the Council of Ministers building in the Kremlin and replaced by the Russian tricolour. The next day the USSR Supreme Soviet met for a final session. The mere two dozen deputies who turned up were, however, not enough to constitute a quorum, and those who met in the funereal atmosphere were therefore unable to agree to a formal dissolution. Soviet power had begun in earnest with an assembly guttering out in the midwinter darkness; its ending was not dissimilar. At midnight on 31 December 1991 the Union of Soviet Socialist Republics ceased to exist as a juridical entity, and Mikhail Gorbachev become a private citizen. The experiment begun amidst such high hopes in October 1917 had been wound up. The Communist Party had held power for three-quarters of a century, yet communism remained as remote as the planet Pluto; and there was a widespread feeling that, despite all the upheavals and sacrifices, even the more modest goal of socialism still lay beyond reach.

That was a damning verdict, given that achieving socialism and then communism had been the Bolsheviks' whole *raison d'être*. That alone had justified their dictatorship. That alone justified the most sustained and far-reaching exercise in social engineering ever known. But far from taking Russia to socialism, the party had taken it on a wild-goose chase whose outcome was misery, oppression, and previously unimagined forms of exploitation. The Bolshevik experiment had proved to be an unmitigated failure. Or so at least the matter looked as the regime and then the Soviet state itself fell apart, as pictures of Nicholas II were hawked in the streets and monuments to Communist Party worthies were toppled or defaced.

Yet the fiasco of the ending should not blind us to the party's achievements. It had conquered power and held onto it contrary to the predictions of almost all non-Bolsheviks. It had used the fearsome powers of the Soviet state to transform the country for good as well as for ill. It had persuaded the great majority of Soviet citizens that they and it together had indeed built socialism. Until manifest decline set in in the 1970s, many non-Marxist observers in the west were impressed by the regime's achievements and reckoned that it had a fair chance of creating a just and prosperous, if not a communist, society. The history of the socialist experiment in Russia is one of ultimate failure; but it is also a history of astounding interim success.

2

The Bolsheviks' success owed a great deal to the skill with which they adapted Marxism to the distinctive and very unwestern circumstances of Russia. The vanguard party was the vital element in this adaptation. Thanks to that, Lenin and a small group of colleagues were able to seize and then hold on to power in the face of widespread and sustained hostility. Without this grafting onto Marxism of statist and authoritarian elements taken from Russia's own political tradition, there would have been no October Revolution. Yet pre-October Bolshevism had been no more than partially and patchily assimilated to the Russian heritage, and its authoritarian elements mingled with rationalist, internationalist and libertarian ones preserved from its Marxist source. Post-October, these non-Russian elements would be rapidly eroded. Lenin, however, made environmental and conjunctural concessions (as we might call them) with reluctance, and in the final months of his life he struggled to look beyond these compromises and to etch for posterity what was necessary for the creation of an – admittedly distant – proper socialist society.

Lenin's adaptation had substituted the party for the missing proletariat and the party elite for the inadequately prepared party masses. The effect was to place power at the outset in the hands of a small group; but Lenin's assumption was that, as socialist consciousness spread, so the bounds of the effective political nation would broaden until they embraced the whole population. For the time being, 'democracy' would extend no further than the party elite – but at that level it would be, and was, real enough.

Developments after Lenin's death did not, however, go as he had anticipated. The evolution was not from oligarchy to democracy and thence to statelessness, but, on the contrary, from oligarchy to autocracy and to an extreme of statefulness. Stalin, who despite his Georgian origins embodied the Russian cultural heritage more completely than any of his rivals, emerged as the dominant figure, and he encouraged and benefited from a much closer convergence between socialism and traditional values than Lenin for one would have tolerated. The idea had even been mooted before the end of the 1930s of the state continuing to exist under communism – of a *communist* state. Russia might have been Bolshevized, but Bolshevism was becoming heavily russified. In the person of Stalin, this tsar in a buttoned-up communist tunic, Russian tradition was having its revenge upon those Bolsheviks who had dreamed of purging their country of its dark heritage and making it part of an international socialist community.

Not that even the most enlightened Bolsheviks had stood for pluralism or liberal democracy. On the contrary, Bolsheviks of all shades had laid heavy emphasis on the need for unity. The party would speak with a single voice, which would reflect Marxist science and at the same time embody the will – the *true* will – of the people. Those who opposed it would therefore be doubly at fault, since they would be opposing both science and the people. However, by the 1930s the voice of the party had become the voice of a single, all-powerful individual. Admittedly, Stalin, unlike the tsars, denied that he possessed any authority in his own person, and he humbly presented himself as no more than the instrument of party and people. The hypocrisy of this self-abasement was, however, pointed up by the utterly unBolshevik cult of his person. No tsar had been so adulated; no tsar had exercised such power over so many.

Stalin's emergence as Leader disposed of what little democracy remained within the party (it had long since disappeared outside it). Stalinism likewise put an end to Bolshevik rationalism and enlightenment. For the cult of Stalin, and the associated cult of Lenin, were pseudo-religions which harnessed to the party's cause instincts that the Bolsheviks had wanted to suppress and had seen as utterly inimical to socialism. From now on, the public proceedings of the party and the actions and utterances of its leaders had a ritualized, stylized and semi-hieratic character. The intention of this heavy ritualism was clear: to instil awe into the simple-minded and to elicit their complete and unthinking obedience. The party's truths were not only scientific but sacred; dissent from them was, therefore, worse than stupidity – it was heresy.

Patriarchal and pseudo-religious autocracy was naturally enough accompanied by a strong reassertion of traditional collectivism and anti-individualism. Everyone had to act as his brother's – his comrade's – keeper. The pursuit of goals unrelated or contrary to the party's goals and any behaviour not explicitly sanctioned by the community were impermissible. Draconian curbs on the individual were given a more powerful and more incessantly preached justification than ever before. Deviants were portrayed as enemies who threatened the Soviet people, their socialist achievements and their march towards communism; the duty of every honest citizen was to unmask and help to crush them. These traitors were either agents of the west or moral degenerates who had been contaminated by its influence. Bolshevik internationalism had long since vanished, of course; Stalin made the utmost use of a deep-seated insecurity towards the west and the xenophobia that fed on it, just as he exploited to the full traditional collectivism, religiosity and patriarchalism.

The Bolsheviks had aimed to transform their backward country out of recognition, creating a socialist society in which very little that was distinctively Russian remained. In the mid-1930s Stalin declared that the socialist goal had been achieved; but what passed as a socialist society had taken on a distinctively Russian colouring, had indeed to a remarkable degree adopted the 'socialist' values of traditional village life. This acculturation did much to make Stalin's dominant position among the party leaders impregnable; it also explained the regime's success in turning indifference or hostility among its subjects into unforced loyalty or even an enthusiastic willingness to carry out its orders.

By its very success as a modernizing agent, however, Stalinist socialism in time made itself anomalous. The old, peasant, uneducated Russia gave way to a Russia that was urban and educated and had a considerable middle class. Khrushchev's attempt in the immediate post-Stalin era to bring the model of socialism into line with the new realities proved premature. But by the 1980s the Stalinist model had become wildly inappropriate to the country's social and cultural profile. Moreover, the hypercentralized economic system, which in the 1930s had achieved astonishing feats of primary industrialization, was now failing badly, and its inability to measure up to the needs of a more sophisticated economy posed a clear threat to the regime's long- if not its short-term survival.

It was against this background that Gorbachev and his colleagues began a major reform of the economic and political systems and a radical rethink of the nature of socialism. The essential preliminary was to break the power of an entrenched, highly conservative oligarchy; in this the reformers succeeded quite beyond the expectations of any Sovietologist, thanks largely to fervent support from much of the middle class. Their reform programme emerged in fact as a charter for the ambitious and the talented. It offered freedom and an opportunity to better themselves to people who had outgrown the dependency culture of the village, resented being tightly corralled by the state, and had, or so it seemed, everything to gain and very little to lose from democracy and the market. The new socialism could not, of course, be presented as a decisive break with the old; the reforms were glossed, rather, as a development from original Bolshevism and, in particular, a return to its long-neglected democratism.

This appeal to tradition was not simply a matter of tactics: the reformers were justifiably enough drawing attention to the elements in early Bolshevism that pointed in the direction not of Stalinism but of all-round fulfilment of the individual person. They emphasized Lenin's reflective and self-critical side, his awareness of what socialism really required, his troubling sense of the discrepancy between socialist ideals and Soviet reality. Lenin's Marxist libertarianism had, however, coexisted uneasily with a stronger strain of authoritarianism; in conflicts between the two it was generally authoritarian solutions that prevailed, and within a few years of his death the conflict had been resolved definitively in authoritarianism's favour. In putting the case for a democratic socialism with its roots in Bolshevik tradition, the reformers were, therefore, emphasizing unrealized Bolshevik ideals as against the realities that had overwhelmed those ideals. They were in fact rediscovering that side of Bolshevism which had proved incompatible with Soviet power and which had had to be sacrificed in order to secure the regime against its enemies. Reforms pursued under the auspices of a 'return to Lenin' would, as it happened, have the entirely unintended effect of cutting the Lenin phase of Russian history short; and it was perhaps a fitting irony that the house that Lenin had built should be demolished in the end with help from the original builder – by the publicizing of those sides of his political personality that were subversive of Soviet power, that he himself had partially suppressed, and that Soviet posterity had then blotted out completely.

The reformers continued to pay obeisance to Lenin and early Bolshevism until the end, but by the final months of the Gorbachev government this had become little more than a ritual formality. Theirs was a movement of democratic socialism dedicated to parliamentary democracy and welfare capitalism, and its proponents saw the creative, self-determining individual, rather than the will of the collective embodied in the state, as the motor of general wellbeing. Moreover, by the 1990s the movement had lost, perhaps even deliberately cut, its moorings to Russian tradition, and all those aspects of socialism that derived from the Russian cultural heritage had been eliminated. The ideas that inspired the reformers were taken almost wholly from the west; and the constituency they had appealed to, at first with notable success, was the derussified sector of the middle class.

By this stage, however, even intellectuals and would-be entrepreneurs were becoming disillusioned with the new socialism. They, too, were suffering from the economic collapse; they, too, were alarmed by the breakdown of law and order; they, too, were mortified by the loss of empire and great-power status. Those who fought against the plotters in August 1991 fought for Yeltsin rather than for Gorbachev – for a liberal, free-market Russia rather than for a socialist one. The new socialism had in fact withered and died after the briefest of heydays; it had become conceptually nebulous, its promises had proved specious, its associations were increasingly negative. As for the old socialism, that had a continuing appeal to the working class and to apparatchiks who had failed to grab the spoils of de-statification, but for the time being it was discredited.

Symbols of the party's hegemony had been largely swept away before the Soviet Union came to an end. Moscow indeed acquired a whole mortuary of toppled monuments to communist worthies. There was one communist, however, who was spared the general contempt. Monuments to Lenin were cast down in the outlying republics, but in the Russian heartland the founder of the Soviet state continued, for many at least, to be touched by sanctity. And not only did he still stand in many of the squares of Russia; his body was left unmolested in the mausoleum Stalin had built to deify him. A motley group of authoritarians and utopians loudly protested their enduring loyalty to him – their very diversity saying something about the conflicting elements he had managed to reconcile within the party and within himself. Lenin's survival amidst the debris of the Bolshevik experiment seemed to confirm that he was bigger than the party, bigger than his followers, a true god among the demi-gods. It suggested, too, that with his contradictions and his passionate extremism he had expressed something authentically Russian. And as Russia of the 1990s struggled to come to terms with capitalism and democracy, his continued presence in that sombre landscape was a reminder of how little of socialism had yet been achieved there.

Notes

Introduction

1. Teodor Shanin, ed., *Late Marx and the Russian Road: Marx and the 'Peripheries of Capitalism'* (London, 1983), p. 119.
2. D. Mackenzie Wallace, *Russia*, 9th edn (London, n.d.), p. 126.
3. Karl Marx, 'Critique of the Gotha Programme', Karl Marx Friedrich Engels, *Collected Works* (47 vols, London, 1975–93), vol. 24, p. 87.
4. V.I. Lenin, *Collected Works* (45 vols, London, 1960–70), vol. 33, pp. 460–502. See also note 35 to Chapter 3 .
5. Martin Malia, *The Soviet Tragedy: A History of Socialism in Russia, 1917–1991* (New York, 1994); Andrzej Walicki, *Marxism and the Leap to the Kingdom of Freedom: The Rise and Fall of the Communist Utopia* (Stanford, 1995).
6. Malia, *The Soviet Tragedy*, p. 225.
7. Ibid., pp. 313, 498.
8. Walicki, *Marxism and the Leap to the Kingdom of Freedom*, p. 541.
9. Malia, *The Soviet Tragedy*, p. 155.
10. Moshe Lewin, *Political Undercurrents in Soviet Economic Debates: From Bukharin to the Modern Reformers* (London, 1975), esp. p. 124. Republished in 1991 as *Stalinism and the Seeds of Soviet Reform* (London and Armonk, NY).

1 Before Lenin

1. A. Herzen ['Iskander'], *Polyarnaya zvezda na 1856* (London, 1856), p. VII.
2. Teodor Shanin, ed., *Late Marx and the Russian Road: Marx and the 'Peripheries of Capitalism'* (London, 1983), p. 187.
3. Andrzej Walicki, *Legal Philosophies of Russian Liberalism* (Oxford, 1987), p. 63.
4. Alexander Herzen, *From the Other Shore and The Russian People and Socialism*, tr. by Moura Budberg, introduced by Isaiah Berlin (London, 1956), p. 188.
5. Ibid., pp. 12, 135, 134.
6. August von Haxthausen, *Studies on the Interior of Russia*, ed. by S. Frederick Starr (Chicago, 1972).
7. Georgi Plekhanov, *Selected Philosophical Works* (5 vols, Moscow, 1976–81), vol. 1, p. 344.
8. Ibid., p. 96.
9. Karl Marx Friedrich Engels, *Collected Works*, vol. 6, p. 497.
10. In his introduction of 1895 to Marx's *The Class War in France 1848 to 1850*: ibid., vol. 27, esp. p. 520.
11. Shanin, *Late Marx and the Russian Road*, pp. 99 and 124.
12. Ibid., p. 116.

13. Ibid., pp. 111–13.
14. Ibid., pp. 110, 112, 135.
15. *Lenin: Biography proposed by the Marx-Engels-Lenin Institute, Moscow* (Moscow, n.d.), p. 7.

2 The Vision, 1890–1917

1. V.I. Lenin, *Collected Works* (45 vols, London 1960–70), vol. 1, p. 159; this edition is henceforth cited as *Lenin*.
2. *Lenin*, vol. 5, p. 447.
3. Pavel Akselrod. Cited in Bertram D. Wolfe, *Three Who Made a Revolution* (London, 1956), p. 249.
4. *Lenin*, vol. 5, p. 474.
5. Ibid., p. 467.
6. Isaac Deutscher, *The Prophet Armed. Trotsky: 1879–1921* (New York and London, 1954), p. 90.
7. *Lenin*, vol. 2, pp. 340–1.
8. *Lenin*, vol. 5, p. 512.
9. *Lenin*, vol. 1, p. 191.
10. *Lenin*, vol. 3, pp. 177–8, 181.
11. *Lenin*, vol. 19, p. 244.
12. *Lenin*, vol. 20, pp. 422, 423.
13. *Lenin*, vol. 11, p. 410; vol. 9, pp. 236–7.
14. *Lenin*, vol. 28, p. 233.
15. *Lenin*, vol. 10, p. 245.
16. Ibid., pp. 155–6.
17. Ibid., p. 63.
18. *Lenin*, vol. 21, p. 216; vol. 23, p. 253.
19. Teodor Shanin, ed., *Late Marx and the Russian Road* (London, 1983), pp. 53–5.
20. *Lenin*, vol. 24, p. 24.
21. *Lenin*, vol. 23, p. 330.
22. *Lenin*, vol. 24, p. 22.
23. Ibid., p. 242.
24. Ibid., pp. 21–4.
25. *Lenin*, vol. 23, p. 324.
26. *Lenin*, vol. 25, pp. 393–4.
27. Ibid., p. 404.
28. Ibid., pp. 126, 114.
29. Ibid., pp. 468–9.
30. *Lenin*, vol. 26, p. 106.
31. Ibid., pp. 23, 19.
32. Ibid., p. 67.
33. Ibid., pp. 19, 67, 191–2.
34. Ibid., p. 188.
35. Ibid., p. 188.
36. Robert Service, *Lenin: A Political Life*, vol. 2: *Worlds in Crisis* (London, 1991), p. 274.

37. John Reed, *Ten Days that Shook the World* (Harmondsworth, 1966), p. 55.
38. N.N. Sukhanov, *The Russian Revolution 1917: A Personal Record,* ed. and tr. by Joel Carmichael (Oxford, 1955), p. 635.

3 The Realization, 1917–24

1. *Lenin,* vol. 33, pp. 480, 475.
2. *Lenin,* vol. 26, p. 472.
3. *Lenin,* vol. 27, pp. 89–90, 99, 291.
4. Ibid., p. 147.
5. *Lenin,* vol. 29, p. 420.
6. *Lenin,* vol. 27, p. 147.
7. Ibid., p. 291.
8. *Lenin,* vol. 26, pp. 239, 297, 365.
9. *Lenin,* vol. 28, p. 56.
10. *Lenin,* vol. 27, p. 436.
11. *Lenin,* vol. 26, p. 449.
12. Richard Pipes, ed., *The Unknown Lenin: From the Secret Archive* (New Haven and London, 1996), p. 98.
13. Ronald Gregor Suny, *The Making of the Georgian Nation* (London, 1989), p. 202.
14. Karl Kautsky, *Georgia: A Social-Democratic Peasant Republic: Impressions and Observations* (London, 1921), p. 8.
15. *Lenin,* vol. 32, p. 160.
16. Ibid., p. 317.
17. Suny, *The Making of the Georgian Nation,* pp. 214–15.
18. Jeremy Smith, *The Bolsheviks and the National Question, 1917–23* (Basingstoke, 1999), p. 193.
19. *Lenin,* vol. 28, pp. 139–40.
20. *Lenin,* vol. 29, p. 183.
21. *Lenin,* vol. 26, p. 401.
22. On this see *Lenin,* vol. 26, pp. 457, 464; vol. 27, pp. 89–90.
23. *Lenin,* vol. 32, p. 199.
24. *Lenin,* vol. 27, p. 135.
25. *Lenin,* vol. 32, p. 343; vol. 33, p. 62.
26. Ibid., pp. 169, 246.
27. Ibid., p. 258.
28. *Lenin,* vol. 33, p. 109.
29. Ibid., p. 290.
30. Ibid., p. 326.
31. Ibid., p. 468.
32. Ibid., pp. 470, 474–5, 285.
33. *Lenin,* vol. 31, p. 423.
34. *Lenin,* vol. 33, pp. 39–40, 225.
35. The fourth Russian edition of Lenin's works, from which the *Collected Works* is derived, omits certain of Lenin's final writings. The missing items can be found in the fifth Russian edition: *Polnoe sobranie sochinenii* (55 vols, Moscow, 1958–65). The reference to 'that truly Russian person …' comes in vol. 45, p. 357.

36. Ibid., pp. 361–2.
37. Ibid., pp. 345, 346.
38. Ibid., pp. 343, 346.
39. *Lenin*, vol. 33, p. 485.
40. Ibid., pp. 463–5.
41. Ibid., pp. 474, 475.
42. Ibid., pp. 474, 475, 476, 480.
43. The label 'political testament' would also, however, be applied more narrowly to his 'Letter to the Congress' of 23 and 24 December 1922 and the addendum on Stalin of 4 January 1923. The whole question of the 'testament' is discussed in Yevgeny Plimak, *Politicheskoe zaveshchanie V.I. Lenina: istoki, sushchnost', vypolnenie* (Moscow, 1988).
44. The best account of Lenin's final phase remains Moshe Lewin's *Lenin's Last Struggle* (London, 1969).
45. V.I. Lenin, *Polnoe sobranie sochinenii*, vol. 45, p. 356.
46. Ibid., p. 607.
47. Martin Malia, *The Soviet Tragedy* (New York, 1994), pp. 133–6; Andrzej Walicki, *Marxism and the Leap to the Kingdom of Freedom* (Stanford, 1995), pp. 391–7.
48. V.I. Lenin, *Polnoe sobranie sochinenii*, vol. 48, p. 234.
49. Walicki, *Marxism and the Leap to the Kingdom of Freedom*, p. 405.
50. *Lenin*, vol. 33, p. 442.

4   After Lenin, 1924–29

1. Nina Tumarkin, *Lenin Lives!: The Lenin Cult in Soviet Russia* (Cambridge, Mass., 1983), p. 212.
2. J.V. Stalin, *Works* (13 vols, Moscow, 1952–5), vol. 6, pp. 47–8; this edition is henceforth cited as *Stalin*.
3. *Stalin*, vol. 6, pp. 54–66.
4. N.I. Bukharin, *Put' k sotsializmu* (Novosibirsk, 1990), p. 60.
5. *Lenin*, vol. 33, p. 474.
6. Bukharin, *Put' k sotsializmu*, p. 108.
7. *Stalin*, vol. 8, pp.14–17.
8. *Stalin*, vol. 6, pp. 394, 395.
9. *Stalin*, vol. 8, p. 67.
10. *Stalin*, vol. 12, pp. 147, 176.
11. Ibid., pp. 37–8, 39–41.
12. Ibid., p. 40.
13. N.I. Bukharin, *Izbrannye proizvedeniya*, ed. by G.L. Smirnov (Moscow, 1988), pp. 399 and 417.
14. Ibid., p. 419.
15. *Stalin*, vol. 12, p. 25.
16. For Lenin on Machiavelli, see Richard Pipes, ed., *The Unknown Lenin: From the Secret Archive* (New Haven and London, 1996), p. 153.

5 Stalin's Socialism, 1929–1953

1. *History of the Communist Party of the Soviet Union (Bolsheviks): Short Course* (Moscow, 1943), p. 305; henceforth cited as *Short Course*.
2. *Stalin*, vol. 13, p. 43.
3. Leon Trotsky, *The Revolution Betrayed*, tr. by Max Eastman (London, 1937), p. 272.
4. J.V. Stalin, *Problems of Leninism* (Peking, 1976), p. 938; henceforth cited as *Problems*.
5. *Stalin*, vol. 13, p. 6.
6. *Stalin*, vol. 13, p. 215.
7. N. Bukharin and E. Preobrazhensky, *The ABC of Communism*, tr. by Eden and Cedar Paul (Harmondsworth, 1969), p. 119.
8. *Stalin*, vol. 13, p. 215.
9. *Problems*, p. 806.
10. Ibid., pp. 806–7, 821.
11. See his remarks to the Seventeenth Party Congress: *Stalin*, vol. 12, especially p. 380.
12. *Problems*, pp. 929 and 931.
13. Ibid., p. 932.
14. Ibid., p. 935.
15. *Stalin*, vol. 13, pp. 59, 363, 121.
16. Trotsky, *The Revolution Betrayed*, pp. 132, 235.
17. Milovan Djilas, *The New Class: An Analysis of the Communist System* (London, 1957).
18. *Stalin*, vol. 13, pp. 341, 343; *Problems*, p. 907.
19. *Stalin*, vol. 12, pp. 304, 305; *Problems*, p. 783.
20. *Stalin*, vol. 13, p. 41.
21. Alec Nove, *An Economic History of the USSR 1917–1991* (London, 1992), p. 210,
22. *Stalin*, vol. 13, p. 342.
23. See, for instance, *Problems*, p. 784.
24. *Short Course*, p. 363.
25. *Problems*, p. 891.
26. T.H. Rigby, *The Changing Soviet System: Mono-Organisational Socialism from its Origins Until Gorbachev's Restructuring* (Aldershot, 1990), ch. 4.
27. *Short Course*, p. 352.
28. See, for instance, the interview with Emile Ludwig in which Stalin allowed the comparison with Peter the Great to be floated and then modestly disclaimed it: *Stalin*, vol. 13, pp. 106–7.
29. Anatolii Rybakov, *Children of the Arbat*, tr. by Harold Shukman (London, 1988), pp. 205–7.
30. Alexander Solzhenitsyn, *The Gulag Archipelago 1918–1956*, tr. by Thomas P. Whitney (3 vols, London 1974–8), vol. I, p. 505.
31. Evgenia S. Ginzburg, *Into the Whirlwind*, tr. by Paul Stevenson and Manya Harari (Harmondsworth, 1968), p. 281.
32. See Robert C. Tucker, 'Stalinism as Revolution from Above', in Robert C. Tucker, ed., *Stalinism* (New York, 1977), p. 104.
33. *Stalin*, vol. 12, p. 379.

34. *Problems*, p. 825.
35. Ibid., pp. 804, 805.
36. Vladimir Bukovsky, *To Build a Castle: My Life as a Dissident*, tr. by Michael Scammell (London, 1978), p. 83.
37. Robert Conquest, *The Great Terror: A Reassessment* (London, 1990), p. 314.
38. Dmitri Volkogonov, *Stalin: Triumph and Tragedy*, ed. and tr. by Harold Shukman (London, 1991), p. 564.

6 Onward to Communism, 1953–64

1. *Khrushchev Remembers*, tr. and ed. by Strobe Talbott (2 vols, London, 1971 and 1974), vol. I, pp. 572, 559–60.
2. Ibid., p. 595.
3. Ibid., pp. 560–5.
4. Ibid., pp. 46, 343.
5. *KPSS v resolyutsiyakh i resheniyakh s'ezdov, konferentsii i plenumov tsk* (15 vols, Moscow, 1983–9), vol. 9, p. 90.
6. Leo Gruliow, ed., *Current Soviet Policies III: The Documentary Record of the Extraordinary 21st Congress of the Communist Party of the Soviet Union* (New York, 1960), p. 43.
7. O. Kuusinen ed., *Fundamentals of Marxism-Leninism* (Moscow, 1961); henceforth cited as *Fundamentals*.
8. *The Road to Communism: Documents of the 22nd Congress of the Communist Party of the Soviet Union, October 17–31 1961* (Moscow, n.d.), p. 313; henceforth cited as *The Road*.
9. *Fundamentals*, p. 849.
10. *The Road*, pp. 232–40.
11. Ibid., p. 512.
12. Ibid., p.114.
13. Ibid., pp. 154, 568.
14. Ibid., pp. 566–7.
15. *Fundamentals*, pp. 832, 833.
16. *The Road*, p. 114.
17. Ibid., p. 538.
18. Ibid., pp. 240, 209, 530, 544.
19. Ibid., p. 260.
20. Ibid., p. 252.
21. *Fundamentals*, p. 840.
22. Fedor Burlatsky, *Khrushchev and the First Russian Spring*, translated by Daphne Skillen (London, 1992), pp. 25–6.
23. *Fundamentals*, p. 83.
24. *The Road*, p. 550.
25. *Fundamentals*, p. 738.
26. *The Road*, p. 583; *Fundamentals*, p. 843.
27. *Fundamentals*, p. 846.
28. T.H. Rigby, *Communist Party Membership in the USSR, 1917–1964* (Princeton, 1968), p.300.
29. *Fundamentals*, p. 846.

30. Burlatsky, *Khrushchev and the First Russian Spring*, p. 200.
31. *Khrushchev Remembers*, vol. 2, p. 108; vol. 1, p. 353 .
32. Sergei Khrushchev, *Khrushchev on Khrushchev* (Boston, 1990), p. 14.
33. The charges against him are reconstructed in Robert V. Daniels, *A Documentary History of Communism* (2 vols, London, 1985), vol. 1, pp. 349–54.
34. *KPSS v resolyutsiyakh i resheniyakh s'ezdov, konferentsii i plenumov tsk*, vol. 10 (Moscow, 1968), p. 418.
35. *Khrushchev on Khrushchev*, p. 154.

7   A Problem of Credibility, 1964–85

1. G.N. Volkov ed., *The Basics of Marxist-Leninist Theory* (Moscow, 1982), p. 178; henceforth cited as *The Basics*.
2. On this, see Alfred B. Evans Jr., 'Developed Socialism in Soviet Ideology', *Soviet Studies*, 29 (July 1977) pp. 409–28.
3. *The Basics*, pp. 179, 183.
4. Aryeh L. Unger, *Constitutional Developments in the USSR: A Guide to the Soviet Constitutions* (London, 1986), p. 234.
5. *The Basics*, p. 251.
6. Ibid., p. 183.
7. Ibid., pp. 182–3.
8. See, for instance, Stephen F. Cohen, *Rethinking the Soviet Experience* (New York, 1985), p. 181.
9. Andrei Amalrik, *Will the Soviet Union Survive until 1984?*, ed. by Hilary Sternberg (Harmondsworth, 1980), p. 37.
10. Rudolf L. Tokes, *Dissent in the USSR: Politics, Ideology and People* (Baltimore, 1975), pp. 423–4.
11. *The Basics*, p. 181.
12. Abel Aganbegyan, *The Challenge: Economics of Perestroika*, ed. by Michael Barratt Brown (London, 1988), p. 3; *Moving the Mountain: Inside the Perestroika Revolution*, tr. by Helen Szamuely (London, 1989), p. 155.
13. *Lenin*, vol. 29, p. 427.
14. Seweryn Bialer, *The Soviet Paradox: External Expansion, Internal Decline* (London, 1986), pp. 75, 169–170.
15. Edward L. Keenan, 'Muscovite Political Folkways', *Russian Review*, 45 (April 1986) pp. 115–82.
16. Alexander Zinoviev, *The Reality of Communism*, tr. by Charles Janson (London, 1984), pp. 59, 246.
17. *The Basics*, p. 256.
18. Yu.V. Andropov, *Izbrannye rechi i stat'i*, 2nd edn (Moscow, 1983), p. 238.
19. Ibid., pp. 234–5, 235, 238.
20. Ibid., p. 245.
21. Ibid., pp. 243, 244.
22. For instance, G.A. Arbatov, *Zatyanuvsheesya vyzdorovlenie (1953–1985 gg.): svidetel'stvo sovremennika* (Moscow, 1991), pp. 323, 332.

8 The Alternative Tradition

1. Vladimir Lakshin, *Solzhenitsyn, Tvardovsky and 'Novy Mir'* (Cambridge, Mass., 1980), p. 66.
2. See Ota Sik, *The Third Way: Marxist-Leninist Theory and Modern Industrial Society,* translated by Marion Sling, (London, 1976) and *For A Humane Economic Democracy* (New York, 1985). Sik's 'Third Way' ideas would be adopted and adapted, with little or no acknowledgement, by 'New Labour' theorists in Britain in the 1990s.
3. For instance, A. Birman, 'Sut' reformy', *Novyi mir,* December 1968, p. 187; N. Petrakov, 'Upravlenie ekonomikoi i ekonomicheskie interesy', *Novyi mir,* August 1970, pp. 196–7.
4. A. Birman, 'Samaya blagodarnaya zadacha', *Novyi mir,* December 1969, p. 179.
5. A. Birman, 'Prodolzhenie razgovora', *Novyi mir,* May 1966, p. 190.
6. Though Ota Sik, for one, would soon be thinking the unthinkable!
7. Ota Sik, *Ekonomika, interesy, politika* (Moscow, 1964).
8. For Sik's own comments on the controversy, see *The Third Way,* p. 45.
9. V. Shubkin, 'O konkretnykh issledovaniyakh sotsial'nykh protsessov', *Kommunist,* 1965, no. 3 (February), p. 51.
10. N. Petrakov, 'Upravlenie ekonomikoi i ekonomicheskie interesy', *Novyi mir,* August 1970, p. 175.
11. Ibid., p. 176.
12. Cited from Moshe Lewin, *Political Undercurrents in Soviet Economic Debates: From Bukharin to the Modern Reformers* (London, 1975), p. 231.
13. A. Birman, 'Samaya blagodarnaya zadacha', *Novyi mir,* December 1969, p. 180.
14. O. Latsis, 'Net isklyucheniya bez pravila', *Novyi mir,* April 1967, p. 167.
15. V. Nemchinov, 'Sotsialisticheskoe khozyaistvovanie i planirovanie proizvodstva', *Kommunist,* no. 5 (March 1964), p. 84.
16. Shubkin, 'O konkretnykh issledovaniyakh', p. 49.
17. Birman, 'Samaya blagodarnaya zadacha', p. 175.
18. N. Petrakov, 'Potreblenie i effektivnost' proizvodstva', *Novyi mir,* June 1971, pp. 198–9.
19. Zdenek Mlynar, 'Il mio compagno di studi, Mikhail Gorbaciov', *L'Unita* (Rome), 9 April 1985, p. 9; Mikhail Gorbachev, *Memoirs* (London, 1996), pp. 81–2.
20. Zdenek Mlynar, 'Problems of Political Leadership and the New Economic System', *World Marxist Review,* vol. 8 (December 1965), p. 62.
21. Ibid., pp. 59, 63.
22. Wlodzimierz Brus, *The Market in a Socialist Economy,* translated by Angus Walker (London, 1972), p. 6; first published in Poland in 1964.
23. N. Petrakov, 'Upravlenie ekonomikoi', p. 184.
24. A. Birman, 'Samaya blagodarnaya zadacha', pp. 179–80, 180–1.
25. Andrei D. Sakharov, *Sakharov Speaks,* ed. Harrison E. Salisbury (London, 1974), pp. 120 and 121.
26. N.I. Bukharin, *Put' k sotsializmu* (Novosibirsk, 1990), pp. 28–9, 48–9, 53–4, 60–1.

27. Roy A. Medvedev, *On Socialist Democracy*, tr. and ed. by Ellen de Kadt (London, 1975), pp. 46, 102, 103, 106.
28. Roy Medvedev, *On Soviet Dissent: Interviews with Piero Ostellino*, tr. by William A. Packer (New York, 1980), pp. 73, 110.
29. Medvedev, *On Soviet Dissent*, p. 138; Medvedev, *On Socialist Democracy*, p. 313.
30. Lewin, *Political Undercurrents in Soviet Economic Debates*, pp. 352, 353.
31. Ibid., p. 352.
32. Yelizaveta Drabkina, *Zimnyi pereval* (Moscow, 1990); the first half appeared in *Novy Mir* for October 1968 (pp. 3–93), but publication was then cut off.
33. Ibid., p. 362.
34. Ibid., p. 363.
35. Mikhail Shatrov, *Izbrannoe* (Moscow, 1982), p. 257.
36. Ibid., pp. 277, 320, 289.
37. Roy Medvedev, *Let History Judge: The Origin and Consequences of Stalinism*, tr. by Colleen Taylor, 1st edn (London, 1976).
38. Ibid., pp. 360, 362.
39. Roy A. Medvedev, *Political Essays*, tr. by Tamara Deutscher (Nottingham, 1976), p. 67.
40. Medvedev, *On Soviet Dissent*, p. 92.
41. Moshe Lewin, *Lenin's Last Struggle* (London, 1969), p. 17.
42. Birman, 'Samaya blagodarnaya zadacha', p. 176.
43. Gennadi Lisichkin, *Socialism: An Appraisal of Prospects* (Moscow, 1989), p. 70.
44. A.P. Butenko, 'Protivorechiya razvitiya sotsializma kak obshchestvennogo stroya', *Voprosii filosofii*, October 1982, pp. 16–29, at p. 27.
45. Ibid., pp. 22–3.
46. 'The Novosibirsk Report', *Survey*, 28 (Spring 1984), pp. 66–108.
47. Ibid., pp. 90, 106, 108.
48. Ibid., pp. 97, 102, 98.
49. B.M. Kurashvili, 'Ob'ektivnye zakony gosudarstvennogo upravleniya', *Sovetskoe gosudarstvo i pravo*, October 1983, p. 44.
50. Feliks Kuznetsov, 'V krivom zerkale', *Novyi mir*, December 1983, pp. 240, 241.
51. A. Birman, 'Mysli posle plenuma', *Novyi mir*, December 1965, p. 194.

9 A New Socialism, 1985–91

1. This view was given its most authoritative expression by Seweryn Bialer. See his *The Soviet Paradox: External Expansion, Internal Decline* (London, 1986), esp. p. 143.
2. There were of course some exceptions. Most notable was Archie Brown, who in a series of articles argued that Gorbachev's reformism had to be taken seriously. See, for instance, 'Gorbachev: New Man in the Kremlin', *Problems of Communism*, 32, no. 3 (1985), pp. 1–23. Archie Brown's work on Gorbachev culminated with *The Gorbachev Factor* (Oxford, 1996).
3. See, in addition to *The Soviet Tragedy*, 'To the Stalin Mausoleum', *Daedalus*, Winter 1990, pp. 295–340 (published under the pseudonym 'Z'), and 'Leninist Endgame', *Daedalus*, Spring 1992, pp. 57–76.

4. Andrzej Walicki, *Marxism and the Leap to the Kingdom of Freedom* (Stanford, 1995), pp. 538 and 555.
5. Ibid., pp. 548, 549, 550, 551–2.
6. Zdenek Mlynar, 'Il mio compagno di studi, Mikhail Gorbaciov', *L'Unita* (Rome), 9 April 1985.
7. *Pravda*, 12 February 1990; Tatyana Zaslavskaya, *The Second Socialist Revolution: An Alternative Socialist Strategy* (London, 1990), p. xi; *The Guardian*, 28 February 1990.
8. As Eduard Shevardnadze said to Gorbachev in 1984: *Pravda*, 1 December 1990, p. 1.
9. G.R. Urban, ed., *Communist Reformation: Nationalism, Internationalism and Change in the World Communist Movement* (London, 1979), pp. 138–9.
10. Fedor Burlatsky, 'Kakoi sotsializm narodu nuzhen?', *Literaturnaya gazeta*, 20 April 1988, p. 2.
11. Yury F. Afanas'ev, ed., *Inogo ne dano: sud'by perestroiki* (Moscow, 1988).
12. Ye. Ambartsumov, ibid., p. 88.
13. M.S. Gorbachev, *Perestroika i novoe myshlenie dlya nashei strany i dlya vsego mira* (Moscow, 1987), p. 39.
14. The decline of communism is reflected in the index to Gorbachev's *Izbrannye rechi i stat'i* (*Selected Speeches and Articles*), 6 vols (Moscow, 1987–9). The first volume, covering the years 1967 to 1983, contained 28 references to 'communism' or 'communist construction'. By volume three, which covered the period October 1985 to July 1986, the number of such references had fallen to 12; and in volume six (December 1987 to October 1988) there were a mere two references.
15. Gorbachev, *Perestroika*, p. 96.
16. *Pravda*, 28 January 1987, p. 3.
17. Ibid., 29 June 1988, p. 4. For a detailed discussion of this subject, see John Gooding, 'Gorbachev and Democracy', *Soviet Studies*, April 1990, pp. 195–231.
18. *Izvestiya*, 8 March 1989, p. 2.
19. *Pravda*, 1 July 1988, p. 8.
20. Gorbachev, *Perestroika*, pp. 99, 102.
21. *Pravda*, 19 February 1988, p. 2.
22. Ibid., 29 June 1988, p. 4.
23. M.S. Gorbachev, *Oktyabr' i perestroika: revolyutsiya prodolzhaetsya* (Moscow, 1987), p. 84.
24. *Pravda*, 8 January 1989, p. 4 ; ibid., 19 June 1989, p. 2.
25. Ibid., 19 February 1988, p. 2; 30 November 1988, p. 1; 27 January 1987, p. 3.
26. Ibid., 19 February 1988, p. 2.
27. G. Arbatov and Ye. Batalov, 'Politicheskaya reforma i evolyutsiya Sovetskogo gosudarstva', *Kommunist*, no. 4, (March 1989), p. 45.
28. *Pravda*, 27 April 1989, p. 1 ; 24 February 1989, p. 2.
29. See R.W. Davies, 'Soviet Economic Reform in Historical Perspective', in Catherine Merridale and Chris Ward., eds., *Perestroika: The Historical Perspective* (London, 1991), pp. 129–30. Also, R.W. Davies, *Soviet History in the Gorbachev Revolution* (London, 1989), pp. 28–34.
30. I. Klyamkin and A. Migranyan, 'Nuzhna "zheleznaya ruka?"', *Literaturnaya gazeta*, 16 August 1989, p. 10.

31. Yu.F. Afanas'ev in *Pravda*, 17 September 1989, p. 2.
32. Igor Klyamkin, 'Kakaya ulitsa vedet k khramu?', *Novyi mir*, November 1987, pp. 158–9.
33. L. Popkova, 'Gde pyshnee pirogi?', *Novyi mir*, May 1987, pp. 240 and 239.
34. See, for instance, Vasilii Selyunin, 'Istoki', *Novyi mir*, May 1988, p. 185–6.
35. A. Tsipko, 'Istoki stalinizma', *Nauka i zhizn'*, nos. 11–12, 1988; nos. 1–2, 1989.
36. Ibid., Ocherk 2, 'Prevratnosti "chistogo sotzializma"', *Nauka i zhizn*, no. 12, 1988, pp. 40–8, esp. p. 46.
37. Nina Andreeva, 'Ne mogu postupatsya printsipami', *Sovetskaya Rossiya*, 13 March 1988, p. 3.
38. *Izvestiya TsK KPSS*, no. 6, 1990, p. 69.
39. Tatyana Zaslavskaya, 'O strategii sotsial'nogo upravleniya perestroiki', Yu.F. Afanas'ev, ed., *Inogo ne dano* (Moscow, 1988), pp. 9–50, esp. p. 18.
40. *Pravda*, 21 April 1990, p. 2.
41. V.K. Mesyats, *Pravda*, 6 February 1990, p. 3.
42. I.T. Frolov, *Pravda*, 17 March 1990, p. 3.
43. *Pravda*, 16 March 1990, p. 2.
44. Ibid., 31 May 1989, p. 2; ibid., 26 November 1989, p. 1.
45. V.I. Mironenko, *Pravda*, 9 February 1990, p. 2.
46. *Pravda*, 13 February 1990, p. 3; ibid., 17 March 1990, p. 7.
47. *Pravda*, 22 April 1989, p. 1; ibid., 3 July 1991, p. 2; ibid., 15 July 1990, p. 3.
48. *Pravda*, 27 July 1991, p. 1; ibid., 8 August 1991, p. 3.
49. *Pravda*, 19 February 1988, p. 2; M.S. Gorbachev, 'Sotsialisticheskaya ideya i revolyutsionnaya perestroika', ibid., 26 November 1989, p. 2; ibid., 3 July 1991, p. 1.
50. *Izvestiya TsK KPSS*, February 1991, no. 2, pp. 50–1.
51. *Izvestiya* 2 July 1991, p. 2; *Sovetskaya Rossiya*, 3 August 1991, p, 1.
52. See Tatyana Zaslavskaya, *The Second Socialist Revolution: An Alternative Socialist Strategy*, tr. by Susan Davies with Jenny Warren (London, 1990).
53. *Komsomol'skaya pravda*, 30 October 1990, p. 2.
54. M. Shatrov, *Dal'she ... Dal'she ... Dal'she!: diskussiya vokrug odnoi p'esy* (Moscow, 1989), p. 64.
55. V. Selyunin, 'Istoki', *Novyi mir*, May 1989, pp. 162–89.
56. *Literaturnaya gazeta*, 17 January 1990, pp. 3, 5.
57. V. Grossman, 'Vse techet', *Oktyabr'*, June 1989, p. 93.
58. Vladimir Soloukhin, *Chitaya Lenina* (Frankfurt-am-Main, 1989), pp. 42–3, reprinted in Russia in *Rodina*, October 1989; 'Rasstavanie s bogom', *Ogonek*, no. 51, December 1990, p. 30.
59. For example, E. Radzinsky, *Argumenty i fakty*, no. 46, 17–23 November 1990, pp. 6–7.
60. Sergei S. Debov, *Pravda*, 27 October 1989, p. 8
61. See Ligachev in *Pravda*, 11 July 1990, p. 5, and in *Sovetskaya Rossiya*, 6 February 1991, p. 3.
62. *Pravda*, 24 October 1990, p. 1.
63. *Moskovskiye novosti*, 4 November 1990, pp. 8–9 ; *Pravda*, 3 January 1991, p. 3; *Izvestiya Tsk KPSS*, February 1991, pp. 50–1.
64. 'Prostite nas, Vladimir Il'ich!', *Pravda*, 21 January 1991, pp. 1, 3.
65. Ibid., p. 1.

66. Ibid., p. 3.
67. V.V. Chertkov, 'Zhestokii vozhd', *Dialog,* 1991, no. 2 (January), p. 45.

Conclusion

1 Mikhail Gorbachev, *The August Coup: The Truth and the Lessons* (London, 1991), p. 38.

Bibliography

This guide to further reading, arranged chapter by chapter, makes no claim to be comprehensive, but contains those books and articles in English which I have found especially useful, plus a small number of key texts in Russian.

Introduction

James H. Billington, *The Icon and the Axe: An Interpretive History of Russian Culture* (London, 1966).

James H. Billington, *Fire in the Minds of Men: Origins of the Revolutionary Faith* (London, 1980).

Jerome Blum, *Lord and Peasant in Russia: From the Ninth to the Nineteenth Centuries* (Princeton, N.J., 1961).

R.N. Carew Hunt, *The Theory and Practice of Communism: An Introduction* (Harmondsworth, 1971).

Michael Cherniavsky, *Tsar and People: Studies in Russian Myths* (New Haven, 1961).

Robert V. Daniels, *The End of the Communist Revolution* (London, 1993).

Alfred B. Evans, *Soviet Marxism-Leninism. The Decline of an Ideology* (Westport, 1993).

August von Haxthausen, *Studies on the Interior of Russia*, ed. S. Frederick Starr (Chicago, 1972)

Geoffrey Hosking, *Russia: People and Empire 1552–1917* (London, 1997).

Leszek Kolakowski, *Main Currents of Marxism* (3 vols, Oxford, 1978).

Walter Laqueur, *The Dream that Failed: Reflections on the Soviet Union* (New York, 1994).

Moshe Lewin, *Russia/USSR/Russia: The Drive and Drift of a Superstate* (New York, 1995).

George Lichtheim, *A Short History of Socialism* (London, 1983).

Martin Malia, *The Soviet Tragedy: A History of Socialism in Russia* (New York, 1994).

Tim McDaniel, *The Agony of the Russian Idea* (Princeton, 1996).

David McLellan, *Marxism after Marx: An Introduction* (London, 1979).

Alfred G. Meyer, *Marxism* (Cambridge, Mass., 1970).

P.N. Milyukov, *Ocherki po istorii russkoi kultury*, vol. 3: *Natsionalizm i yevropeizm* (Paris, 1930).

John Plamenatz, *German Marxism and Russian Communism* (London, 1954).

Geroid Tanquary Robinson, *Rural Russia under the Old Regime* (New York, 1961).

Mark Sandle, *A Short History of Soviet Socialism* (London, 1999).

James P. Scanlan, *Marxism in the USSR* (Ithaca, 1985).

Teodor Shanin, *Russia as a 'Developing Society'* (London, 1985).

Robert C. Tucker, *The Marxian Revolutionary Idea* (London, 1970).

Adam B. Ulam, *The Unfinished Revolution: An Essay on the Sources of Influence of Marxism and Communism* (London, 1960).

Lazar Volin, *A Century of Russian Agriculture* (Cambridge, Mass., 1970).
Wayne S. Vucinich, ed., *The Peasant in Nineteenth-Century Russia* (Stanford, 1968).
Andrzej Walicki, *Marxism and the Leap to the Kingdom of Freedom: The Rise and Fall of the Communist Utopia* (Stanford, 1997).
Donald Mackenzie Wallace, *Russia* (London, n.d.).
Anthony Wright, *Socialisms: Theories and Practices* (Oxford, 1987).
Alexander Yanov, *The Russian Challenge and the Year 2000* (Oxford, 1987).

1 Before Lenin

Edward Acton, *Alexander Herzen and the Role of the Intellectual Revolutionary* (Cambridge, 1979).
Samuel H. Baron, *Plekhanov: The Father of Russian Marxism* (London, 1963).
James H. Billington, *Mikhailovsky and Russian Populism* (Oxford, 1958).
Theodore Dan, *The Origins of Bolshevism* (London, 1964).
Isaac Deutscher, *Lenin's Childhood* (London, 1970).
Abbott Gleason, *Young Russia: The Genesis of Russian Radicalism in the 1860s* (Chicago, 1983).
Leopold H. Haimson, *The Russian Marxists and the Origins of Bolshevism* (London, 1955).
Alexander Herzen, *From the Other Shore and The Russian People and Socialism*, with an introduction by Isaiah Berlin (London, 1956).
E. Lampert, *Sons against Fathers: Studies in Russian Radicalism and Revolution* (Oxford, 1965).
Martin Malia, *Alexander Herzen and the Birth of Russian Socialism 1812 – 1855* (London, 1961).
Georgi Plekhanov, *Selected Philosophical Works* (5 vols, Moscow, 1976 – 81).
Philip Pomper, *Peter Lavrov and the Russian Revolutionary Movement* (Chicago, 1972).
Teodor Shanin, ed., *Late Marx and the Russian Road: Marx and the 'Peripheries of Capitalism'* (London, 1983).
Rolf Theen, *Lenin: Genesis and Development of a Revolutionary* (London, 1974).
Franco Venturi, *Roots of Revolution: A History of the Populist and Socialist Movements in Nineteenth-Century Russia*, with an introduction by Isaiah Berlin (London, 1960).
Franco Venturi, *Studies in Free Russia* (Chicago, 1982).
Andrzej Walicki, *The Controversy over Capitalism: Studies in the Social Philosophy of the Russian Populists* (Oxford, 1969).
William F. Woehrlin, *Chernyshevski: The Man and the Journalist* (Cambridge, Mass., 1971).

2 The Vision, 1890–1917

Jonathan Frankel, 'Lenin's Doctrinal Revolution of April 1917', *Journal of Contemporary History*, 4 (1969), pp. 117–42.
Neil Harding, *Lenin's Political Thought* (2 vols, London, 1977 and 1981).
Neil Harding, *Leninism* (London, 1996).

Esther Kingston-Mann, *Lenin and the Problem of Marxist Peasant Revolution* (New York, 1983).

David Lane, *Leninism: A Sociological Interpretation* (Cambridge, 1984).

V.I. Lenin, *Collected Works* (45 vols, London, 1960–70).

V.I. Lenin, *Polnoe sobranie sochinenii* (55 vols, Moscow, 1958–65).

Lenin: Biography Proposed by the Marx-Engels-Lenin Institute, Moscow (Moscow, n.d.).

Richard Pipes, ed.,*The Unknown Lenin: From the Secret Archive* (New Haven, 1996).

A.J. Polan, *Lenin and the End of Politics* (London, 1984).

Philip Pomper, *Lenin, Trotsky and Stalin: The Intelligentsia and Power* (New York, 1990).

Robert Service, *Lenin: A Political Life* (3 vols, London, 1985, 1991, and 1995).

Robert Service, *Lenin: A Biography* (London, 2000).

Alexander Solzhenitsyn, *Lenin in Zurich* (London, 1976).

Donald W. Treadgold, *Lenin and His Rivals: The Struggle for Russia's Future, 1898–1906* (London, 1955).

Adam Ulam, *Lenin and the Bolsheviks: The Intellectual and Political History of the Triumph of Communism in Russia* (London, 1969).

Dimitri Volkogonov, *Lenin: Life and Legacy* (London, 1994).

Bertram D. Wolfe, *Three Who Made A Revolution* (London, 1956).

* * * *

Edward Acton, *Rethinking the Russian Revolution* (London, 1990).

Edward Acton, Vladimir Cherniaev, and William G. Rosenberg, eds, *Critical Companion to the Russian Revolution 1914–1921* (London, 1997).

Oskar Anweiler, *The Soviets: Russian Workers', Peasants' and Soldiers' Councils, 1905–1921* (New York, 1974).

Isaac Deutscher, *Trotsky* (3 vols, London, 1954, 1959, and 1963).

Paul Dukes, *October and the World: Perspectives on the Russian Revolution* (London, 1979).

John Dunn, *Modern Revolutions* (2nd edn, Cambridge, 1989).

Marc Ferro,*The Russian Revolution of February 1917* (London, 1972).

Marc Ferro, *October 1917: A Social History of the October Revolution* (London, 1980).

Orlando Figes, *A People's Tragedy: The Russian Revolution 1891–1924* (London, 1996).

Sheila Fitzpatrick, *The Russian Revolution* (2nd edn, Oxford, 1994).

Michael T. Florinsky, *The End of the Russian Empire* (New Haven, 1931).

Ziva Galili, *The Menshevik Leaders in the Russian Revolution: Social Realities and Political Strategies* (Princeton, 1989).

Israel Getzler, *Martov* (Cambridge, 1967).

Neil Harding, ed., *Marxism in Russia: Key Documents 1879–1906* (Cambridge, 1983).

Tsuyoshi Hasegawa, *The February Revolution: Petrograd 1917* (Seattle, 1981).

George Katkov, *Russia 1917: The February Revolution* (London, 1967).

J.L.H. Keep, *The Rise of Social Democracy in Russia* (Oxford, 1969).

John Keep, *The Russian Revolution: A Study in Mass Mobilisation* (London, 1976).

Baruch Knei-Paz, *The Social and Political Thought of Leon Trotsky* (Oxford, 1978).

David Lane, *The Roots of Russian Communism* (Assen and London, 1975).

Rosa Luxemburg,*The Russian Revolution*, ed. Bertram D. Wolfe (Ann Arbor, 1962).

J.P. Nettl, *Rosa Luxemburg* (2 vols, Oxford, 1976).
Richard Pipes, ed., *Revolutionary Russia* (Cambridge, Mass., 1968).
Richard Pipes, *Struve: Liberal on the Left, 1870–1905* (Cambridge, Mass., 1970).
Richard Pipes,*The Russian Revolution 1899–1919* (London, 1990).
Alexander Rabinowitch, *The Bolsheviks Come to Power: The Revolution of 1917 in Petrograd* (New York, 1976).
Oliver H. Radkey, *The Agrarian Foes of Bolshevism: Promise and Default of the Russian Socialist Revolutionaries, February to October 1917* (New York, 1958).
Christopher Read, *From Tsar to Soviets: The Russian People and their Revolution, 1917–1921* (London, 1996).
John Reed, *Ten Days That Shook the World* (Harmondsworth, 1966).
Leonard Schapiro, *The Communist Party of the Soviet Union* (2nd edn, London, 1970).
Leonard Schapiro, *1917: The Russian Revolution and the Origins of Present-Day Communism* (London, 1984).
Teodor Shanin, *Russia 1905–07: Revolution as a Moment of Truth* (London, 1986).
Harold Shukman, ed., *The Blackwell Encyclopedia of the Russian Revolution* (Oxford, 1988).
Theda Skocpol, *States and Social Revolutions: A Comparative Analysis of France, Russia and China* (Cambridge, 1979).
S.A. Smith, *Red Petrograd: Revolution in the Factories* (Cambridge, 1983).
N.N. Sukhanov, *The Russian Revolution 1917: A Personal Record*, ed. by Joel Carmichael (Oxford, 1955).
Ronald Grigor Suny, 'Towards a Social History of the October Revolution', *American Historical Review*, 88 (1983), pp. 31–52.
Leon Trotsky, *The History of the Russian Revolution* (London, 1965).
James D. White, *The Russian Revolution 1917–1921: A Short History* (London, 1995).
Allan Wildman, *The Making of a Workers' Revolution: Russian Social Democracy, 1891–1903* (Chicago, 1967).

3 The Realization, 1917–24

N.I. Bukharin and E. Preobrazhensky, *The ABC of Communism* (Harmondsworth, 1969).
Jane Burbank, *Intelligentsia and Revolution: Russian Views of Bolshevism* (New York, 1986).
E.H. Carr, *A History of Soviet Russia* (14 vols, London, 1950–78).
E.H. Carr, *The Russian Revolution from Lenin to Stalin, 1917–1929* (London, 1980).
Stephen F. Cohen, *Rethinking the Soviet Experience* (New York, 1985).
Robert V. Daniels, *The Conscience of the Revolution: Communist Opposition in Soviet Russia* (Cambridge, Mass., 1960).
Samuel Farber, *Before Stalin: The Rise and Fall of Soviet Democracy* (Cambridge,1990).
Orlando Figes, *Peasant Russia, Civil War: The Volga Countryside in Revolution (1917–1921)* (Oxford, 1989).
Israel Getzler, *Kronstadt, 1917–1921: The Fate of a Soviet Democracy* (Cambridge, 1983).

Geoffrey Hosking, *A History of the Soviet Union 1917–1991* (London, 1992).

Karl Kautsky, *Georgia: A Social-Democratic Peasant Republic* (London, 1921).

Peter Kenez, *The Birth of the Propaganda State: Soviet Methods of Mass Mobilization, 1917–1929* (Cambridge, 1985).

Diane P. Koenker, William G. Rosenberg and Ronald Grigor Suny, eds, *Party, State and Society in the Russian Civil War* (Bloomington, 1989).

Moshe Lewin, *Lenin's Last Struggle* (London, 1969).

Marcel Liebman, *Leninism under Lenin* (London, 1975).

Silvana Malle, *The Economic Organization of War Communism 1918–1921* (Cambridge, 1985).

Mary McAuley, *Bread and Justice: State and Society in Petrograd 1917–1922* (Oxford, 1991).

Mary McAuley, *Soviet Politics 1917–1991* (Oxford, 1992).

Peter Nettl, *The Soviet Achievement* (London, 1967).

Alec Nove, *An Economic History of the Soviet Union 1917–1991* (London, 1992).

Richard Pipes, *Russia Under the Bolshevik Regime 1919–1924* (London, 1994).

Richard Pipes, *The Formation of the Soviet Union* (Cambridge, Mass., 1997).

Yevgeny Plimak, *Politicheskoe zaveshchanie V.I. Lenina: istoki, sushchnost', vypolnenie* (Moscow, 1988).

Oliver H. Radkey, *Russia Goes to the Polls: Elections to the All-Russian Constituent Assembly, 1917* (Ithaca, 1989).

Thomas F. Remington, *Building Socialism in Bolshevik Russia: Ideology and Industrial Organization, 1917–1921* (Pittsburgh, 1984).

T.H. Rigby, *Communist Party Membership in the USSR, 1917–1967* (Princeton, N.J., 1968).

T.H. Rigby, *Lenin's Government: Sovnarkom, 1917–1922* (Cambridge, 1979).

Richard Sakwa, *Soviet Communists in Power: A Study of Moscow During the Civil War, 1918–1921* (London, 1988).

Leonard Schapiro, *The Origin of the Communist Autocracy: Political Opposition in the Soviet State: First Phase, 1917–1922* (London, 1955).

Victor Serge, *Memoirs of a Revolutionary 1901–1941* (Oxford, 1963).

Robert Service, *The Bolshevik Party in Revolution: A Study in Organisational Change, 1917–1923* (London, 1979).

Jeremy Smith, *The Bolsheviks and the National Question 1917–1923* (London, 1999).

Ronald Gregor Suny, *The Making of the Georgian Nation* (London, 1989).

H.G. Wells, *Russia in the Shadows* (London, 1921).

Stephen White, *The Bolshevik Poster* (New Haven, 1988).

4   After Lenin, 1924–29

N.I. Bukharin, *Selected Writings on the State and the Transition to Socialism*, ed. Richard B. Day (Nottingham, 1982).

Stephen F. Cohen, *Bukharin and the Bolshevik Revolution: A Political Biography 1888–1938* (London, 1974).

V.P. Danilov, *Rural Russia under the New Regime*, ed. Orlando Figes (Bloomington, 1988).

Alexander Erlich, *The Soviet Industrialization Debate, 1924–1928* (Cambridge, Mass., 1960).

Sheila Fitzpatrick, *Education and Social Mobility in the Soviet Union, 1921–1934* (Cambridge, 1979).

Sheila Fitzpatrick, Alexander Rabinowitch and Richard Stites, eds, *Russia in the Era of NEP* (Bloomington, 1990).

Sheila Fitzpatrick, *The Cultural Front: Power and Culture in Revolutionary Russia* (Ithaca, 1992).

Graeme Gill, *Origins of the Stalinist Political System* (Cambridge, 1990).

A. Kemp-Welch, ed., *The Ideas of Nikolai Bukharin* (Oxford, 1992).

Christel Lane, *The Rites of Rulers: Ritual in Industrial Society – The Soviet Case* (Cambridge, 1981).

Anna Larina, *This I Cannot Forget* (London, 1993).

Moshe Lewin, *The Making of the Soviet System: Essays in the Social History of Interwar Russia* (London, 1985).

Lars T. Lih, Oleg V. Naumov and Oleg V. Khlevniuk, eds, *Stalin's Letters to Molotov, 1926–1936* (New Haven, 1996).

Catherine Merridale, *Moscow Politics and the Rise of Stalin* (London, 1990).

Michael Mirski, *The Mixed Economy: NEP and Its Lot* (Copenhagen, 1984).

Roger Pethybridge, *The Social Prelude to Stalinism* (London, 1974).

Roger Pethybridge, *One Step Backwards, Two Steps Forward: Soviet Society and Politics under the New Economic Policy* (Oxford, 1990).

Michal Reiman, *The Birth of Stalinism* (Bloomington, 1987).

Lewis H. Siegelbaum, *Soviet State and Society between Revolutions, 1918–1929* (Cambridge, 1992).

J.V. Stalin, *Works* (13 vols, London, 1952–5).

J.V. Stalin, *Problems of Leninism* (Peking, 1976)

Robert C. Tucker, *Stalin as Revolutionary, 1879–1929* (New York, 1973).

Nina Tumarkin, *Lenin Lives! The Lenin Cult in Soviet Russia* (2nd edn, Cambridge, Mass., 1997).

5 Stalin's Socialism, 1929–53

Giuseppe Boffa, *The Stalin Phenomenon* (Ithaca, 1992).

Robert Conquest, *The Harvest of Sorrow: Soviet Collectivization and the Terror-Famine* (London, 1986)

Robert Conquest, *The Great Terror: A Reassessment* (London, 1990).

Robert Conquest, *Stalin: Breaker of Nations* (London, 1991).

R.W. Davies, *The Industrialization of Soviet Russia: Socialist Offensive* (London, 1989).

R.W. Davies, *The Industrialization of Soviet Russia: Soviet Collective Farm, 1929–38* (London, 1989).

Sarah Davies, *Popular Opinion in Stalin's Russia: Terror, Propaganda and Dissent, 1934–1941* (Cambridge, 1997).

Isaac Deutscher, *Stalin: A Political Biography* (London, 1967).

Milovan Djilas, *The New Class: An Analysis of the Communist System* (London, 1957).

Donald Filzer, *Soviet Workers and Stalinist Industrialization* (London, 1986).

Sheila Fitzpatrick, ed., *Cultural Revolution in Russia, 1928–1931* (Bloomington, 1978)

Sheila Fitzpatrick, *Stalin's Peasants: Resistance and Survival in the Russian Village after Collectivization* (Oxford, 1994).

J. Arch Getty, *Origins of the Great Purges: The Soviet Communist Party Reconsidered, 1933–1938* (Cambridge, 1985).

J. Arch Getty and Roberta T. Manning, *Stalinist Terror: New Perspectives* (Cambridge, 1993).

Evgenia Ginzburg, *Into the Whirlwind* (Harmondsworth, 1968).

History of the Communist Party of the Soviet Union (Bolsheviks): Short Course (Moscow, 1939).

Joseph Stalin: A Short Biography Proposed by the Marx-Engels-Lenin Institute, Moscow (London, 1950).

Ian Kershaw and Moshe Lewin, eds, *Stalinism and Nazism: Dictatorships in Comparison* (Cambridge, 1997).

Hiroaki Kiromiya, *Stalin's Industrial Revolution: Politics and Workers, 1928–1932* (Cambridge, 1988).

Stephen Kotkin, *Magnetic Mountain: Stalinism as a Civilization* (Berkeley, 1995).

Moshe Lewin, *Russian Peasants and Soviet Power: A Study of Collectivization* (London, 1968).

Nadezhda Mandelshtam, *Hope Against Hope* (Harmondsworth, 1975).

Roy Medvedev, *Let History Judge: The Origins and Consequences of Stalinism* (New York, 1971).

Roy Medvedev, *On Stalin and Stalinism* (Oxford, 1979).

Alec Nove, *Stalinism and After: The Road to Gorbachev* (Boston, 1989).

Alec Nove, ed., *The Stalin Phenomenon* (London, 1993).

T.H. Rigby, *The Changing Soviet System: Mono-Organisational Socialism from its Origins until Gorbachev's Restructuring* (Aldershot, 1990).

Anatoli Rybakov, *Children of the Arbat* (London, 1988).

Alexander Solzhenitsyn, *The Gulag Archipelago 1918–1956* (3 vols, London, 1974–8).

Nikolai Timasheff, *The Great Retreat: The Growth and Decline of Communism in Russia* (New York, 1946).

Leon Trotsky, *The Revolution Betrayed: What Is the Soviet Union and Where Is It Going?* (London, 1964).

Robert C. Tucker, *The Soviet Political Mind: Stalinism and Post-Stalin Change* (2nd edn, London, 1972).

Robert C. Tucker, ed., *Stalinism: Essays in Historical Interpretation* (New York, 1977).

Robert C. Tucker, *Stalin in Power: the Revolution from Above, 1928–1941* (New York, 1990).

Lynn Viola, *The Best Sons of the Fatherland: Workers in the Vanguard of Soviet Collectivization* (Oxford, 1987).

Dmitri Volkogonov, *Stalin: Triumph and Tragedy* (London, 1991).

Chris Ward, ed., *The Stalinist Dictatorship* (London, 1998).

Chris Ward, *Stalin's Russia* (2nd edn, London, 1999).

Sidney and Beatrice Webb, *Soviet Communism: A New Civilisation* (3rd edn, London, 1944).

6 Onward to Communism, 1953–64

George W. Breslauer, *Khrushchev and Brezhnev as Leaders: Building Authority in Soviet Politics* (London, 1982).
Archie Brown, ed., *Political Leadership in the Soviet Union* (London, 1989).
Vladimir Bukovsky, *To Build a Castle: My Life as a Dissenter* (London, 1978).
Fedor Burlatsky, *Khrushchev and the First Russian Spring* (London, 1991).
Stephen F. Cohen, Alexander Rabinowitch and Robert Sharlet, eds, *The Soviet Union since Stalin* (London, 1980).
Edward Crankshaw, *Khrushchev's Russia* (2nd edn, Harmondsworth, 1962).
Edward Crankshaw, *Khrushchev: A Biography* (London, 1966).
Current Soviet Policies III: The Documentary Record of the Extraordinary 21st Congress of the Communist Party of the Soviet Union (New York, 1960).
Donald Filzer, *The Khrushchev Era* (London, 1993)
Edith Rogovin Frankel, *Novy Mir: A Case Study in the Politics of Literature, 1952–58* (Cambridge, 1981).
Mark Frankland, *Khrushchev* (Harmondsworth, 1966).
Ronald J. Hill, 'The "All-People's State" and "Developed Socialism"', in Neil Harding, ed., *The State and Socialist Society* (London, 1984), pp. 104–28.
Jerry Hough and Merle Fainsod, *How the Soviet Union is Governed* (Cambridge, Mass., 1979).
John L.H. Keep, *Last of the Empires: A History of the Soviet Union, 1945–1991* (Oxford, 1995).
Nikita Khrushchev, *Khrushchev Remembers*, ed. and tr. by Strobe Talbott (2 vols, London, 1971 and 1974).
Sergei Khrushchev, *Khrushchev on Khrushchev* (Boston, 1990).
Amy Knight, *Beria: Stalin's First Lieutenant* (Princeton, N.J., 1993).
O. Kuusinen, ed., *Fundamentals of Marxism-Leninism* (London, 1961).
Wolfgang Leonhard, *The Kremlin since Stalin* (Oxford, 1962)
Carl A. Linden, *Khrushchev and the Soviet Leadership 1957–1964* (Baltimore, 1966).
Martin McCauley, ed., *Khrushchev and Khrushchevism* (London, 1987).
Martin McCauley, *Nikita Sergeievich Khrushchev* (London, 1991).
Roy and Zhores Medvedev, *Khrushchev: The Years in Power* (Oxford, 1977).
Boris Pasternak, *Doctor Zhivago* (London, 1958).
Roger Pethybridge, *A Key to Soviet Politics: The Crisis of the Anti-Party Group* (New York, 1962).
Michael Scammell, *Solzhenitsyn: A Biography* (London, 1985).
Leonard Schapiro, ed., *The USSR and the Future: An Analysis of the New Program of the CPSU* (New York, 1963).
Alexander Solzhenitsyn, *One Day in the Life of Ivan Denisovich* (Harmondsworth, 1963).
Alexander Solzhenitsyn, *The Oak and the Calf: Sketches of Literary Life in the Soviet Union* (London, 1980).
The Road to Communism: Documents of the 22nd Congress of the Communist Party of the Soviet Union, October 17–31 1961 (Moscow, n.d.).
William J. Tompson, *Khrushchev: A Political Life* (London, 1994).
Yevgeny Yevtushenko, *A Precocious Autobiography* (London, 1963).

7 A Problem of Credibility, 1964–85

Abel Aganbegyan, *The Challenge: Economics of Perestroika*, ed. Michael Barratt Brown (London, 1988).

Andrei Amalrik, *Will the Soviet Union Survive until 1984?* (Harmondsworth, 1980).

Yu.V. Andropov, *The Teaching of Karl Marx and Some Questions of Building Socialism in the USSR* (Moscow, 1983).

G.A. Arbatov, *Zatyanuvsheesya vyzdorovlenie (1953–1985 gg.): Svidetel'stvo sovremennika* (Moscow, 1991).

Seweryn Bialer, *The Soviet Paradox: External Expansion, Internal Decline* (London, 1986).

Archie Brown and Michael Kaiser, eds, *The Soviet Union since the Fall of Khrushchev* (2nd edn, London, 1978).

L.G. Churchward, *Soviet Socialism: Social and Political Essays* (London, 1987).

Stephen F. Cohen, ed., *An End to Silence: Uncensored Opinion in the Soviet Union* (New York, 1982).

John Dornberg, *Brezhnev: The Masks of Power* (London, 1974).

Alfred B. Evans, Jr, 'Developed Socialism in Soviet Ideology', *Soviet Studies*, 29 (1977), pp. 409–28.

Marshall. I. Goldman, *USSR in Crisis: The Failure of an Economic System* (New York, 1983).

Ronald J. Hill and Peter Frank, *The Soviet Communist Party* (London, 1981).

Jerry F. Hough, *Soviet Leadership in Transition* (Washington, D.C., 1980).

Edward L. Keenan, 'Muscovite Political Folkways', *Russian Review*, 45 (1986), pp. 115–82.

Basile Kerblay, *Modern Soviet Society* (London, 1988).

R. Kosolapov, *Developed Socialism: Theory and Practice* (Moscow, 1982).

Zhores Medvedev, *Andropov: His Life and Death* (Oxford, 1984).

John W. Parker, *Kremlin in Transition*, vol. 1: *From Brezhnev to Chernenko* (London, 1991).

Peter Reddaway, ed., *Uncensored Russia: The Human Rights Movement in the Soviet Union* (London, 1972).

Abraham Rothberg, *The Heirs of Stalin: Dissidence and the Soviet Regime* (Ithaca, 1972).

Joshua Rubenstein, *Soviet Dissidents: Their Struggle for Human Rights* (London, 1981).

George Saunders, ed., *Samizdat: Voices of the Soviet Opposition* (New York, 1974).

G. Shakhnazarov, *The Destiny of the World: The Socialist Shape of Things to Come* (Moscow, 1979).

Marshall S. Shatz, *Soviet Dissent in Historical Perspective* (Cambridge, 1980).

Alexander Solzhenitsyn, *Letter to Soviet Leaders* (London, 1974).

Rudolf L. Tokes, ed., *Dissent in the USSR: Politics, Ideology and People* (Baltimore, 1975).

Aryeh L. Unger, *Constitutional Development in the USSR: A Guide to the Soviet Constitutions* (London, 1986).

G.N. Volkov, ed., *The Basics of Marxist-Leninist Theory* (Moscow, 1982).

Stephen White, *Political Culture and Soviet Politics* (London, 1979).

Alexander Zinoviev, *The Reality of Communism* (London, 1984).

8 The Alternative Tradition

Ronald Amann, 'Towards a New Economic Order: The Writings of B.P. Kurashvili', *Détente*, no. 8 (1987), pp. 8–10.

Rudolph Bahro, *The Alternative in Eastern Europe* (London, 1978).

Wlodzimierz Brus, *The Market in a Socialist Economy* (London, 1972).

Stephen F. Cohen, *Rethinking the Soviet Experience: Politics and History since 1917* (New York, 1985).

Stephen F. Cohen, 'The Afterlife of Nikolai Bukharin', in N.I. Bukharin, *Selected Writings on the State and the Transition to Socialism*, ed. Richard B. Day (Nottingham, 1982).

Yelizaveta Drabkina, *Zimnyi pereval* (Moscow, 1990).

M. Ellman, 'Economic Reform in the Soviet Union', *PEP Broadsheets*, vol. 35 (1969), pp. 283–371.

Edith Rogovin Frankel, *Novy Mir: A Case Study in the Politics of Literature, 1952–58* (Cambridge, 1981).

Michael Glenny, ed., *Novy Mir: A Selection, 1925–1967* (London, 1972).

Philip Hanson, 'The Novosibirsk Report: A Comment', *Survey*, 28 (1984), pp. 83–7.

Geoffrey Hosking, *The Awakening of the Soviet Union* (London, 1990).

Boris Kagarlitsky, *The Thinking Reed: Intellectuals and the Soviet State, 1917 to the Present* (London, 1988).

Vladimir Lakshin, *Solzhenitsyn, Tvardovsky and 'Novy Mir'* (Cambridge, Mass., 1980).

Moshe Lewin, *Lenin's Last Struggle* (London, 1969).

Moshe Lewin, *Political Undercurrents in Soviet Economic Debates: From Bukharin to the Modern Reformers* (London, 1975).

Moshe Lewin, *The Gorbachev Phenomenon: A Historical Interpretation* (London, 1988).

Roy Medvedev, *Let History Judge: The Origins and Consequences of Stalinism* (New York, 1971).

Roy Medvedev, *On Socialist Democracy*, ed. Ellen de Kadt (London, 1975).

Roy Medvedev, *On Stalin and Stalinism* (Oxford, 1979).

Roy Medvedev, *On Soviet Dissent: Interviews with Piero Ostellino* (New York, 1980).

Roy Medvedev, *Leninism and Western Socialism* (London, 1981).

Roy Medvedev, *Political Essays* (Nottingham, 1976).

Roy Medvedev, *The October Revolution* (London, 1979).

Zdenek Mlynar, 'Problems of Political Leadership and the New Economic System', *World Marxist Review*, vol. 8 (December 1965), pp. 58–63.

Richard Pipes, 'Can the Soviet Union Reform?', *Foreign Affairs*, 63 (1984), pp. 47–61.

Andrei Sakharov, *Sakharov Speaks*, ed. Harrison E. Salisbury (London, 1974).

Mikhail Shatrov, *The Bolsheviks and Other Plays* (London, 1990).

Ota Sik, *The Third Way: Marxist-Leninist Theory and Modern Industrial Society* (London, 1976).

H. Gordon Skilling and Franklyn Griffiths, eds., *Interest Groups in Soviet Politics* (Princeton, N.J., 1971).

Pekka Sutela, *Economic Thought and Economic Reform in the Soviet Union* (Cambridge, 1991).

Tatyana Zaslavskaya, 'The Novosibirsk Report', *Survey*, 28 (1984), pp. 88–108.
Tatyana Zaslavskaya, *The Second Socialist Revolution: An Alternative Socialist Strategy* (London, 1990).

9 A New Socialism, 1985–91

Yury F. Afanas'ev, ed., *Inogo ne dano: sud'by perestroiki* (Moscow, 1988).
Abel Aganbegyan, *Moving the Mountain: Inside the Perestroika Revolution* (London, 1989).
Anders Aslund, *Gorbachev's Struggle for Economic Reform* (2nd edn, London, 1991).
Seweryn Bialer, ed., *Politics, Society and Nationality in Gorbachev's Russia* (Boulder, 1989).
Archie Brown, 'Gorbachev: New Man in the Kremlin', *Problems of Communism*, 32, no. 3 (1985), pp. 1–23.
Archie Brown, 'Political Science in the USSR', *International Political Science Review*, 7 (1986), pp. 443–81.
Archie Brown, *The Gorbachev Factor* (Oxford, 1996).
Timothy J. Colton, *The Dilemma of Reform in the Soviet Union* (2nd edn, New York, 1986).
Current Soviet Policies IX: The Documentary Record of the 27th Congress of the Communist Party of the Soviet Union (Columbus, 1986).
Anthony D'Agostino, *Gorbachev's Revolution, 1985–1991* (London, 1998).
Alexander Dallin and Gail W. Lapidus, eds, *The Soviet System: From Crisis to Collapse* (2nd edn, Boulder, 1994).
R.W. Davies, *Soviet History in the Gorbachev Revolution* (London, 1989).
John B. Dunlop, *The Rise of Russia and the Fall of the Soviet Union* (Princeton, N.J., 1993).
Michael Ellman and Vladimir Kontorovich, eds, *The Disintegration of the Soviet Economic System* (London, 1992).
Graeme Gill, *The Rules of the Communist Party of the Soviet Union* (London, 1988).
Graeme Gill, *The Collapse of a Single Party System* (Cambridge, 1994).
Marshall I. Goldman, *What Went Wrong With Perestroika* (New York, 1991).
Mikhail Gorbachev, *Perestroika: New Thinking for Our Country and the World* (London, 1987).
Mikhail Gorbachev, *The August Coup:The Truth and the Lessons* (London, 1991).
Mikhail Gorbachev, *Memoirs* (London, 1996).
Andrei Grachev, *Final Days: The Inside Story of the Collapse of the Soviet Union* (Boulder, 1995).
Philip Hanson, *From Stagnation to Catastroika* (London, 1992).
Edward A. Hewett, *Reforming the Soviet Economy* (Washington, D.C., 1988).
Ronald J. Hill and Jan Ake Dellenbrandt, eds, *Gorbachev and Perestroika: Towards A New Socialism?* (Aldershot, 1989).
Jerry Hough, *Gorbachev and the West: The Politics of Reform* (2nd edn, New York, 1990).
Boris Kagarlitsky, *The Disintegration of the Monolith* (London, 1992).
Steven Kull, *Burying Lenin: The Revolution in Soviet Ideology and Foreign Policy* (Boulder, 1992).

David Lane, *Soviet Society under Perestroika* (2nd edn, London, 1992).
Walter Laqueur, *The Long Road to Freedom: Russia and Glasnost* (London, 1989).
Yegor Ligachev, *Inside Gorbachev's Kremlin* (Boulder, 1996).
Roy Medvedev and Giuletto Chiesa, *Time of Change: An Insider's View of Russia's Transformation* (London, 1991).
Catherine Merridale and Chris Ward, eds, *Perestroika: The Historical Perspective* (London, 1991).
John Miller, *Mikhail Gorbachev and the End of Soviet Power* (London, 1993).
John Morrison, *Boris Yeltsin: From Bolshevik to Democrat* (Harmondsworth, 1991).
Alec Nove, *Glasnost in Action: Cultural Renaissance in Russia* (Boston, 1989).
E.A. Rees, *The Soviet Communist Party in Disarray* (London, 1992).
David Remnick, *Lenin's Tomb: The Last Days of the Soviet Empire* (London, 1993).
Philip G. Roeder, *Red Sunset: The Failure of Soviet Politics* (Princeton, N.J., 1994).
Richard Sakwa, *Gorbachev and His Reforms 1985–1990* (Hemel Hempstead, 1990).
Richard Sakwa, *Russian Politics and Society* (London, 1993).
Mark Sandle, 'The Final Word: The Draft Party Programme of July/August 1991', *Europe-Asia Studies,* 48 (1996), pp. 1131–50.
Victor Sergeyev and Nikolai Biryukov, *Russia's Road to Democracy* (Aldershot, 1993).
Vladimir Shlapentokh, *Soviet Ideologies in the Period of Glasnost: Responses to Brezhnev's Stagnation* (New York, 1988).
Vladimir Shlapentokh, 'The XXVII Congress – A Case Study of the Shaping of a New Party Ideology', *Soviet Studies,* 40 (1988), pp. 1–20.
Nikolai Shmelev, *The Turning-Point* (London, 1990).
Christopher Smart, 'Gorbachev's Lenin: The Myth in Service to Perestroika', *Studies in Comparative Communism,* 23 (1990), pp. 5–21.
Graham Smith, ed., *The Nationalities Question in the Soviet Union* (London, 1990).
Hedrick Smith, *The New Russians* (London, 1990).
Vladimir Soloukhin, *Chitaya Lenina* (Frankfurt-am-Main, 1989)
Jonathan Steele, *Eternal Russia* (2nd edn, London, 1995).
Ronald Grigor Suny, *The Revenge of the Past: Nationalism, Revolution and the Collapse of the Soviet Union* (Stanford, 1993).
Terry L. Thompson, *Ideology and Policy: The Political Uses of Doctrine in the Soviet Union* (Boulder, 1989).
A. Tsipko, 'Istoki stalinizma', *Nauka i zhizn',* nos. 11–12, 1988, nos. 1–2, 1989.
Robert C. Tucker, *Political Culture and Leadership in the Soviet Union: From Lenin to Gorbachev* (Brighton, 1987).
Michael E. Urban, *More Power to the Soviets: The Democratic Revolution in the USSR* (Aldershot, 1990).
Stephen White, 'The New Programme and Rules of the CPSU', *The Journal of Communist Studies,* 2 (1986), pp. 182–191.
Stephen White, *After Gorbachev* (4th edn, Cambridge, 1993).
Alexander Yakovlev, *The Fate of Marxism in Russia* (New Haven, 1993).
Boris Yeltsin, *Against the Grain: An Autobiography* (London, 1990).
'Z', 'To The Stalin Mausoleum', *Daedalus,* 119 (1990), pp. 295–340.

Index

Bukharin, Nikolai – *continued*
Communism, 122; *Notes of an
Economist*, 110; *The Political
Testament of Lenin*, 111;
downfall, 111, 113; show-trial,
135; Roy Medvedev on, 196;
'the Bukharin alternative' and
'Bukharinism', 104, 226; cult and
rehabilitation, 226
Butenko, Anatoly, 203–4

capitalism, 7, 50; Herzen and, 20;
Marx on, 30, 31; Lenin on, 42–3,
85; Bukharin and, 102, 104;
under War Communism, 79;
under NEP, 85; Stalin on, 197,
123, 126, 129; Khrushchev and,
150; popular attitudes towards,
181; 'alternative' ideas about,
191, 195, 207; reappraised during
perestroika, 217, 221–2, 252;
Gorbachev endorses, 233
Castro, Fidel, 154
Chernenko, Konstantin, 186
Chernyshevsky, Nikolai, 20; on
commune, 23–4; Lenin and, 34
'children of the Twentieth Congress',
213
China, 141, 153, 154, 169
church, *see* Orthodox Church,
Russian
civil war, Russian (1918–20), 12, 64
collectivization, collective farms, 10,
108, 113, 118–20, 130; Marx on,
31; Lenin and, 115; Khrushchev
and, 158
command economy, the, 122, 133,
188, 223
Committees of Poor Peasants, 69
commune, *see* mir,
Communist Party of the Soviet Union
(CPSU) [*earlier* All-Union
Communist Party (Bolsheviks);
Russian Communist Party
(Bolsheviks); Russian Social-
Democratic Labour Party
(Bolsheviks)]; composition, 87,
98, 113, 136, 143, 208; size, 78,
162; and communism, 11, 13,

175–6; as dictatorship, 12, 14, 78,
83, 133, 145; democracy within
12, 78, 83, 86–7; ban on factions,
83; monopoly, 71, 104, 173, 175,
186, 196, 216, 217, 220, 232;
Central Committee of
Bolshevik/Communist Party, 57,
74, 89, 93, 108, 147, 169, 232;
Central Control Commission,
89–90; under Khrushchev, 161–2;
1961 Programme, 152, 155, 157,
159, 160, 236; divided over Stalin
question, 151; under Brezhnev,
173, 175, 183; declining influence
of, 180–1, 205–6; 19th
Conference (1988), 214, 216;
conservatism within, 172, 173,
206; 'alternative' thinkers and,
188, 196–7, 200, 206, 207; feuding within, 225, 229–30, 239;
'red-brown alliance', 230; loses
privileged position, 233; banned
in Russia, 246–7; verdict on Soviet
experiment, 248; *see also*
Bolsheviks, Bolshevism;
Congresses of the Communist
Party; Politburo
Congresses of the Communist Party:
8th (1919), 76; 10th (1921), 81,
83; 12th (1923), 89 ;13th (1924),
93; 17th (1934), 129; 18th
(1939), 121, 124; 20th (1956),
93, 147, 213; 21st (1959), 152;
22nd (1961), 150, 151, 152, 166;
27th (1986), 236
Congress of People's Deputies of the
USSR, 216, 226
Congress of Soviets, *see* soviets
Constituent Assembly: as envisaged
by Lenin before 1917, 49;
elections to, 58–9, 67–8, 77; Roy
Medvedev on, 201
constitutions, Soviet: 1918 ,76; 1936,
123, 132–3; 1977, 175, 186, 232
cooperatives, 84, 85, 90, 103;
Bukharin and, 102, 104; in
perestroika period, 215, 222
Council of People's Commissars, 83
Cuba, 154, 169

Machine Tractor Stations (MTSs), 119
Macmillan, Harold, 154
Makharadze, Pilipe, 74
Malenkov, Georgy, 146, 151
Malia, Martin, 16–18, 92, 210
market, the: during War
    Communism, 79; Bukharin and,
    102, 221; 'market socialism' ,18,
    190, 194, 226, 233; perestroika
    and, 18, 215, 221, 233; Ligachev
    on, 229; 'marketeers', 230
Marx, Karl, Marxism, 6, 10–11; and
    phases of communist society, 10,
    12; and dictatorship of the
    proletariat, 11, 47; and Russia, 2,
    24, 30–1; and nationalities
    question, 45; *The Communist
    Manifesto*, 28, 45; *Capital*, 21, 30;
    Lenin and, 7–8, 13, 32, 34–5;
    Herzen and, 19, 20, 21; Stalin
    and, 124–5; Andropov and, 184;
    perestroika and, 233, 236, 238;
    Malia and Walicki on, 16–18
Marxism-Leninism, 12, 17, 148, 150,
    167, 175; rejected, 225, 231
Marxists, Russian: problems of, 6;
    and populism, 20; disregard
    Marx on Russia, 31, 32; and
    peasants, 42; and nationalities,
    45–6
Mdivani, Budu, 74
Medvedev, Roy: ideas, 195–7; and
    Bukharin, 196; and 'party-
    democrats', 197; *On Socialist
    Democracy*, 198; on Stalinism,
    200; joins Central Committee,
    213
Mensheviks, Menshevism, 6, 7;
    origins, 37; how different from
    Bolsheviks, 7, 37, 39–40, 42; and
    1905, 6, 36, 39; and Provisional
    Government, 53; and *April
    Theses*, 53; and Second Congress
    of Soviets, 58; in Georgia, 72–3;
    excluded from politics, 77;
    liquidated as party, 83
middle class, bourgeoisie, 19, 80; in
    tsarist Russia, 28, 29; Soviet
    equivalent, 15; Khrushchev

against ,165; suffers from wage
    equalizing, 165, 176–7, 208;
    receptive to 'alternative'
    approach, 208; increasing
    influence within party, 209;
    support for perestroika
    movement and democracy, 227,
    230, 239, 246, 251, 252;
    abandons socialism, 225, 237,
    252; resists August 1991 coup,
    246
Mikhailovsky, Nikolai, 21
mir, 2–4; Herzen on, 19–20, 23;
    Chernyshevsky on, 23–4; Marx
    and, 24, 30–1; Russian Marxists
    and, 42; resilience, 43; abolished,
    119
Mlynar, Zdenek: ideas, 193–4; and
    Gorbachev, 193, 209, 212; on
    Prague Spring, 213
Molotov, Vyacheslav, 146, 151
Moscow: soviet, 53; university, 193,
    211; and Shatrov's *The
    Bolsheviks*, 199; Yeltsin and, 216,
    227; Muscovites and Lenin, 243,
    253
'movement to the people', the, 24–5

nationalities, question of: Lenin on,
    45–6, 70–2; right of self-
    determination, 66, 137, 224;
    Stalin and, 137–9; Khrushchev
    and, 158, 166; idea of Soviet
    nationality, 178–9; failure of
    Lenin's nationalities project, 178,
    179; 'alternative' thinkers and,
    197, 206; during perestroika
    period, 223–4, 227, 235; Russian
    nationalism, 224, 227, 229–30;
    new Union treaty, 234
Nemchinov, V.S., 189, 193
NEP (New Economic Policy), 82–3,
    83–4, 94, 112, 116, 142; Lenin
    and, 10, 16, 82–3, 84, 85, 112;
    party resentment against, 101,
    112; Left Opposition and, 101–2;
    Bukharin's defence of, 102–4,
    110; problems of, 103, 104;
    abandoned 110; Alternative

NEP (New Economic Policy) –
continued
Tradition and ,198, 199, 201;
perestroika and, 213–14, 221,
223, 226; Gorbachev on, 218,
231–2
Nicholas II, Emperor, 241–2, 248
Nove, Alec, 130
Novozhilov, V.V., 189, 191
Novy Mir, 187, 198, 205

October Revolution, *see* revolutions,
Russian
Old Bolsheviks, 78, 98, 99, 121, 136,
198, 199; Lenin as, 97; Bukharin
as, 105, 110
'Old Guard' (of Bolsheviks), 78, 87,
228
oligarchy, 94, 171, 249, 251; as
'natural' form of Russian
government, 182
Ordzhonikidze, Sergo: and Georgia,
73, 75, 88, 91, 92
Orthodox Church, Russian, 119, 157,
163; revival during perestroika,
217, 242
'outer empire', the, 223, 230

Pasternak, Boris, 164–5
peasants, 1–5; and individual
farming, 3; and 'movement to
the people', 24; Marx and
Marxists on, 30–1; as potential
proletarians, 7, 42–3; numbers,
28, 29; conditions prior to1917,
28, 29, 43–4; differentiation
among, 43–4, 69, 103; and
Bolsheviks, 54, 68–9, 80; peasant
soviet movement, 54, 58; and
cooperatives, 102, 103; Left
Opposition and, 102; Bukharin
and, 102–3, 107; Stalin and, 108,
109, 118–20; and
collectivization, 10, 108, 112–13,
118–20; private plots, 119, 164;
famine of 1932–3, 130–1;
Khrushchev and, 158, 163;
conditions under Brezhnev, 176;
Klyamkin on 'peasant Russia's'

demise, 225; *see also* Committees
of Poor Peasants; collectivization
People's Will, 26; Marx and, 30, 32;
Lenin and, 32, 36, 38
perestroika, chapter 9 *passim*; success,
211; myths of, 18; Zdenek
Mlynar and, 193; *see also*
reformers of perestroika period
'permanent revolution', 47, 106
Pestel, Pavel, 25
Petrakov, Nikolai, 191, 193, 194
Petrograd Soviet, 51, 53
Pinochet, General Augusto, 223
Plekhanov, Georgy: as 'father' of
Russian Marxism, 27, 32; and the
People's Will, 26; and capitalism,
27; and bourgeois revolution, 29;
and socialist revolution, 27–8;
Marxist orthodoxy of, 27, 32
pluralism, 219, 236
Poland: Red Army defeated in, 70;
and de-Stalinization, 151;
Solidarity movement, 203;
'alternative' thinkers and, 203
Politburo, 83, 89, 94, 149, 174, 217,
228, 233
Popkova, L., 226
populism, populists, 19–24; and
Marx, 21; and liberalism, 21; and
mir, 23–4; 'movement to the
people', 24–5
Prague Spring, the, 197, 213
Pravda, 53, 134, 150, 233, 247;
launches new cult of Lenin, 243
Preobrazhensky, Yevgeny, 101, 102,
122
privatization, 234, 235
profit motive, the, 172, 190
proletariat, *see* working class
property, private: peasants and, 2;
Gorbachev on, 215, 233;
Ligachev on, 229; sale of land,
217
Provisional Government of 1917, 9,
52, 247
purges of 1930s, the, 124, 128, 132,
134–5, 149, 198, 199

Reagan, Ronald, 182